MICROSOFT
Word 2000
Introductory Concepts and Techniques

Gary B. Shelly
Thomas J. Cashman
Misty E. Vermaat

COURSE TECHNOLOGY
ONE MAIN STREET
CAMBRIDGE MA 02142

Thomson Learning™

SHELLY
CASHMAN
SERIES®

Australia   Canada   Denmark   Japan   Mexico   New Zealand   Philippines
Puerto Rico   Singapore   South Africa   Spain   United Kingdom   United States

Asia (excluding Japan)
Thomson Learning
60 Albert Street, #15-01
Albert Complex
Singapore 189969

Japan
Thomson Learning
Palaceside Building 5F
1-1-1 Hitotsubashi, Chiyoda-ku
Tokyo 100 0003 Japan

Australia/New Zealand
Nelson/Thomson Learning
102 Dodds Street
South Melbourne, Victoria 3205
Australia

Latin America
Thomson Learning
Seneca, 53
Colonia Polanco
11560 Mexico D.F. Mexico

South Africa
Thomson Learning
Zonnebloem Building,
Constantia Square
526 Sixteenth Road
P.O. Box 2459
Halfway House, 1685
South Africa

Canada
Nelson/Thomson Learning
1120 Birchmount Road
Scarborough, Ontario
Canada M1K 5G4

UK/Europe/Middle East
Thomson Learning
Berkshire House
168-173 High Holborn
London, WC1V 7AA United Kingdom

Spain
Thomson Learning
Calle Magallanes, 25
28015-MADRID
ESPANA

TRADEMARKS

Course Technology and the Open Book logo are registered trademarks and CourseKits is a trademark of Course Technology.

SHELLY CASHMAN SERIES ® and **Custom Edition** ® are trademarks of Thomson Learning. Some of the product names and company names used in this book have been used for identification purposes only and may be trademarks or registered trademarks of their respective manufacturers and sellers. Thomson Learning and Course Technology disclaim any affiliation, association, or connection with, or sponsorship or endorsement by, such owners.

DISCLAIMER

Course Technology reserves the right to revise this publication and make changes from time to time in its content without notice.

PHOTO CREDITS: Microsoft Word 2000 *Project 2, pages* WD 2.2-3 Space photograph, Courtesy of Digital Stock; *Project 3, pages* WD 3.2-3 Classified listing, pen and glasses, hand on mouse, woman in business suit, Courtesy of PhotoDisc, Inc.; Albert Einstein and signature, Courtesy of the American Institute of Physics.

ISBN 0-7895-4684-1

1 2 3 4 5 6 7 8 9 10   BC   04 03 02 01 00

MICROSOFT

Word 2000

Introductory Concepts and Techniques

C O N T E N T S

● PROJECT 3

USING A WIZARD TO CREATE A RESUME
AND CREATING A COVER LETTER WITH A TABLE

● WEB FEATURE

CREATING WEB PAGES USING WORD

● APPENDIX A

MICROSOFT WORD 2000 HELP SYSTEM   WD A.1

● APPENDIX B

PUBLISHING OFFICE WEB PAGES
TO A WEB SERVER   WD B.1

● APPENDIX C

RESETTING THE WORD MENUS
AND TOOLBARS   WD C.1

● APPENDIX D

MICROSOFT OFFICE USER SPECIALIST
CERTIFICATION PROGRAM   WD D.1

Preface

The Shelly Cashman Series® offers the finest textbooks in computer education. We are proud of the fact that our Microsoft Office 4.3, Microsoft Office 95, and Microsoft Office 97 textbooks have been the most widely used books in education. Each edition of our Office textbooks has included innovations, many based on comments made by the instructors and students who use our books. The Microsoft Office 2000 books continue with the innovation, quality, and reliability that you have come to expect from the Shelly Cashman Series.

Office 2000 is the most significant upgrade ever to the Office suite. Microsoft has enhanced Office 2000 in the following areas: (1) interface changes; (2) application-specific features; (3) multi-language pack; (4) round tripping HTML files back to an Office 2000 application; (5) collaboration; and (6) new applications. Each one of these enhancements is discussed in detail.

In our Office 2000 books, you will find an educationally sound and easy-to-follow pedagogy that combines a step-by-step approach with corresponding screens. All projects and exercises in this book are designed to take full advantage of the Office 2000 enhancements. The popular Other Ways and More About features offer in-depth knowledge of Office 2000. The project openers provide a fascinating perspective on the subject covered in the project. The project material is developed carefully to ensure that students will see the importance of learning Office 2000 applications for future course work.

Objectives of This Textbook

Microsoft Word 2000: Introductory Concepts and Techniques is intended for a course that covers a brief introduction to Microsoft Word 2000. No experience with a computer is assumed, and no mathematics beyond the high school freshman level is required. The objectives of this book are:

- To teach the fundamentals of Microsoft Word 2000.
- To expose students to practical examples of the computer as a useful tool
- To acquaint students with the proper procedures to create documents suitable for course work, professional purposes, and personal use
- To develop an exercise-oriented approach that allows learning by example.
- To encourage independent study, and help those who are working alone.

The Shelly Cashman Approach

Features of the Shelly Cashman Series Office 2000 books include:

- **Project Orientation:** Each project in the book presents a practical problem and complete solution in an easy-to-understand approach.
- **Screen-by-Screen, Step-by-Step Instructions:** Each of the tasks required to complete a project is identified throughout the development of the project. The steps are accompanied by full-color screens.
- **Thoroughly Tested Projects:** Every screen in the book is correct because it is produced by the author only after performing a step, resulting in unprecedented quality.

1. Click Border button on Tables and Borders toolbar
2. On Format menu click Borders and Shading, click Borders tab, click Bottom button in Preview area, click OK button

Data and Statistics

When researching for a paper, you may need to access data, graphs of data, or perform statistical computations on data. For more information on statistical formulas and available data and graphs, visit the Word 2000 More About Web page (www.scsite.com/wd2000/more.htm) and then click Data and Statistics.

- **Other Ways Boxes and Quick Reference Summary:** Word 2000 provides a variety of ways to carry out a given task. The Other Ways boxes displayed at the end of most of the step-by-step sequences specify the other ways to do the task completed in the steps. Thus, the steps and the Other Ways box make a comprehensive reference unit. A Quick Reference Summary is available on the Web that summarizes the way specific tasks can be completed.

- **More About Feature:** These marginal annotations provide background information that complements the topics covered, adding depth and perspective.

- **Integration of the World Wide Web:** We have integrated the World Wide Web into the students' Word 2000 learning experience in different ways. For example, we have added (1) More Abouts that send students to Web sites for up-to-date information and alternative approaches to tasks; (2) a MOUS information Web page and a MOUS map Web page so students can better prepare for the Microsoft Office Use Specialist (MOUS) Certification examinations; (3) a Word 2000 Quick Reference Summary Web page that summarizes the ways to complete tasks (mouse, menu, shortcut menu, and keyboard); and (4) project reinforcement Web pages in the form of true/false, multiple choice, and short answer questions, and other types of student activities.

Organization of This Textbook

Microsoft Word 2000: Introductory Concepts and Techniques provides detailed instruction on how to use Word 2000. The material is divided into three projects, a Web Feature, and four Appendices.

Project 1 - Creating and Editing a Word Document In Project 1, students are introduced to Word terminology and the Word window by preparing an announcement. Topics include starting and quitting Word; entering text; checking spelling while typing; saving a document; selecting; changing the font and font size of text; centering, right-aligning, and formatting text in bold and italic; undoing commands and actions; inserting clip art into a document; resizing a graphic; printing a document; opening a document; correcting errors; and using the Word Help system.

Project 2 – Creating a Research Paper In Project 2, students use the MLA style of documentation to create a research paper. Topics include changing margins; adjusting line spacing; using a header to number pages; entering text using Click and Type; first-line indenting paragraphs; using Word's AutoCorrect feature; adding a footnote; modifying a style; inserting a symbol; inserting a manual page break; creating a hanging indent; creating a text hyperlink; sorting paragraphs; moving text; finding a synonym; counting words in a document; and checking spelling and grammar at once.

Project 3 – Using a Wizard to Create a Resume and Creating a Cover Letter with a Table In Project 3, students create a resume using Word's Resume Wizard and then create a cover letter with a letterhead. Topics include personalizing the resume; adding color to characters; setting and using tab stops; collecting and pasting; adding a bottom border; creating and inserting an AutoText entry; creating a bulleted list while typing; inserting a Word table; entering data into a Word table; and formatting a Word table. Finally, students prepare and print an envelope address.

Web Feature – Creating Web Pages Using Word In the Web Feature, students are introduced to creating Web pages. Topics include saving the resume created in Project 3 as a Web page; creating a Web page using the Web Page Wizard; resizing a Web page frame; editing a hyperlink; and editing a Web page from your browser.

Appendices Appendix A presents a detailed step-by-step introduction to the Microsoft Word Help system. Students learn how to use the Office Assistant and the Contents, Answer Wizard, and Index sheets in the Help window. Appendix B describes how to publish Office Web pages to a Web server. Appendix C shows students how to reset the menus and toolbars. Appendix D introduces students to the Microsoft Office User Specialist (MOUS) Certification program.

End-of-Project Student Activities

A notable strength of the Shelly Cashman Series Office 2000 books is the extensive student activities at the end of each project. Well-structured student activities can make the difference between students merely participating in a class and students retaining the information they learn. The activities in the Shelly Cashman Series Word 2000 books include the following.

- **What You Should Know** A listing of the tasks completed within a project together with the pages where the step-by-step, screen-by-screen explanations appear. This section provides a perfect study review for students.

- **Project Reinforcement on the Web** Every project has a Web page (www.scsite.com/ off2000/reinforce.htm). The Web page includes true/false, multiple choice, and short answer questions, and additional project-related reinforcement activities that will help students gain confidence in their Word 2000 abilities.

- **Apply Your Knowledge** This exercise requires students to open and manipulate a file on the Data Disk for the Office 2000 books. To obtain a copy of the Data Disk, follow the instructions on the inside back cover of this textbook.

- **In the Lab** Three in-depth assignments per project require students to apply the knowledge gained in the project to solve problems on a computer.

- **Cases and Places** Up to seven unique case studies that require students to apply their knowledge to real-world situations.

Shelly Cashman Series Teaching Tools

A comprehensive set of Teaching Tools accompanies this textbook in the form of a CD-ROM. The CD-ROM includes an Instructor's Manual and teaching and testing aids. The CD-ROM (ISBN 0-7895-4636-1) is available through your Course Technology representative or by calling one of the following telephone numbers: Colleges and Universities, 1-800-648-7450; High Schools, 1-800-824-5179; and Career Colleges, 1-800-477-3692. The contents of the CD-ROM are listed below.

- **Instructor's Manual** The Instructor's Manual is made up of Microsoft Word files. The files include lecture notes, solutions to laboratory assignments, and a large test bank. The files allow you to modify the lecture notes or generate quizzes and exams from the test bank using your own word processing software. Where appropriate, solutions to laboratory assignments are embedded as icons in the files. When an icon appears, double-click it and the application will start and the solution will display on the screen. The Instructor's Manual includes the following for each project: project objectives; project overview; detailed lesson plans with page number references; teacher notes and activities; answers to the end-of-project exercises; test bank of 110 questions for every project (25 multiple-choice, 50 true/false, and 35 fill-in-the-blank) with page number references; and transparency references. The transparencies are available through the Figures in the Book. The test bank questions are numbered the same as in Course Test Manager. Thus, you can print a copy of the project test bank and use the printout to select your questions in Course Test Manager.

- **Figures in the Book** Figures and tables in the textbook are available in Figures in the Book.

- Course Test Manager Course Test Manager is a powerful testing and assessment package that enables instructors to create and print tests from the large test bank. Instructors with access to a networked computer lab (LAN) can administer, grade, and track tests online. Students also can take online practice tests, which generate customized study guides.

- Course Syllabus Any instructor who has been assigned a course at the last minute knows how difficult it is to come up with a course syllabus. For this reason, sample syllabi are included for each of the Office 2000 products that can be customized easily to a course.

- Lecture Success System Lecture Success System files are for use with the application software, a personal computer, and projection device to explain and illustrate the step-by-step, screen-by-screen development of a project in the textbook without entering large amounts of data.

- Instructor's Lab Solutions Solutions and required files for all the In the Lab assignments at the end of each project are available.

- Lab Tests/Test Outs Tests that parallel the In the Lab assignments are supplied for the purpose of testing students in the laboratory on the material covered in the project or testing students out of the course.

- Project Reinforcement True/false, multiple choice, and short answer questions, and additional project-related reinforcement activities for each project help students gain confidence in their Office 2000 abilities.

- Student Files All the files that are required by students to complete the Apply Your Knowledge exercises are included.

- Interactive Labs Eighteen hands-on interactive labs that take students from ten to fifteen minutes each to step through help solidify and reinforce mouse and keyboard usage and computer concepts. Student assessment is available.

Acknowledgments

The Shelly Cashman Series would not be the leading computer education series without the contributions of outstanding publishing professionals. First, and foremost, among them is Becky Herrington, director of production and designer. She is the heart and soul of the Shelly Cashman Series, and it is only through her leadership, dedication, and tireless efforts that superior products are made possible. Becky created and produced the award-winning Windows series of books.

Under Becky's direction, the following individuals made significant contributions to these books: Doug Cowley, production manager; Ginny Harvey, series specialist and developmental editor; Ken Russo, senior Web designer; Mike Bodnar, associate production manager; Mark Norton, Web designer; Stephanie Nance, graphic artist and cover designer; Marlo Mitchem, Chris Schneider, and Hector Arvizu, graphic artists; Jeanne Black and Betty Hopkins, Quark experts; Lyn Markowicz, copy editor; Kim Kosmatka, proofreader; Cristina Haley, indexer; Sarah Evertson of Image Quest, photo researcher; and Susan Sebok and Ginny Harvey, contributing writers.

Special thanks go to Richard Keaveny, managing editor; Jim Quasney, series consultant; Lora Wade, product manager; Meagan Walsh, associate product manager; Francis Schurgot, Web product manager; Tonia Grafakos, associate Web product manager; Scott Wiseman, online developer; Rajika Gupta, marketing manager; and Erin Bennett, editorial assistant.

Gary B. Shelly
Thomas J. Cashman
Misty E. Vermaat

MICROSOFT

Word 2000

Microsoft **Word 2000**

Microsoft Word 2000

P R O J E C T

1

Creating and Editing a Word Document

You will have mastered the material in this project when you can:

O B J E C T I V E S

- Start Word
- Describe the Word window
- Zoom page width
- Change the default font size of all text
- Enter text into a document
- Check spelling as you type
- Scroll through a document
- Save a document
- Select text
- Change the font of selected text
- Change the font size of selected text
- Bold selected text
- Right-align a paragraph
- Center a paragraph
- Undo commands or actions
- Italicize selected text
- Underline selected text
- Insert clip art into a document
- Resize a graphic
- Print a document
- Open a document
- Correct errors in a document
- Use Microsoft Word Help
- Quit Word

Wobbling Words

Help for the Spelling Challenged

" *My spelling is Wobbly.*
It's good spelling, but it Wobbles,
and the letters get in the wrong places. "

Winnie-the-Pooh

N o wonder Pooh has a difficult time trying to spell words correctly. If he pronounces the words bough, cough, rough, though, and through, he realizes that despite the fact they all end with the letters, ough, they all are pronounced quite differently.

If you share Pooh's spelling dilemma, you are not alone. Most people have difficulty remembering how to spell some words. One study reports 20 percent of writers do not spell well because they cannot visualize words. Even remembering the simple rules such as, i before e except after c, does not offer much assistance because of the slew of exceptions such as the words, weird science.

A spelling error in a flyer distributed on campus, a resume sent to a potential employer, or an e-mail message forwarded to an associate

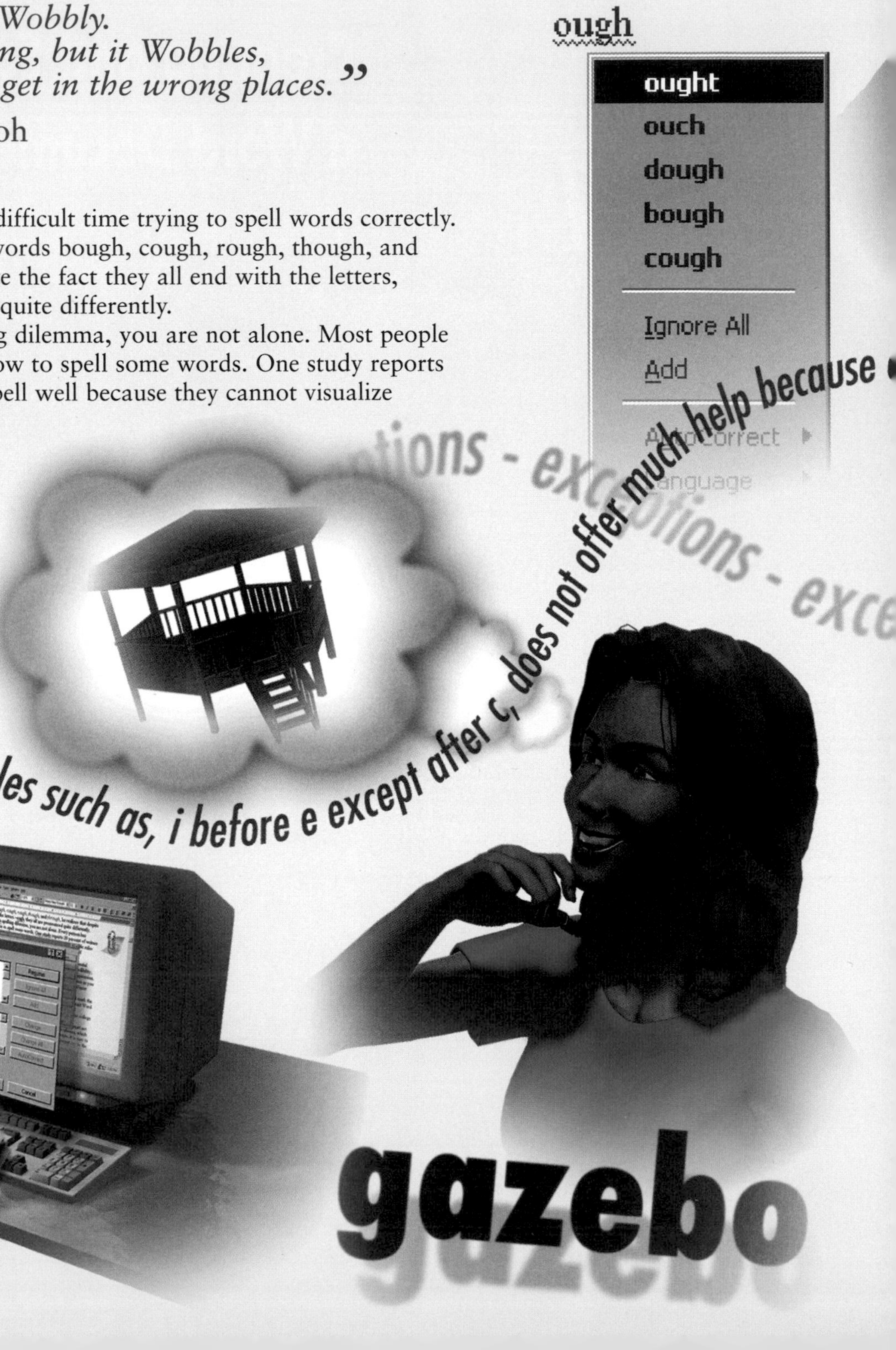

ough

| ought |
| ouch |
| dough |
| bough |
| cough |
| Ignore All |
| Add |
| AutoCorrect |
| Language |

gazebo

dolphin

däl-fən

homophones

bough,

cough,

rough,

slew of exceptions, such as, weird and s

could lessen your credibility, cause a reader to doubt the accuracy of your statements, and leave a negative impression. In this project, Microsoft Word will check your typing for possible spelling errors as you create an announcement for the Student Government Association's upcoming winter break ski trip at Summit Peak Resort.

If you type a word that does not appear in Word's dictionary, Word will flag the possible error with a wavy red underline. If the spelling is correct, you can instruct Word to ignore the flagged word. If it is misspelled, the spelling feature will offer a list of suggested corrections. Despite this assistance from the spelling checker, one study indicates college students repeatedly ignore or override the flagged words.

Word's spelling checker is a useful alternative to a dictionary, but you must not rely on it 100 percent. It will not flag commonly misused homophones, which are words that are pronounced alike but are spelled differently. For example, it is easy to confuse the homophones in the sentence, The Web site contains an incorrect cite to the reference materials discussing regaining sight after experiencing blindness.

Then what is a spelling-challenged writer to do? English teachers emphasize that you can learn to spell better, but not by strictly memorizing long lists or having someone mark all the errors in a paper. Instead, you need to try the following strategies to improve awareness of spelling difficulties.

First, identify error patterns. For example, do you misspell the same words repeatedly? If so, write them in a list and have a friend dictate them to you. Then write the words again. If you involve your senses, hear the words spelled correctly, and then visualize the words, you increase your awareness of the problem.

Next, always consult a dictionary when you are uncertain of a word's spelling. Note the word's etymology — its origin and history. For example, the word, science, originated from the Latin word, scientia, a form of the verb to know.

As you proofread, read from right to left. Use a pencil to point at each word as you say it aloud.

Using Microsoft Word's spelling checker and a good dictionary should enhance your spelling skills, and stop your words from *Wobbling*.

Microsoft Word 2000

Creating and Editing a Word Document

P R O J E C T

1

C A S E   P E R S P E C T I V E

Jackie Peterson is this year's Activities Chairperson for the Student Government Association (SGA) at Hilltop Community College. Each year, the Activities Chairperson coordinates vacation plans for the winter break and then prepares fliers announcing the exciting plans. SGA members post these announcements in locations throughout the school, print them in the school newspaper, and mail them to each student.

Because of Jackie's avid love of skiing and snowboarding, she attempts to locate a ski resort in the Midwest designed to accommodate all tastes and budgets. She succeeds! Summit Peak Resort has over 5,200 acres of groomed slopes and pristine lakes for skiing, sledding, snowboarding, ice skating, and ice fishing.

As a Marketing major, you have learned the guidelines for designing announcements. Jackie asks for your assistance with this assignment. You recommend using large, bold characters for the headline and title. To attract attention to the announcement, you suggest including a graphic of a skier sailing down the slopes. Together, you begin designing the announcement.

What Is Microsoft Word 2000?

Microsoft Word is a full-featured word processing program that allows you to create professional looking documents such as announcements, letters, resumes, and reports, and revise them easily. You can use Word's desktop publishing features to create high-quality brochures, advertisements, and newsletters. Word also provides many tools that enable you to create Web pages with ease. From within Word, you even can place these Web pages directly on a Web server.

Word has many features designed to simplify the production of documents. With Word, you easily can include borders, shading, tables, graphics, pictures, and Web addresses in your documents. You can instruct Word to create a template, which is a form you can use and customize to meet your needs. While you are typing, Word can perform tasks automatically. For example, Word can detect and correct spelling and grammar errors in a variety of languages. Word also can format text such as headings, lists, fractions, borders, and Web addresses as you type them. Word's thesaurus allows you to add variety and precision to your writing. Within Word, you can e-mail a copy of your Word document to an e-mail address.

Project One — Summit Peak Announcement

To illustrate the features of Word, this book presents a series of projects that use Word to create documents similar to those you will encounter in academic and business environments. Project 1 uses Word to produce the announcement shown in Figure 1-1.

Feel the Thrill...
...Seize the Slopes!

headline

graphic of skier

body title

SUMMIT PEAK RESORT

Summit Peak is the *largest* ski resort in the country. Breathtaking mountains provide more than 5,200 acres of groomed slopes and pristine lakes for skiing, sledding, snowboarding, ice skating, and ice fishing.

Summit Peak offers a range of vacation packages for every taste and budget, from traditional ski lodges to luxurious condominiums. Add transportation, meals, lift tickets, gear, and lessons for an exceptional value.

body copy

Call (970) 555-SNOW for reservations.

FIGURE 1-1

More About
Word 2000
For more information on the features of Microsoft Word 2000, visit the Word 2000 More About Web page (www.scsite.com/wd2000/more.htm) and then click Microsoft Word 2000 Features.

The announcement informs students about exciting vacation packages offered by Summit Peak Resort during winter break. The announcement begins with a headline that is followed by a graphic of a skier. Below the graphic of the skier is the body title, SUMMIT PEAK RESORT, followed by the body copy that consists of a brief paragraph about the resort and another paragraph about the vacation packages. Finally, the last line of the announcement lists the resort's telephone number. The appearance of the text and graphic in the announcement is designed to catch the attention of the reader.

Starting Word

Follow these steps to start Word, or ask your instructor how to start Word for your system.

 To Start Word

1 **Click the Start button on the taskbar and then point to New Office Document.**

The programs on the Start menu display above the Start button (Figure 1-2). The New Office Document command is highlighted on the Start menu. A **highlighted command** *displays as light text on a dark background.*

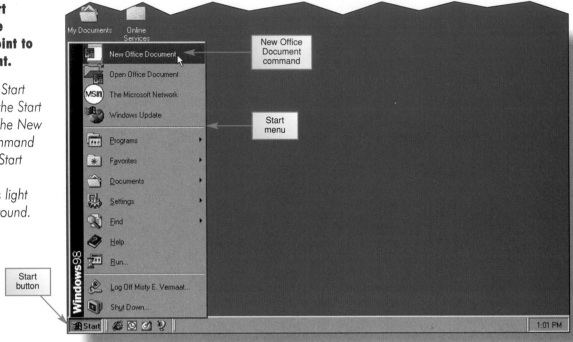

FIGURE 1-2

2 **Click New Office Document. If necessary, click the General tab when the New Office Document dialog box first displays. Point to the Blank Document icon.**

Office displays several icons in the General sheet in the New Office Document dialog box (Figure 1-3). The icons are large because the Large Icons button is selected. Each icon represents a different type of document you can create in Microsoft Office.

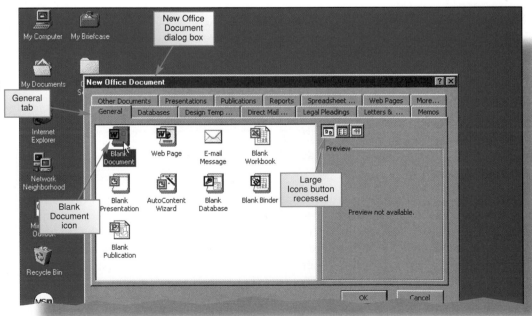

FIGURE 1-3

3 **Double-click the Blank Document icon.**

Office starts Word. While Word is starting, the mouse pointer changes to the shape of an hourglass. After a few moments, an empty document titled Document1 displays in the Word window (Figure 1-4).

4 **If the Word window is not maximized, double-click its title bar to maximize it. If the Office Assistant displays, right-click it and then click Hide on the shortcut menu. If your screen differs from Figure 1-4, click View on the menu bar and then click Normal.**

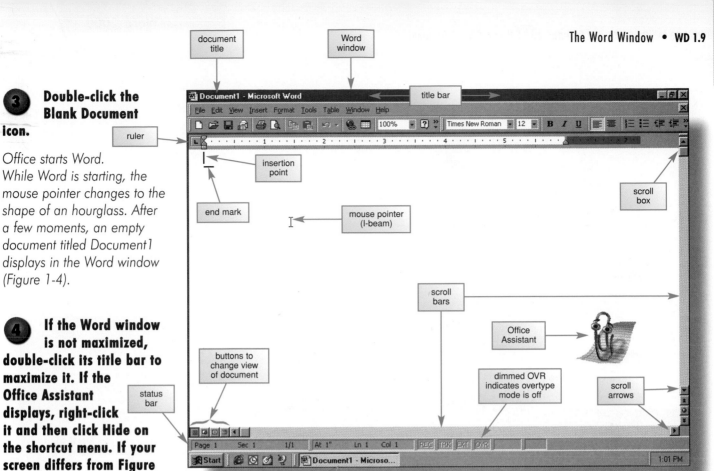

FIGURE 1-4

The Windows taskbar at the bottom of the screen displays the Word program button, indicating the Word program is open.

The Word Window

The **Word window** (Figure 1-4) consists of a variety of components to make your work more efficient and documents more professional. The following sections discuss these components.

Document Window

The document window displays text, tables, graphics, and other items as you type or insert them into a document. Only a portion of your document, however, displays on the screen at one time. You view the portion of the document displayed on the screen through the **document window** (Figure 1-5 on the next page).

Other Ways

1. Right-click Start button, click Open, double-click New Office Document, click General tab, double-click Blank Document icon

2. Click New Office Document button on Microsoft Office Shortcut Bar, click General tab, double-click Blank Document icon

3. On Start menu point to Programs, click Microsoft Word

FIGURE 1-5

The document window contains several elements commonly found in other applications, as well as some elements unique to Word. The main elements of the Word document window are the insertion point, end mark, mouse pointer, rulers, scroll bars, and status bar (see Figure 1-4 on the previous page).

INSERTION POINT The **insertion point** is a blinking vertical bar that indicates where text will be inserted as you type. As you type, the insertion point moves to the right and, when you reach the end of a line, it moves downward to the next line. You also can insert graphics, tables, and other items at the location of the insertion point.

END MARK The **end mark** is a short horizontal line that indicates the end of your document. Each time you begin a new line, the end mark moves downward.

MOUSE POINTER The **mouse pointer** becomes different shapes depending on the task you are performing in Word and the pointer's location on the screen. The mouse pointer in Figure 1-4 has the shape of an I-beam. Other mouse pointer shapes are described as they appear on the screen during this and subsequent projects.

RULERS At the top edge of the document window is the **horizontal ruler**. You use the horizontal ruler, sometimes simply called the **ruler**, to set tab stops, indent paragraphs, adjust column widths, and change page margins.

An additional ruler, called the **vertical ruler**, sometimes displays at the left edge of the window when you perform certain tasks. The purpose of the vertical ruler is discussed as it displays on the screen in a later project. If your screen displays a vertical ruler, click View on the menu bar and then click Normal.

SCROLL BARS You use the **scroll bars** to display different portions of your document in the document window. At the right edge of the document window is a vertical scroll bar, and at the bottom of the document window is a horizontal scroll bar. On both the vertical and horizontal scroll bars, the position of the **scroll box** reflects the location of the portion of the document displaying in the document window.

On the left edge of the horizontal scroll bar are four buttons you use to change the view of your document, and on the bottom of the vertical scroll bar are three buttons you can use to scroll through a document. These buttons are discussed as they are used in later projects.

STATUS BAR The status bar displays at the bottom of the document window, above the Windows taskbar. The **status bar** presents information about the location of the insertion point, the progress of current tasks, as well as the status of certain commands, keys, and buttons.

From left to right, the following information displays on the status bar in Figure 1-5: the page number, the section number, the page containing the insertion point followed by the total number of pages in the document, the position of the insertion point in inches from the top of the page, the line number and column number of the insertion point, followed by several status indicators. If you perform a task that requires several seconds (such as saving a document), the status bar displays a message informing you of the progress of the task.

You use the **status indicators** to turn certain keys or modes on or off. Four of these status indicators (REC, TRK, EXT, and OVR) display darkened when on and dimmed when off. For example, the dimmed OVR indicates overtype mode is off. To turn these four status indicators on or off, double-click the status indicator. These status indicators are discussed as they are used in the projects.

The next status indicators display icons as you perform certain tasks. When you begin typing in the document window, a Spelling and Grammar Status icon displays. When Word is saving your document, a Background Save Status icon displays. When you print a document, a Background Print Status icon displays.

When you point to various areas on the status bar, Word displays a ScreenTip to help you identify it. A **ScreenTip** is a short descriptive name of a button, icon, or command associated with the item to which you are pointing.

Menu Bar and Toolbars

The menu bar displays at the top of the screen just below the title bar (Figure 1-6a on the next page). The Standard toolbar and Formatting toolbar are preset to share a single row that displays immediately below the menu bar.

The Horizontal Ruler

If the horizontal ruler does not display on your screen, click View on the menu bar and then click Ruler. To hide the ruler, also click View on the menu bar and then click Ruler.

Scroll Bars

You can use the vertical scroll bar to scroll through multi-page documents. As you drag the scroll box up or down the scroll bar, Word displays a page indicator to the left of the scroll box. If you release the mouse button, Word displays the page referenced by the page indicator in the document window.

Language Mode

If system support for multiple languages was installed on your computer, the status bar also displays the Language mode indicator, which shows the name of the language you are using to create the document.

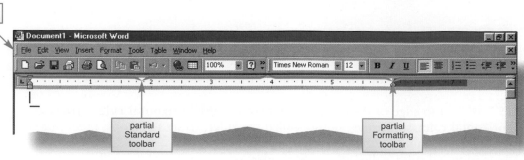

FIGURE 1-6a

MENU BAR The **menu bar** displays the Word menu names. Each menu contains a list of commands you can use to perform tasks such as retrieving, storing, printing, and formatting data in your document. When you click a menu name on the menu bar, a **short menu** displays that lists your most recently used commands (Figure 1-6b). To display a menu, such as the View menu, click the menu name on the menu bar. If you point to a command on a menu with an arrow to its right, a submenu displays from which you choose a command.

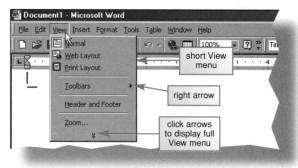

FIGURE 1-6b

If you wait a few seconds or click the arrows at the bottom of the short menu, it expands into a full menu. A **full menu** lists all the commands associated with a menu (Figure 1-6c). You also can display a full menu immediately by double-clicking the menu name on the menu bar. In this book, when you display a menu, always display the full menu using one of these techniques:

1. Click the menu name on the menu bar and then wait a few seconds.
2. Click the menu name and then click the arrows at the bottom of the short menu.
3. Click the menu name and then point to the arrows at the bottom of the short menu.
4. Double-click the menu name.

When a full menu displays, some of the commands are recessed into lighter gray background and some also are unavailable. A recessed command is called a **hidden command** because it does not display on a short menu. As you use Word, it automatically personalizes the short menus for you based on how often you use commands. That is, as you use hidden commands, Word *unhides* them and places them on the short menu. An **unavailable command** displays dimmed, which indicates it is not available for the current selection.

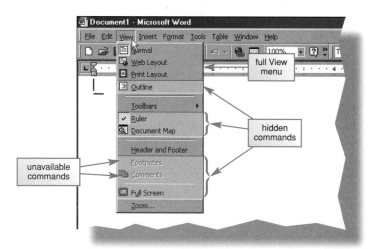

FIGURE 1-6c

TOOLBARS Word has many pre-defined, or built-in, toolbars. A **toolbar** contains buttons, boxes, and menus that allow you to perform tasks more quickly than using the menu bar and related menus. For example, to print a document, you click the Print button on the toolbar. Each button on a toolbar displays an image to help you remember its function. Also, when you point to a button or box on a toolbar, a ScreenTip (the item's name) displays below the mouse pointer (see Figure 1-10 on page WD 1.15).

Two built-in toolbars are the Standard toolbar and the Formatting toolbar. Figure 1-7a illustrates the Standard toolbar and identifies its buttons and boxes. Figure 1-7b illustrates the Formatting toolbar. Each button and box is explained in detail as it is used in the projects throughout the book.

The Standard toolbar and Formatting toolbar are preset to display docked on the same row immediately below the menu bar. A **docked toolbar** is one that is attached to the edge of the Word window. Because both of these toolbars cannot fit entirely on a single row, a portion or all of the Standard toolbar displays on the left of the row and a portion or all of the Formatting toolbar displays on the right (Figure 1-8a). The buttons that display on the toolbar are the more frequently used buttons.

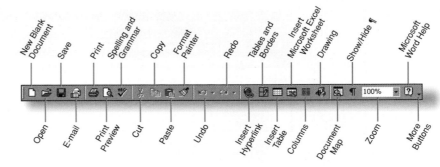

FIGURE 1-7a Standard Toolbar

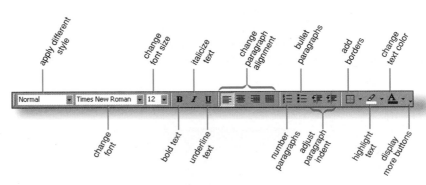

FIGURE 1-7b Formatting Toolbar

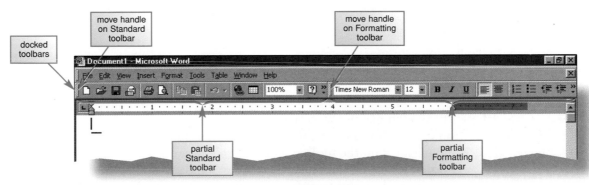

FIGURE 1-8a

To display the entire Standard toolbar, double-click its **move handle**, which is the vertical bar at the left edge of a toolbar. When you display the complete Standard toolbar, only a portion of the Formatting toolbar displays (Figure 1-8b). To display the entire Formatting toolbar, double-click its move handle. When you display the complete Formatting toolbar, only a portion of the Standard toolbar displays (Figure 1-8c on the next page).

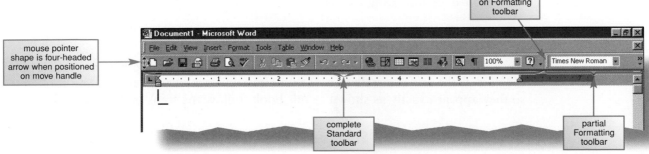

FIGURE 1-8b

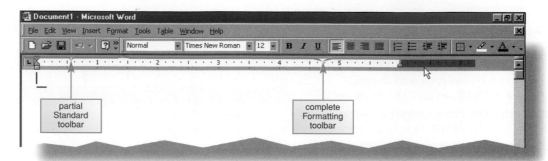

FIGURE 1-8c

An alternative to double-clicking the move handle to display an entire toolbar is to click the More Buttons button at the right edge of the toolbar. When you click a toolbar's **More Buttons** button, Word displays a **More Buttons list** that contains the toolbar's hidden buttons (Figure 1-8d).

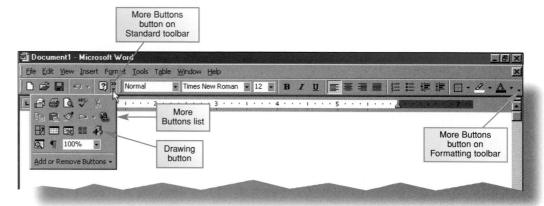

FIGURE 1-8d

As with menus, Word personalizes toolbars. That is, once you click a hidden button in the More Buttons list, Word removes the button from the More Buttons list and places it on the toolbar. For example, if you click the Drawing button in Figure 1-8d, Word displays this button on the Standard toolbar and removes a less frequently used button to make room for the Drawing button. By adapting to the way you work, this intelligent personalization feature of Word is designed to increase your productivity.

Additional toolbars may display on the Word screen, depending on the task you are performing. These additional toolbars display either stacked below the row containing the Standard and Formatting toolbars or floating in the Word window. A **floating toolbar** is not attached to an edge of the Word window. You can rearrange the order of docked toolbars and can move floating toolbars anywhere in the Word window. Later in this book, steps are presented that show you how to float a docked toolbar or dock a floating toolbar.

Resetting Menus and Toolbars

Each project in this book begins with the menu bars and toolbars appearing as they did at the initial installation of the software. To reset your menus and toolbars so they appear exactly as shown in this book, follow the steps in Appendix C.

Displaying the Entire Standard Toolbar

Perform the following step to display the entire Standard toolbar.

To Display the Entire Standard Toolbar

1 **Double-click the move handle on the Standard toolbar.**

Word displays the entire Standard toolbar (Figure 1-9).

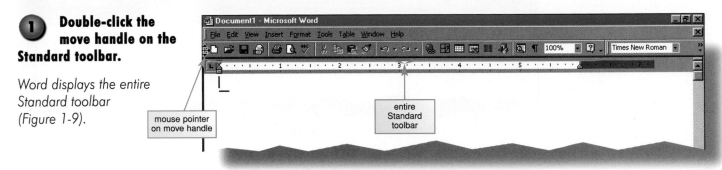

mouse pointer on move handle

entire Standard toolbar

FIGURE 1-9

Zooming Page Width

Depending on your Windows and Word settings, the horizontal ruler at the top of the document window may show more inches or fewer inches than the ruler shown in Figure 1-9. The more inches of ruler that display, the smaller the text will be on the screen. The fewer inches of ruler that display, the larger the text will be on the screen. To minimize eyestrain, the projects in this book display the text as large as possible without extending the right margin beyond the right edge of the document window.

Two factors that affect how much of the ruler displays in the document window are the Windows screen resolution and the Word zoom percentage. The screens in this book use a resolution of 800 x 600. With this resolution, you can increase the preset zoom percentage beyond 100% so that the right margin extends to the edge of the document window. To increase or decrease the size of the displayed characters to a point where both the left and right margins are at the edges of the document window, use the **zoom page width** command as shown in the following steps.

Steps **To Zoom Page Width**

1 **Point to the Zoom box arrow on the Standard toolbar.**

The mouse pointer shape is a left-pointing block arrow when positioned on a toolbar button or box (Figure 1-10). When you point to a toolbar button or box, Word displays a ScreenTip.

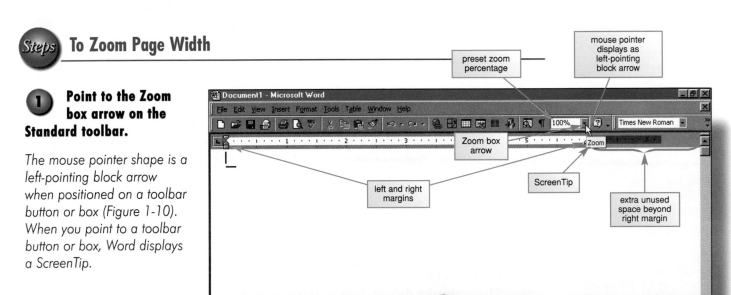

mouse pointer displays as left-pointing block arrow

preset zoom percentage

Zoom box arrow

left and right margins

ScreenTip

extra unused space beyond right margin

FIGURE 1-10

Click the Zoom box arrow.

Word displays a list of available zoom percentages and the Page Width option in the Zoom list (Figure 1-11).

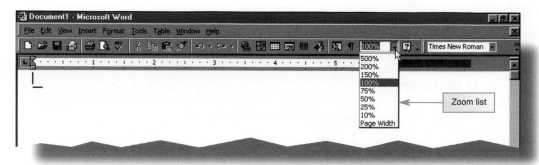

FIGURE 1-11

 Point to Page Width in the Zoom list.

Word highlights Page Width in the Zoom list (Figure 1-12).

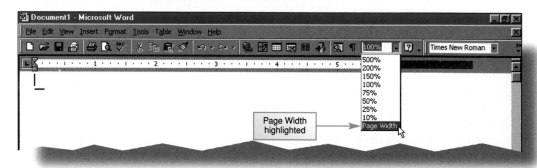

FIGURE 1-12

 Click Page Width.

Word extends the right margin to the right edge of the document window (Figure 1-13).

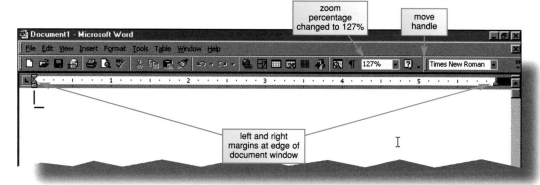

FIGURE 1-13

 Other Ways

1. On View menu click Zoom, select Page Width, click OK button

 **More About**

Zooming

If you want to zoom to a percentage not displayed in the Zoom list, you can click the Zoom box on the Standard toolbar, type the desired percentage, and then press the ENTER key; or click view on the menu bar, click Zoom, and then enter the desired zoom percentage.

If your Zoom list (Figure 1-12) displayed additional options, click View on the menu bar and then click Normal.

The Zoom box in Figure 1-13 displays 127%, which Word computes based on a variety of settings. Your percentage may be different depending on your system configuration.

Changing the Default Font Size

Characters that display on the screen are a specific shape, size, and style. The **font**, or typeface, defines the appearance and shape of the letters, numbers, and special characters. The preset, or **default**, font is Times New Roman (Figure 1-14). **Font size** specifies the size of the characters. Font size is determined by a measurement system called points. A single **point** is about 1/72 of one inch in height. Thus, a character with a font size of ten is about 10/72 of one inch in height.

If Word 2000 is installed on a new computer, then the default font size most likely is 12. If, however, you upgrade from a previous version of Word when installing Word 2000, your default font most likely is 10.

If more of the characters in your document require a larger font size than the default, you easily can change the default font size before you type. In Project 1, many of the characters in the announcement are a font size of 16. Follow these steps to increase the font size before you begin entering text.

Font Size

Many people need to wear reading glasses. Thus, use a font size of at least 12 in your documents. Because an announcement usually is posted on a bulletin board, its font size should be as large as possible so that all potential readers can see the announcement easily.

 To Increase the Default Font Size Before Typing

1 **Double-click the move handle on the Formatting toolbar to display the entire toolbar. Click the Font Size box arrow on the Formatting toolbar and then point to 16.**

A list of available font sizes displays in the Font Size list (Figure 1-14). The available font sizes depend on the current font, which is Times New Roman.

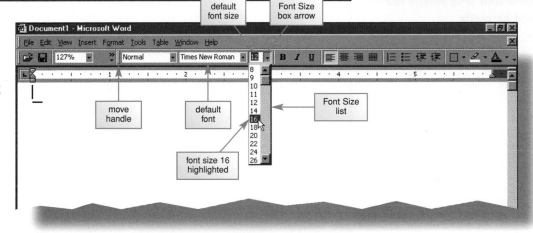

FIGURE 1-14

2 **Click 16.**

The font size for characters in this document changes to 16 (Figure 1-15). The size of the insertion point increases to reflect the new font size.

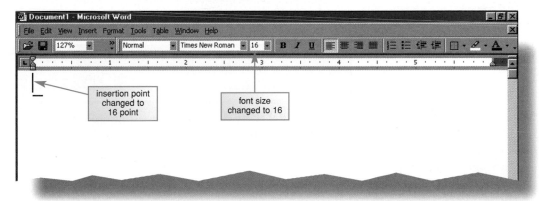

FIGURE 1-15

The new font size takes effect immediately in your document. Word uses this font size for characters you type into this announcement.

Entering Text

To create a document that contains text, you enter the text by typing on the keyboard. The example on the next page explains the steps to enter both lines of the headline of the announcement. These lines will be positioned at the left margin. Later in this project, you will format the headline so that both lines are bold and enlarged and the second line is positioned at the right margin.

Other **Ways**

1. Right-click above end mark, click Font on shortcut menu, click Font tab, select desired font size in Size list, click OK button

2. On Format menu click Font, click Font tab, select desired font size in Size list, click OK button

3. Press CTRL+SHIFT+P, type desired font size, press ENTER

4. Press CTRL+SHIFT+>

Steps **To Enter Text**

 Type Feel the Thrill **and then press the** PERIOD **key (.) three times. If you make an error while typing, press the** BACKSPACE **key until you have deleted the text in error and then retype the text correctly.**

As you type, the insertion point moves to the right (Figure 1-16).

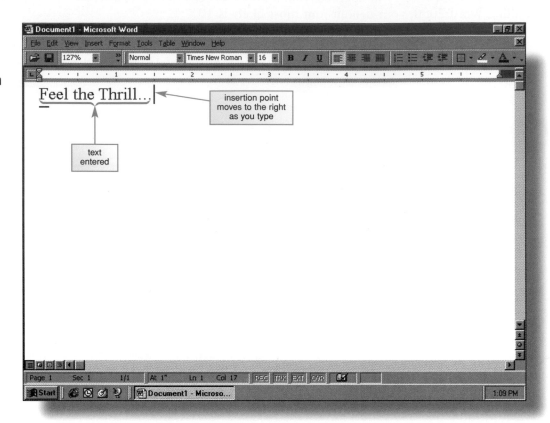

FIGURE 1-16

Press the ENTER **key.**

Word moves the insertion point to the beginning of the next line (Figure 1-17). Notice the status bar indicates the current position of the insertion point. That is, the insertion point currently is on line 2 column 1.

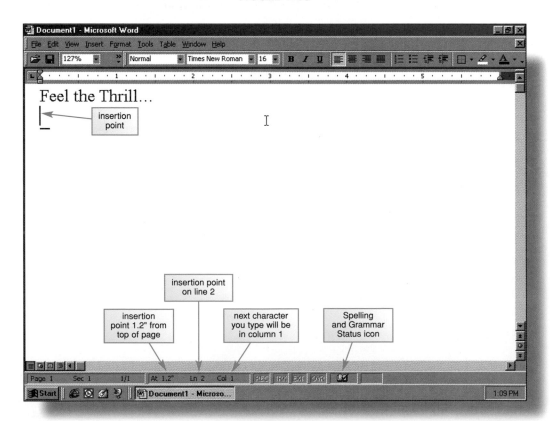

FIGURE 1-17

Press the PERIOD key three times and then type Seize the Slopes! **Press the ENTER key.**

The headline is complete (Figure 1-18). The insertion point is on line 3.

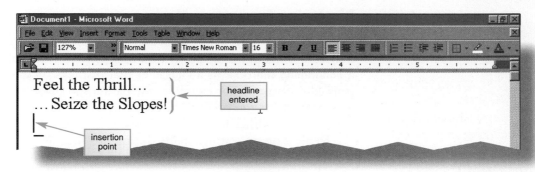

FIGURE 1-18

When you begin entering text into a document, the **Spelling and Grammar Status icon** displays at the right of the status bar (Figure 1-17). As you type, the Spelling and Grammar Status icon shows an animated pencil writing on paper, which indicates Word is checking for possible errors. When you stop typing, the pencil changes to either a red check mark or a red X. In Figure 1-17, the Spelling and Grammar Status icon displays a red check mark.

In general, if all of the words you have typed are in Word's dictionary and your grammar is correct, a red check mark displays on the Spelling and Grammar Status icon. If you type a word not in the dictionary (because it is a proper name or misspelled), a red wavy underline displays below the word. If you type text that may be grammatically incorrect, a green wavy underline displays below the text. When Word flags a possible spelling or grammar error, it also changes the red check mark on the Spelling and Grammar Status icon to a red X. As you enter text into the announcement, your Spelling and Grammar Status icon may show a red X instead of a red check mark. Later in this project, you will check the spelling of these words. At that time, the red X will return to a red check mark.

More About 2000

Entering Text

In the days of typewriters, the letter l was used for both the letter l and the numeral one. Keyboards, however, have both a numeral one and the letter l. Keyboards also have both a numeral zero and the letter o. Be careful to press the correct keyboard character when creating a word processing document.

Entering Blank Lines into a Document

To enter a blank line into a document, press the ENTER key without typing any text on the line. The following example explains how to enter three blank lines below the headline.

 To Enter Blank Lines into a Document

Press the ENTER key three times.

Word inserts three blank lines into your document below the headline (Figure 1-19).

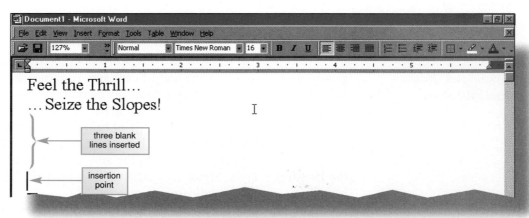

FIGURE 1-19

Displaying Formatting Marks

To indicate where in the document you press the ENTER key or SPACEBAR, you may find it helpful to display formatting marks. A **formatting mark**, sometimes called a **nonprinting character**, is a character that displays on the screen but is not visible on a printed document. For example, the paragraph mark (¶) is a formatting mark that indicates where you pressed the ENTER key. A raised dot (•) shows where you pressed the SPACEBAR. Other formatting marks are discussed as they display on the screen.

Depending on settings made during previous Word sessions, your screen may already display formatting marks (see Figure 1-21). If the formatting marks are not already displaying on your screen, perform the following steps to display them.

 To Display Formatting Marks

1 **Double-click the move handle on the Standard toolbar to display the entire toolbar. Point to the Show/Hide ¶ button on the Standard toolbar (Figure 1-20).**

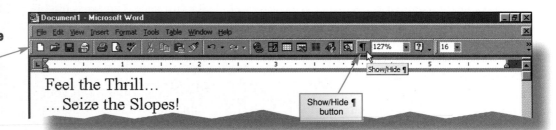

FIGURE 1-20

2 **If it is not already recessed, click the Show/Hide ¶ button.**

Word *recesses*, or pushes in, the Show/Hide ¶ button on the Standard toolbar and displays formatting marks on the screen (Figure 1-21).

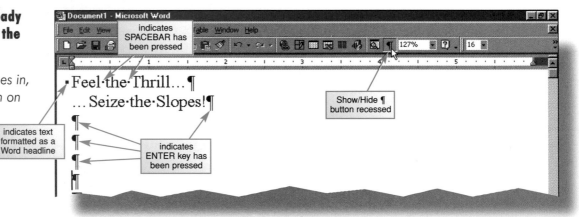

FIGURE 1-21

Other **Ways**

1. On Tools menu click Options, click View tab, click All, click OK button
2. Press CTRL+SHIFT+*

Notice several changes to your Word document window (Figure 1-21). A paragraph mark displays at the end of each line to indicate you pressed the ENTER key. Each time you press the ENTER key, Word creates a new paragraph. Because you changed the font size, the paragraph marks are 16 point. Notice Word places a paragraph mark above the end mark – you cannot delete this paragraph mark. Between each word, a raised dot appears, indicating you pressed the SPACEBAR. A small square at the beginning of the first line in the announcement indicates it is formatted using the Heading 1 style. Styles are discussed in a later project. Finally, the Show/Hide ¶ button is recessed to indicate it is selected.

If you feel the formatting marks clutter your screen, you can hide them by clicking the Show/Hide ¶ button again. It is recommended that you display formatting marks; therefore, the document windows presented in this book show the formatting marks.

Entering More Text

The body title (SUMMIT PEAK RESORT) in the announcement is capitalized. The next step is to enter this body title in all capital letters into the document window as explained below.

TO ENTER MORE TEXT

 1 Press the CAPS LOCK key on the keyboard to turn on capital letters. Verify the CAPS LOCK indicator is lit on your keyboard.

2 Type SUMMIT PEAK RESORT and then press the CAPS LOCK key to turn off capital letters.

3 Press the ENTER key twice.

The body title displays on line 6 as shown in Figure 1-22 below.

Using Wordwrap

Wordwrap allows you to type words in a paragraph continually without pressing the ENTER key at the end of each line. When the insertion point reaches the right margin, Word positions it automatically at the beginning of the next line. As you type, if a word extends beyond the right margin, Word also positions that word automatically on the next line with the insertion point.

Thus, as you enter text using Word, do not press the ENTER key when the insertion point reaches the right margin. Because Word creates a new paragraph each time you press the ENTER key, press the ENTER key only in these circumstances:

1. To insert blank lines into a document
2. To begin a new paragraph
3. To terminate a short line of text and advance to the next line
4. In response to certain Word commands

Perform the following step to become familiar with wordwrap.

More About

Wordwrap

Your printer controls where wordwrap occurs for each line in your document. For this reason, it is possible that the same document could word-wrap on different words if printed on different printers.

Steps **To Wordwrap Text as You Type**

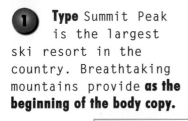 **1** **Type** Summit Peak is the largest ski resort in the country. Breathtaking mountains provide **as the beginning of the body copy.**

Word wraps the word, mountains, to the beginning of line 9 because it is too long to fit on line 8 (Figure 1-22). Your document may wordwrap differently depending on the type of printer you are using.

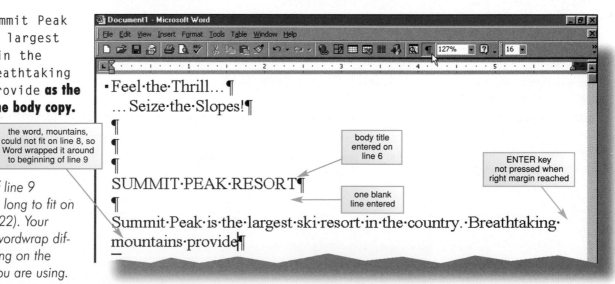

FIGURE 1-22

Checking Spelling Automatically as You Type

As you type text into the document window, Word checks your typing for possible spelling and grammar errors. If a word you type is not in the dictionary, a red wavy underline displays below it. Likewise, if text you type contains possible grammar errors, a green wavy underline displays below the text. In both cases, the Spelling and Grammar Status icon on the status bar displays a red X, instead of a check mark. Although you can check the entire document for spelling and grammar errors at once, you also can check these errors immediately.

To verify that the check spelling as you type feature is enabled, right-click the Spelling and Grammar Status icon on the status bar and then click Options on the shortcut menu. When the Spelling & Grammar dialog box displays, be sure Check spelling as you type has a check mark and Hide spelling errors in this document does not have a check mark.

When a word is flagged with a red wavy underline, it is not in Word's dictionary. A flagged word, however, is not necessarily misspelled. For example, many names, abbreviations, and specialized terms are not in Word's main dictionary. In these cases, you tell Word to ignore the flagged word. As you type, Word also detects duplicate words. For example, if your document contains the phrase, to the the store, Word places a red wavy underline below the second occurrence of the word, the. To display a list of suggested corrections for a flagged word, you right-click it.

In the following example, the word, sledding, has been misspelled intentionally as sleding to illustrate Word's check spelling as you type feature. If you are doing this project on a personal computer, your announcement may contain different misspelled words, depending on the accuracy of your typing.

More *About*

Entering Sentences

Word processing documents use variable character fonts; for example, the letter w takes up more space than the letter i. With these fonts, it often is difficult to determine how many times the SPACEBAR has been pressed between sentences. Thus, the rule is to press the SPACEBAR only once after periods, colons, and other punctuation marks.

Steps **To Check Spelling as You Type**

① Press the SPACEBAR once. Type more than 5,200 acres of groomed slopes and pristine lakes for skiing, sleding, **and then press the SPACEBAR.**

Word flags the misspelled word, sleding, by placing a red wavy underline below it (Figure 1-23). Notice the Spelling and Grammar Status icon on the status bar now displays a red X, indicating Word has detected a possible spelling or grammar error.

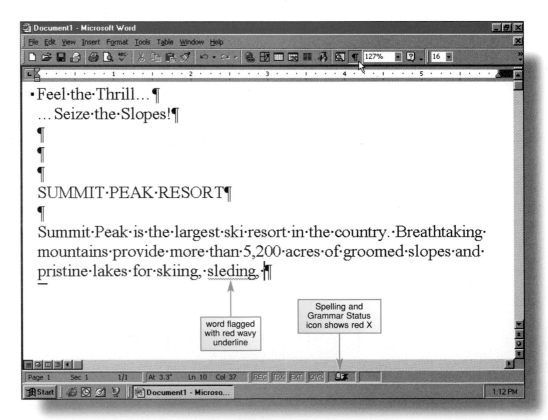

FIGURE 1-23

2 **Position the mouse pointer in the flagged word (sleding, in this case).**

The mouse pointer's shape is an I-beam when positioned in a word (Figure 1-24).

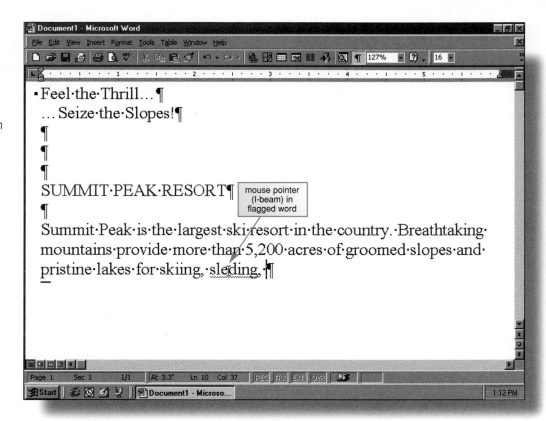

FIGURE 1-24

3 **Right-click the flagged word, sleding. When the shortcut menu displays, point to sledding.**

Word displays a shortcut menu that lists suggested spelling corrections for the flagged word (Figure 1-25).

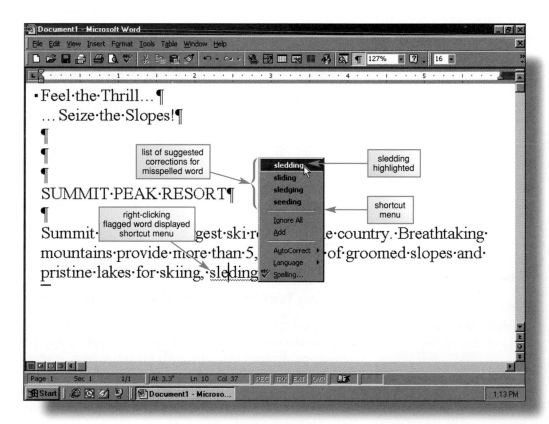

FIGURE 1-25

4 **Click sledding. Press the END key and then type the remainder of the sentence:** snowboarding, ice skating, and ice fishing.

Word replaces the misspelled word with the selected word on the shortcut menu (Figure 1-26). Word replaces the red X with a check mark on the Spelling and Grammar Status icon.

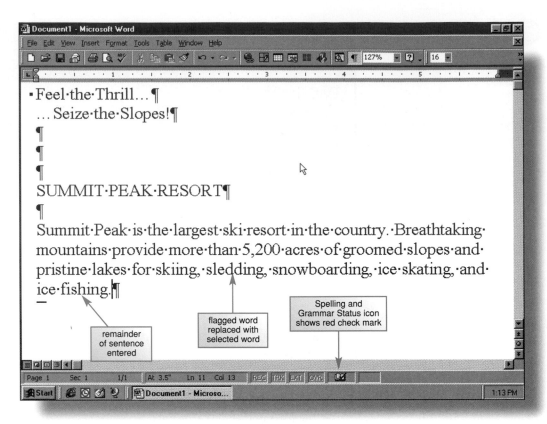

FIGURE 1-26

If the word actually is spelled correctly and, for example, is a proper name, you can right-click it and then click Ignore All on the shortcut menu (Figure 1-25 on the previous page). If, when you right-click the misspelled word, your desired correction is not in the list on the shortcut menu, you can click outside the shortcut menu to make the menu disappear and then retype the correct word, or you can click Spelling on the shortcut menu to display the Spelling dialog box. The Spelling dialog box is discussed in Project 2.

If you feel the wavy underlines clutter your document window, you can hide them temporarily until you are ready to check for spelling errors. To hide spelling errors, right-click the Spelling and Grammar Status icon on the status bar and then click Hide Spelling Errors on the shortcut menu. To hide grammar errors, right-click the Spelling and Grammar Status icon on the status bar and then click Hide Grammatical Errors on the shortcut menu.

Entering Text that Scrolls the Document Window

As you type more lines of text than Word can display in the document window, Word **scrolls** the top portion of the document upward off the screen. Although you cannot see the text once it scrolls off the screen, it remains in the document. You have learned that the document window allows you to view only a portion of your document at one time (Figure 1-5 on page WD 1.10).

Perform the following step to enter text that scrolls the document window.

To Enter Text that Scrolls the Document Window

1 Press the **ENTER** key twice. Type Summit Peak offers a range of vacation packages for every taste and budget, from traditional ski lodges to luxurious condominiums. Add transportation, meals, lift tickets, gear, and lessons for an exceptional value. **Press the ENTER key twice. Type** Call (970) 555-SNOW for reservations.

Word scrolls the headline off the top of the screen (Figure 1-27). Your screen may scroll differently depending on the type of monitor you are using.

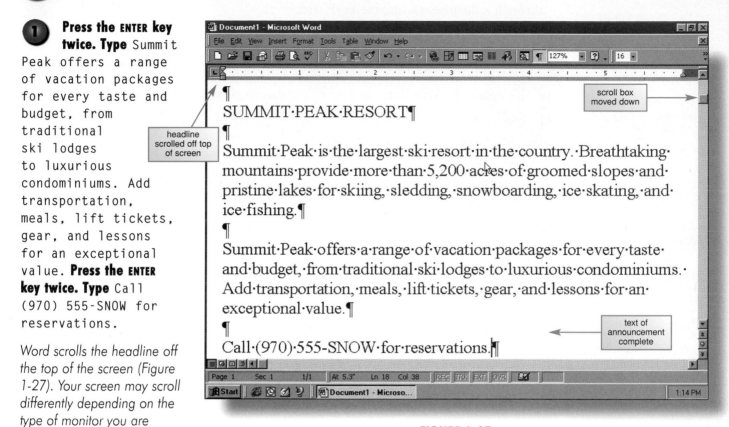

FIGURE 1-27

When Word scrolls text off the top of the screen, the scroll box on the scroll bar at the right edge of the document window moves downward (Figure 1-27). The **scroll box** indicates the current relative location of the insertion point in the document. You may use either the mouse or the keyboard to move the insertion point to a different location in a document.

With the mouse, you use the scroll arrows or the scroll box to display a different portion of the document in the document window, and then click the mouse to move the insertion point to that location. Table 1-1 explains various techniques for vertically scrolling with the mouse.

More *About*

Microsoft IntelliMouse®

For more information on the scrolling with the Microsoft IntelliMouse, visit the Word 2000 More About Web page (www.scsite.com/wd2000/more.htm) and then click Microsoft IntelliMouse.

Table 1-1 Techniques for Scrolling with the Mouse	
SCROLL DIRECTION	**MOUSE ACTION**
Up	Drag the scroll box upward.
Down	Drag the scroll box downward.
Up one screen	Click anywhere above the scroll box on the vertical scroll bar.
Down one screen	Click anywhere below the scroll box on the vertical scroll bar.
Up one line	Click the scroll arrow at the top of the vertical scroll bar.
Down one line	Click the scroll arrow at the bottom of the vertical scroll bar.

When you use the keyboard to scroll, the insertion point moves automatically when you press the appropriate keys. Table 1-2 outlines various techniques to scroll through a document using the keyboard.

Table 1-2   Techniques for Scrolling with the Keyboard

SCROLL DIRECTION	KEY(S) TO PRESS	SCROLL DIRECTION	KEY(S) TO PRESS
Left one character	LEFT ARROW	Down one paragraph	CTRL+DOWN ARROW
Right one character	RIGHT ARROW	Up one screen	PAGE UP
Left one word	CTRL+LEFT ARROW	Down one screen	PAGE DOWN
Right one word	CTRL+RIGHT ARROW	To top of document window	ALT+CTRL+PAGE UP
Up one line	UP ARROW	To bottom of document window	ALT+CTRL+PAGE DOWN
Down one line	DOWN ARROW	Previous page	CTRL+PAGE UP
To end of a line	END	Next page	CTRL+PAGE DOWN
To beginning of a line	HOME	To the beginning of a document	CTRL+HOME
Up one paragraph	CTRL+UP ARROW	To the end of a document	CTRL+END

More About 2000

Saving

When you save a document, you use meaningful file names. A file name can be up to 255 characters, including spaces. The only invalid characters are back-slash (\), slash (/), colon (:), asterisk (*), question mark (?), quotation mark ("), less than symbol (<), greater than symbol (>), and vertical bar (|).

Saving a Document

As you create a document in Word, the computer stores it in memory. If you turn off the computer or if you lose electrical power, the document in memory is lost. Hence, it is mandatory to save on disk any document that you will use later. The following steps illustrate how to save a document on a floppy disk inserted in drive A using the Save button on the Standard toolbar.

Steps **To Save a New Document**

1 **Insert a formatted floppy disk into drive A. Click the Save button on the Standard toolbar.**

Word displays the Save As dialog box (Figure 1-28). The first line from the document displays high-lighted in File name text box as the default file name. With this file name selected, you can change it by immediately typing the new name.

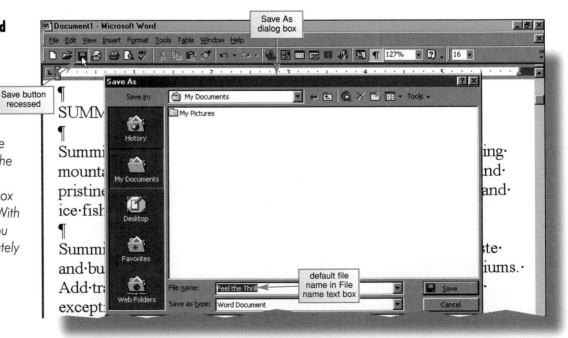

FIGURE 1-28

2 **Type** Summit Peak Announcement **in the File name text box. Do not press the ENTER key after typing the file name.**

The file name, Summit Peak Announcement, displays in the File name text box (Figure 1-29). Notice that the current save location is the My Documents folder. A **folder** is a specific location on a disk. To change to a different save location, you use the Save in box.

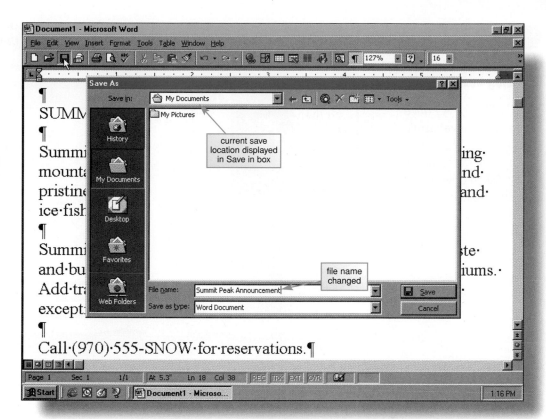

FIGURE 1-29

3 **Click the Save in box arrow and then point to 3½ Floppy (A:).**

A list of the available save locations displays (Figure 1-30). Your list may differ depending on your system configuration.

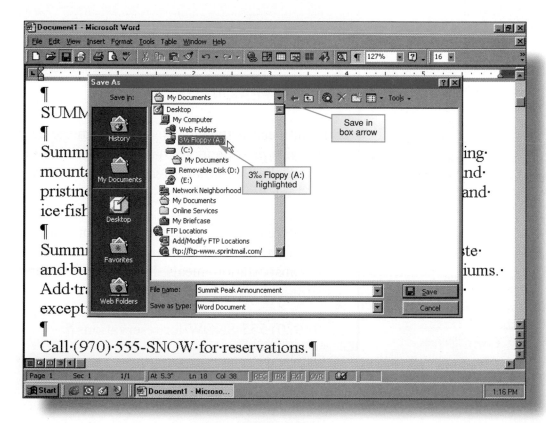

FIGURE 1-30

4 Click 3½ Floppy (A:) and then point to the Save button in the Save As dialog box.

The 3½ Floppy (A:) drive becomes the save location (Figure 1-31). The names of existing files stored on the floppy disk in drive A display. In Figure 1-31, no Word files currently are stored on the floppy disk in drive A.

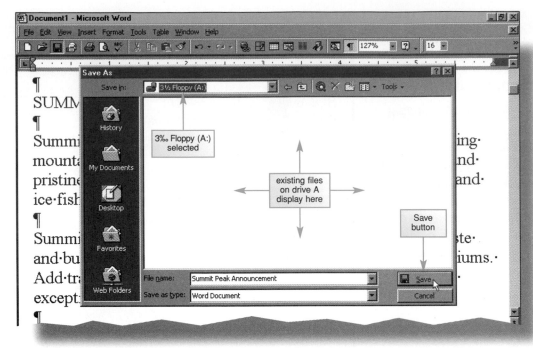

FIGURE 1-31

5 Click the Save button in the Save As dialog box.

Word saves the document on the floppy disk in drive A with the file name Summit Peak Announcement (Figure 1-32). Although the announcement is saved on a floppy disk, it also remains in main memory and displays on the screen.

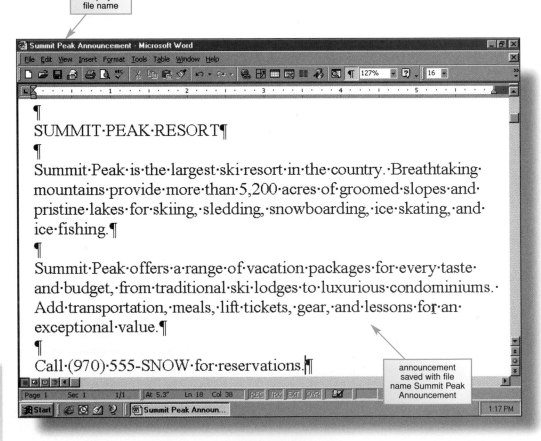

FIGURE 1-32

Formatting Paragraphs and Characters in a Document

The text for Project 1 now is complete. The next step is to format the characters and paragraphs in the announcement. Paragraphs encompass the text up to and including a paragraph mark (¶). **Paragraph formatting** is the process of changing the appearance of a paragraph. For example, you can center or indent a paragraph.

Characters include letters, numbers, punctuation marks, and symbols. **Character formatting** is the process of changing the way characters appear on the screen and in print. You use character formatting to emphasize certain words and improve readability of a document.

With Word, you can format before you type or apply new formats after you type. Earlier, you changed the font size before you typed any text, and then you entered the text. In this section, you format existing text.

Figure 1-33a shows the announcement before formatting the paragraphs and characters. Figure 1-33b shows the announcement after formatting. As you can see from the two figures, a document that is formatted not only is easier to read, but it looks more professional.

More About

Formatting

Character formatting includes changing the font, font style, font size; adding an underline, color, strikethrough, shadow, outline; embossing; engraving; making a superscript or subscript; and changing the case of the letters. Paragraph formatting includes alignment; indentation; and spacing above, below, and in between lines.

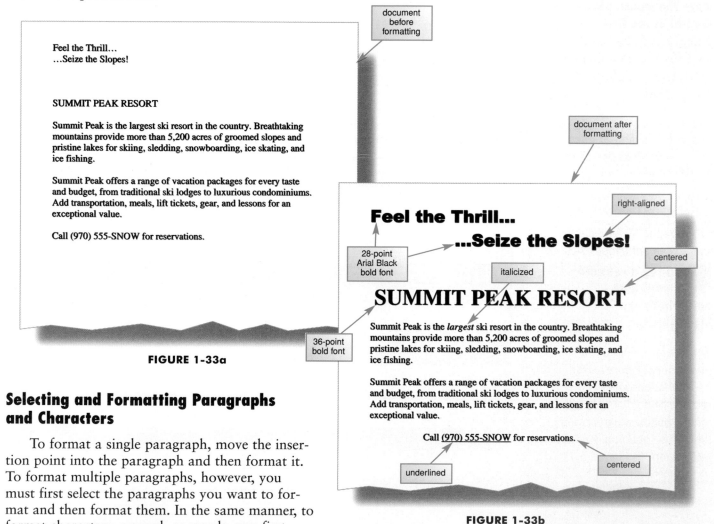

FIGURE 1-33a

FIGURE 1-33b

Selecting and Formatting Paragraphs and Characters

To format a single paragraph, move the insertion point into the paragraph and then format it. To format multiple paragraphs, however, you must first select the paragraphs you want to format and then format them. In the same manner, to format characters, a word, or words, you first must select the characters, word, or words to be formatted and then format your selection.

Selected text is highlighted. That is, if your screen normally displays dark letters on a light background, then selected text displays light letters on a dark background.

Selecting Multiple Paragraphs

The first formatting step in this project is to change the font of the characters in the headline. The headline consists of two separate lines, each ending with a paragraph mark. You have learned that each time you press the ENTER key, Word creates a new paragraph. Thus, the headline actually is two separate paragraphs.

To change the font of the characters in the headline, you must first **select**, or highlight, both paragraphs in the headline as shown in the following steps.

 To Select Multiple Paragraphs

1 Press CTRL+HOME; that is, press and hold the CTRL key, then press the HOME key, and then release both keys. Move the mouse pointer to the left of the first paragraph to be selected until the mouse pointer changes to a right-pointing block arrow.

The mouse pointer changes to a right-pointing block arrow when positioned to the left of a paragraph (Figure 1-34). CTRL + HOME positions the insertion point at the top of the document.

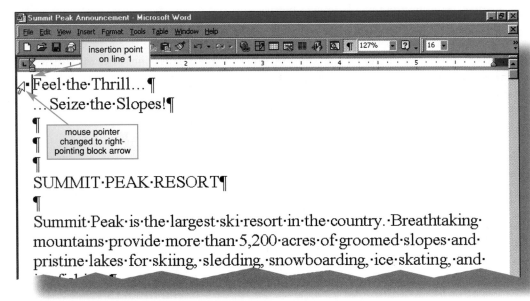

FIGURE 1-34

2 Drag downward until both paragraphs are highlighted.

Word selects both of the paragraphs (Figure 1-35). Recall that dragging is the process of holding down the mouse button while moving the mouse and finally releasing the mouse button.

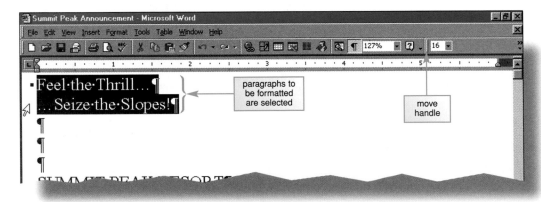

FIGURE 1-35

1. With insertion point at beginning of first paragraph, press CTRL+SHIFT+DOWN ARROW repeatedly

Changing the Font of Selected Text

You have learned that the default font is Times New Roman. Word, however, provides many other fonts to add variety to your documents. Thus, change the font of the headline in the announcement to Arial Black as shown in these steps.

To Change the Font of Selected Text

1 **Double-click the move handle on the Formatting toolbar to display the entire toolbar. While the text is selected, click the Font box arrow on the Formatting toolbar, scroll through the list until Arial Black displays, and then point to Arial Black.**

Word displays a list of available fonts (Figure 1-36). Your list of available fonts may differ, depending on the type of printer you are using.

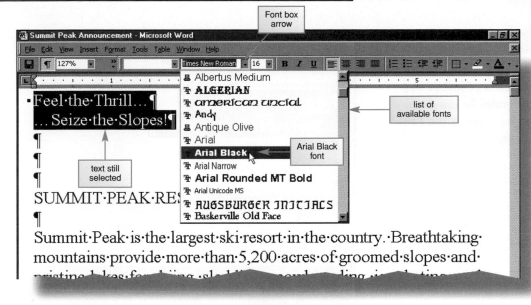

FIGURE 1-36

2 **Click Arial Black.**

Word changes the font of the selected text to Arial Black (Figure 1-37).

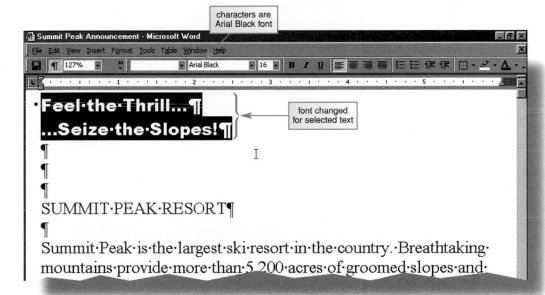

FIGURE 1-37

Changing the Font Size of Selected Text

The next step is to increase the font size of the characters in the selected headline. Recall that the font size specifies the size of the characters. Earlier in this project, you changed the font size for characters in the entire announcement to 16. To give the headline more impact, it has a font size larger than the body copy. Follow the steps on the next page to increase the font size of the headline from 16 to 28 points.

Other Ways

1. Right-click selected text, click Font on shortcut menu, click Font tab, select desired font in Font list, click OK button
2. On Format menu click Font, click Font tab, select desired font in Font list, click OK button
3. Press CTRL+SHIFT+F, press DOWN ARROW key until desired font displays, press ENTER

Steps To Change the Font Size of Selected Text

1 **While the text is selected, click the Font Size box arrow on the Formatting toolbar and then point to the down scroll arrow on the Font Size scroll bar.**

Word displays a list of the available font sizes (Figure 1-38). Available font sizes vary depending on the font and printer driver.

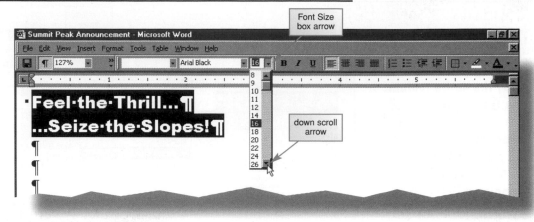

FIGURE 1-38

2 **Click the down scroll arrow on the scroll bar until 28 displays in the list and then point to 28.**

Word highlights 28 in the list (Figure 1-39).

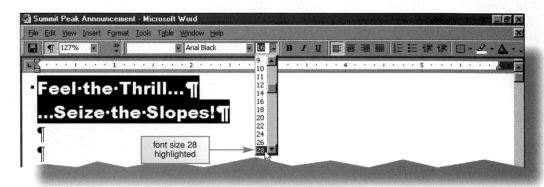

FIGURE 1-39

3 **Click 28.**

Word increases the font size of the headline from 16 to 28 (Figure 1-40). The Font Size box on the Formatting toolbar displays 28, indicating the selected text has a font size of 28.

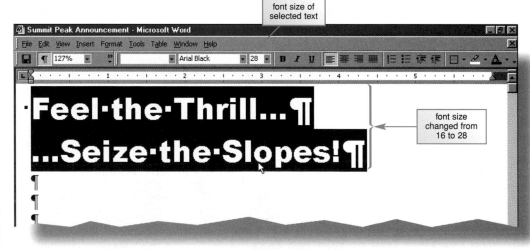

FIGURE 1-40

Other Ways

1. Right-click selected text, click Font on shortcut menu, click Font tab, select desired point size in Size list, click OK button
2. On Format menu click Font, click Font tab, select desired point size in Size list, click OK button
3. Press CTRL+SHIFT+P, type desired point size, press ENTER

Bold Selected Text

Bold characters display somewhat thicker than those that are not bold. To further emphasize the headline of the announcement, perform the following step to bold its characters.

Steps **To Bold Selected Text**

1 **While the text is selected, click the Bold button on the Formatting toolbar.**

Word formats the headline in bold (Figure 1-41). The Bold button is recessed.

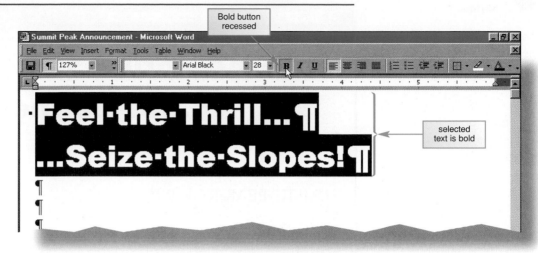

FIGURE 1-41

When the selected text is bold, the Bold button on the Formatting toolbar is recessed. If, for some reason, you wanted to remove the bold format of the selected text, you would click the Bold button a second time.

Right-Align a Paragraph

The default alignment for paragraphs is **left-aligned**; that is, flush at the left edge of the document with uneven right edges. In Figure 1-42, the Align Left button is recessed to indicate the current paragraph is left-aligned.

The second line of the headline, however, is to be **right-aligned**; that is, flush at the right edge of the document with uneven left edges. Recall that the second line of the headline is a paragraph and that paragraph formatting does not require you to select the paragraph prior to formatting. Just position the insertion point in the paragraph to be formatted and then format it accordingly.

Perform the following steps to right-align the second line of the headline.

Other **Ways**

1. Right-click selected text, click Font on shortcut menu, click Font tab, click Bold in Font style list, click OK button

2. On Format menu click Font, click Font tab, click Bold in Font style list, click OK button

3. Press CTRL+B

Steps **To Right-Align a Paragraph**

1 **Click somewhere in the paragraph to be right-aligned. Point to the Align Right button on the Formatting toolbar.**

Word positions the insertion point at the location you clicked (Figure 1-42).

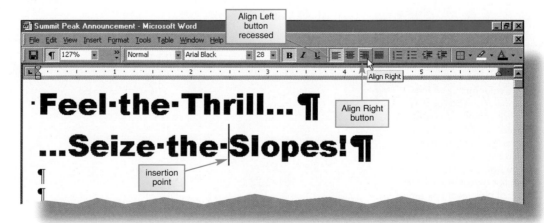

FIGURE 1-42

Click the Align Right button.

The second line of the headline is right-aligned (Figure 1-43). Notice that you did not have to select the paragraph before right-aligning it; paragraph formatting only requires the insertion point be positioned somewhere in the paragraph.

FIGURE 1-43

Other **Ways**

1. Right-click paragraph, click Paragraph on shortcut menu, click Indents and Spacing tab, click Alignment box arrow, click Right, click OK button

2. With insertion point in desired paragraph, on Format menu click Paragraph, click Indents and Spacing tab, click Alignment box arrow, click Right, click OK button

3. Press CTRL+R

When a paragraph is right-aligned, the Align Right button on the Formatting toolbar is recessed. If, for some reason, you wanted to return the selected paragraphs to left-aligned, you would click the Align Left button on the Formatting toolbar.

Center a Paragraph

The body title currently is left-aligned. Perform the following step to **center** it, that is, position the body title horizontally between the left and right margins on the page.

More About Centering

The Center button on the Formatting toolbar centers text horizontally. You also can center text vertically between the top and bottom margins. To do this, click File on the menu bar, click Page Setup, click the Layout tab, click the Vertical alignment box arrow, click Center in the list, and then click the OK button.

To Center a Paragraph

1 **Click somewhere in the paragraph to be centered. Click the Center button on the Formatting toolbar.**

Word centers the body title between the left and right margins (Figure 1-44). The Center button on the Formatting toolbar is recessed, which indicates the paragraph containing the insertion point is centered.

FIGURE 1-44

When a paragraph is centered, the Center button on the Formatting toolbar is recessed. If, for some reason, you wanted to return the selected paragraphs to left-aligned, you would click the Align Left button on the Formatting toolbar.

Undoing Commands or Actions

Word provides an **Undo button** on the Standard toolbar that you can use to cancel your recent command(s) or action(s). For example, if you format text incorrectly, you can *undo* the format and try it again. If, after you undo an action, you decide you did not want to perform the undo, you can use the **Redo button** to undo the undo. Some actions, such as saving or printing a document, cannot be undone or redone.

Perform the steps on the next page to *uncenter* the body title and then re-center it.

Other **Ways**

1. Right-click paragraph, click Paragraph on shortcut menu, click Indents and Spacing tab, click Alignment box arrow, click Centered, click OK button

2. On Format menu click Paragraph, click Indents and Spacing tab, click Alignment box arrow, click Centered, click OK button

3. Press CTRL+E

Steps **To Undo an Action**

1 **Double-click the move handle on the Standard toolbar to display the entire toolbar. Click the Undo button on the Standard toolbar.**

Word left-aligns the body title (Figure 1-45). Word returns the body title to its formatting prior to you issuing the command to center it.

2 **Click the Redo button on the Standard toolbar.**

Word re-applies the center format to the body title (see Figure 1-46).

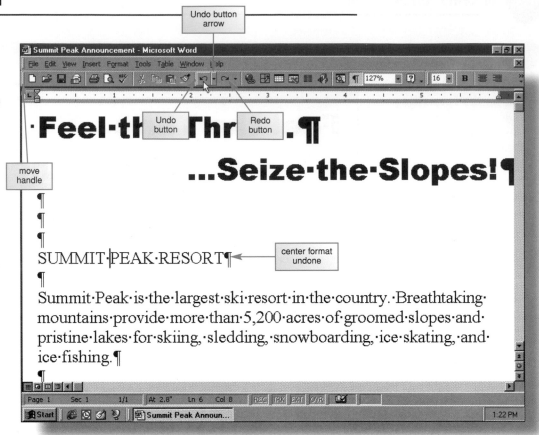

FIGURE 1-45

 Other **Ways**

1. On Edit menu click Undo
2. Press CTRL+Z

You also can cancel a series of prior actions by clicking the Undo button arrow (Figure 1-45) to display the undo actions list and then dragging through the actions you wish to be undone.

Whereas undo cancels an action you did not want to perform, Word also provides a **Repeat command**, which duplicates an action you wish to perform again. For example, if you format a paragraph and wish to format another paragraph the exact same way, you could click in the second paragraph to format and then click Repeat on the Edit menu.

Selecting a Line and Formatting It

The next series of steps selects the body title, SUMMIT PEAK RESORT, and formats the characters in it. First, you select the body title. To select the body title, perform the following step.

Steps To Select a Line

1 **Move the mouse pointer to the left of the line to be selected (SUMMIT PEAK RESORT) until it changes to a right-pointing block arrow and then click.**

The entire line to the right of the mouse pointer is highlighted (Figure 1-46).

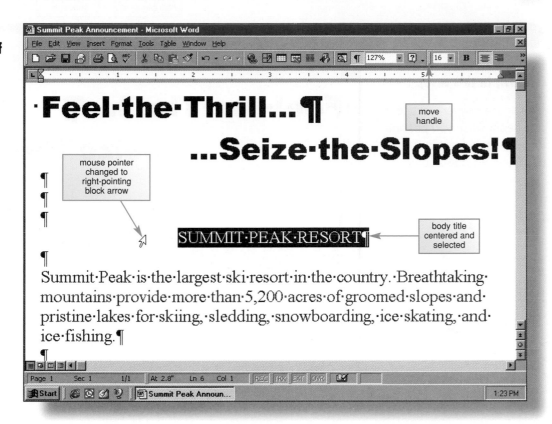

FIGURE 1-46

The next step is to increase the font size of the selected characters to 36 point and bold the selected characters, as explained in the following steps.

TO FORMAT A LINE OF TEXT

1 Double-click the move handle on the Formatting toolbar to display the entire toolbar. While the text is selected, click the Font Size box arrow on the Formatting toolbar and then scroll to 36 in the list. Click 36.

2 Click the Bold button on the Formatting toolbar.

The characters in the body title are enlarged and bold (Figure 1-47 on the next page).

Selecting a Word

To format characters in a word, you must select the entire word first. Follow the steps on the next page to select the word, largest, so you can italicize it.

Other Ways

1. Drag through the line
2. With insertion point at beginning of desired line, press SHIFT+DOWN ARROW

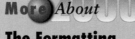

The Formatting Toolbar

Many of the buttons on the Formatting toolbar are toggles; that is, click them once to format the selected text; and click them again to remove the format from the selected text. For example, clicking the Bold button bolds selected text; clicking the Bold button again removes the bold.

To Select a Word

1 **Position the mouse pointer somewhere in the word to be formatted (largest, in this case).**

The mouse pointer's shape is an I-beam when you position it in unselected text in the document window (Figure 1-47).

FIGURE 1-47

2 **Double-click the word to be selected.**

The word, largest, is high-lighted (Figure 1-48). Notice that when the mouse pointer is positioned in a selected word, its shape is a left-pointing block arrow.

FIGURE 1-48

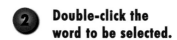

1. Drag through the word
2. With insertion point at beginning of desired word, press CTRL+SHIFT+RIGHT ARROW

Italicize Selected Text

To italicize the word, largest, perform the following step.

 To Italicize Selected Text

1 **With the text still selected, click the Italic button on the Formatting toolbar.**

Word italicizes the text (Figure 1-49). The Italic button on the Formatting toolbar is recessed.

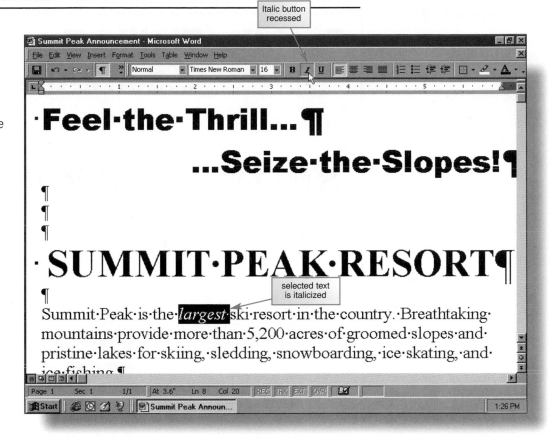

FIGURE 1-49

When the selected text is italicized, the Italic button on the Formatting toolbar is recessed. If, for some reason, you wanted to remove the italics from the selected text, you would click the Italic button a second time, or you immediately could click the Undo button on the Standard toolbar.

Scrolling

Continue formatting the document by scrolling down one screen so the bottom portion of the announcement displays in the document window. Perform the steps on the next page to display the lower portion of the document.

Other Ways

1. Right-click selected text, click Font on shortcut menu, click Font tab, click Italic in Font style list, click OK button

2. On Format menu click Font, click Font tab, click Italic in Font style list, click OK button

3. Press CTRL+I

To Scroll Through the Document

1 **Position the mouse pointer below the scroll box on the vertical scroll bar (Figure 1-50).**

2 **Click below the scroll box on the vertical scroll bar.**

Word scrolls down one screenful in the document (see Figure 1-51). Depending on your monitor type, your screen may scroll differently.

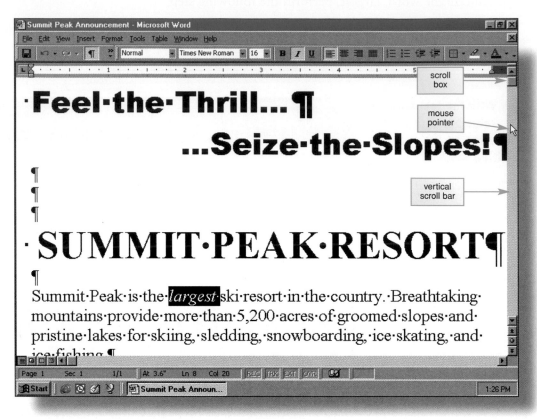

FIGURE 1-50

The next step is to center the last line of the announcement as described in the following steps.

TO CENTER A PARAGRAPH

1 Click somewhere in the paragraph to be centered.

2 Click the Center button on the Formatting toolbar.

Word centers the last line of the announcement (see Figure 1-51).

Selecting a Group of Words

The next step is to underline the telephone number in the last line of the announcement. Because the telephone number contains spaces and other punctuation, Word considers it a group of words. Thus, the telephone number is a group of words. Select the telephone number by performing the following steps.

Steps To Select a Group of Words

1 **Position the mouse pointer immediately to the left of the first character of the text to be selected.**

The mouse pointer, an I-beam, is to the left of the parenthesis in the telephone number (Figure 1-51).

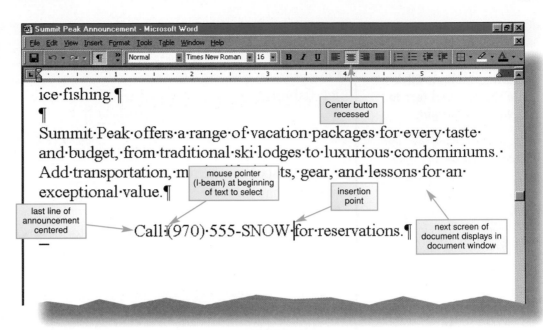

ice·fishing.¶

¶

Summit·Peak·offers·a·range·of·vacation·packages·for·every·taste· and·budget,·from·traditional·ski·lodges·to·luxurious·condominiums.· Add·transportation,·m_____ts,·gear,·and·lessons·for·an· exceptional·value.¶

Center button recessed

mouse pointer (I-beam) at beginning of text to select

insertion point

last line of announcement centered

Call·(970)·555-SNOW·for·reservations.¶

next screen of document displays in document window

FIGURE 1-51

2 **Drag the mouse pointer through the last character of the text to be selected.**

Word highlights the telephone number (Figure 1-52).

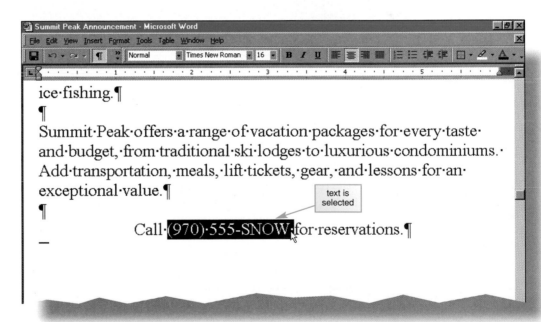

ice·fishing.¶

¶

Summit·Peak·offers·a·range·of·vacation·packages·for·every·taste· and·budget,·from·traditional·ski·lodges·to·luxurious·condominiums.· Add·transportation,·meals,·lift·tickets,·gear,·and·lessons·for·an· exceptional·value.¶

¶

text is selected

Call·(970)·555-SNOW·for·reservations.¶

FIGURE 1-52

Other Ways

1. With insertion point at beginning of first word in the group, press CTRL+SHIFT+RIGHT ARROW until words are selected

Underlining Selected Text

Underlined text prints with an underscore (_) below each character. Like bold, it used to emphasize or draw attention to specific text. Follow the step on the next page to underline the selected telephone number.

Steps To Underline Selected Text

1 **With the text still selected, click the Underline button on the Formatting toolbar. Click inside the selected text to remove the highlight.**

Word underlines the text and positions the insertion point inside the underlined text (Figure 1-53). When the insertion point is inside the underlined text, the Underline button is recessed.

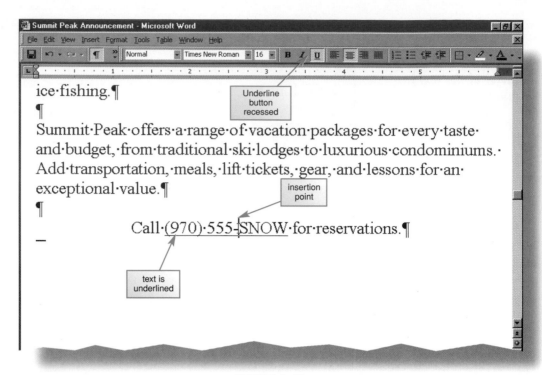

FIGURE 1-53

To remove a highlight, click the mouse. If you click inside the highlight, the Formatting toolbar displays the formatting characteristics of the characters and paragraphs containing the insertion point.

When the selected text is underlined, the Underline button on the Formatting toolbar is recessed. If, for some reason, you wanted to remove the underline from the selected text, you would click the Underline button a second time, or you immediately could click the Undo button on the Standard toolbar.

In addition to the basic underline shown in Figure 1-53, Word has many decorative underlines that are available in the Font dialog box. For example, you can use double underlines, dotted underlines, and wavy underlines. You also can change the color of an underline and instruct Word to underline only the words and not the spaces between the words.

The formatting for the announcement is now complete. The next step is to insert a graphical image into the document and then resize the image.

Inserting Clip Art into a Word Document

Files containing graphical images, also called **graphics**, are available from a variety of sources. Word 2000 includes a series of predefined graphics called **clip art** that you can insert into a Word document. Clip art is located in the **Clip Gallery**, which contains a collection of **clips**, including clip art, as well as photographs, sounds, and video clips. The Clip Gallery contains its own Help system to assist you in locating clips suited to your application.

More About

Clip Galleries

For more information on the clip galleries available for purchase, visit the Word 2000 More About Web page (www.scsite.com/wd2000/more.htm) and then click Clip Galleries.

Inserting Clip Art

The next step in the project is to insert a graphic of a skier into the announcement. Perform the following steps to insert a graphic into the document.

 To Insert Clip Art into a Document

1 **To position the insertion point where you want the clip art to be located, press CTRL+HOME and then press the DOWN ARROW key three times. Click Insert on the menu bar.**

The insertion point is positioned on the second paragraph mark below the headline, and the Insert menu displays (Figure 1-54). Remember that a short menu initially displays, which expands into a full menu after a few seconds.

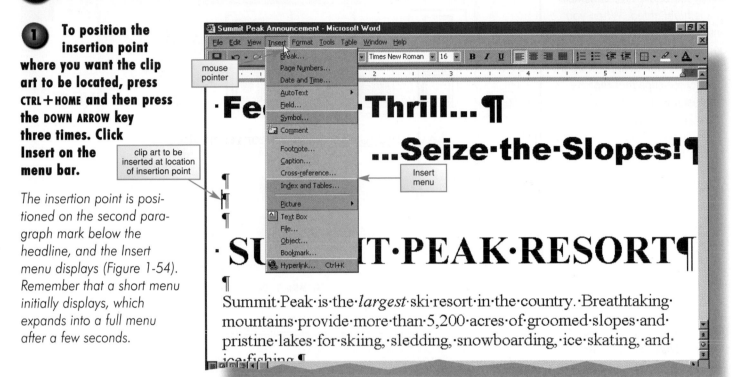

FIGURE 1-54

2 **Point to Picture and then point to Clip Art.**

The Picture submenu displays (Figure 1-55). You have learned that when you point to a command that has a small arrow to its right, Word displays a submenu associated with that command.

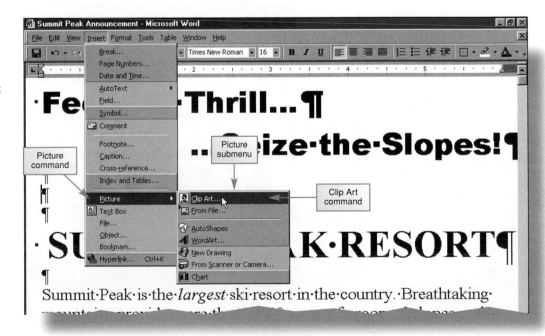

FIGURE 1-55

3 **Click Clip Art. When the Insert ClipArt window opens, click the Search for clips text box.**

Word opens the Insert ClipArt window (Figure 1-56). The text in the Search for clips text box is highlighted. When you enter a description of the desired graphic in this text box, Word searches the Clip Gallery for clips that match the description.

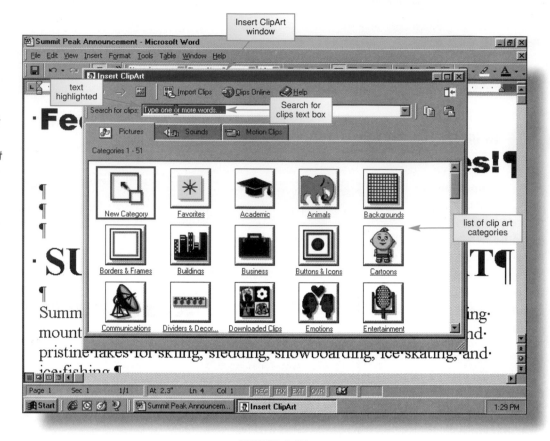

FIGURE 1-56

4 **Type ski and then press the ENTER key.**

A list of clips that match the description, ski, displays (Figure 1-57).

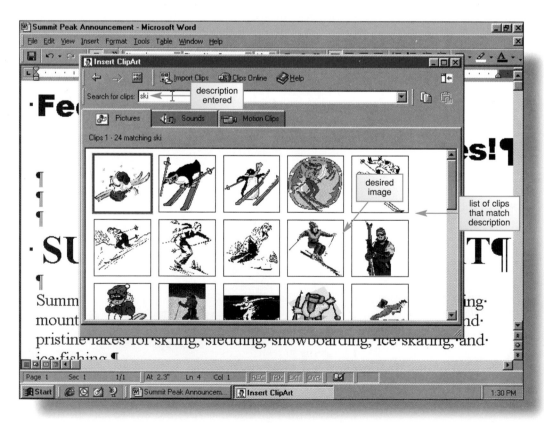

FIGURE 1-57

5 **Click the desired image and then point to the Insert clip button on the Pop-up menu.**

Word displays a Pop-up menu (Figure 1-58). The Pop-up menu contains four buttons: (1) Insert clip, (2) Preview clip, (3) Add clip to Favorites or other category, and (4) Find similar clips.

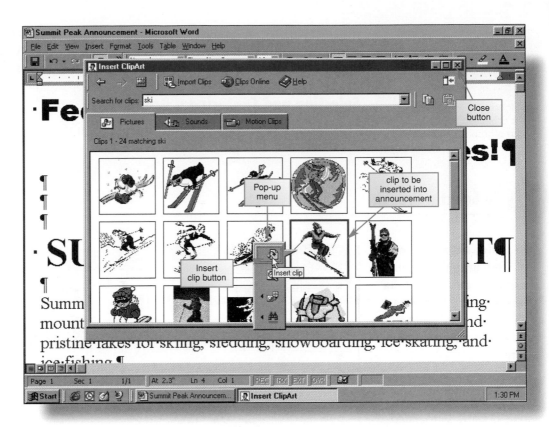

FIGURE 1-58

6 **Click the Insert clip button. Click the Close button at the right edge of the Insert ClipArt window's title bar. Press the UP ARROW key twice to display part of the headline.**

Word inserts the clip into the document at the location of the insertion point (Figure 1-59). The graphic of the skier displays below the headline in the announcement.

FIGURE 1-59

Obtaining Graphics

If you have a scanner or digital camera attached to your computer, Word can insert a graphic directly from these devices.

The clip art in the document is part of a paragraph. Because that paragraph is left-aligned, the clip art also is left-aligned. You can, however, use any of the paragraph alignment buttons on the Formatting toolbar to reposition the clip art.

Selecting and Centering a Graphic

To center a graphic, you first must select it. Perform the following steps to select and then center the graphic.

 **To Select a Graphic**

 Click anywhere in the graphic. If your screen does not display the Picture toolbar, click View on the menu bar, point to Toolbars, and then click Picture.

*Word selects the graphic (Figure 1-60). A selected graphic displays surrounded by a **selection rectangle** that has small squares, called **sizing handles**, at each corner and middle location. You use the sizing handles to change the size of the graphic. When a graphic is selected, the Picture toolbar automatically displays on the screen.*

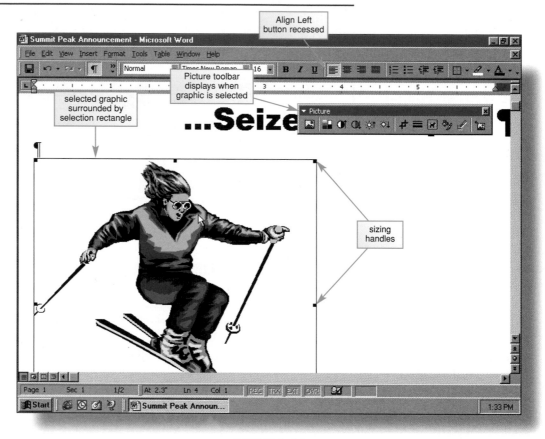

FIGURE 1-60

Graphics

Emphasize a graphic by placing it at the optical center of the page. To determine optical center, divide the page in half horizontally and vertically. The optical center is located one third of the way up the vertical line from the point of intersection of the two lines.

If the Picture toolbar covers the Standard and Formatting toolbars you can drag the title bar of the Picture toolbar to move the toolbar to a different location.

TO CENTER A SELECTED GRAPHIC

 With the graphic still selected, click the Center button on the Formatting toolbar.

Word centers the selected graphic between the left and right margins of the document (see Figure 1-61). The Center button is recessed.

When you center the graphic, Word may scroll down so the graphic is positioned at the top of the document window. The graphic is a little too large for this announcement. The next step is to resize the graphic.

Resizing a Graphic

Once you have inserted a graphic into a document, you easily can change its size. **Resizing** includes both enlarging and reducing the size of a graphic. To resize a graphic, you first must select it. The following steps show how to resize the graphic you just inserted and selected.

Resizing Graphics

When you drag the sizing handles to resize a graphic, you might distort its proportions. To maintain the proportions of the graphic, press the SHIFT key while you drag a corner sizing handle.

 To Resize a Graphic

1 **With the graphic still selected, point to the upper-left corner sizing handle.**

The mouse pointer changes to a two-headed arrow when it is on a sizing handle (Figure 1-61). To resize a graphic, you drag the sizing handles until the graphic is the desired size.

FIGURE 1-61

2 **Drag the sizing handle diagonally toward the center of the graphic until the dotted selection rectangle is positioned approximately as shown in Figure 1-62.**

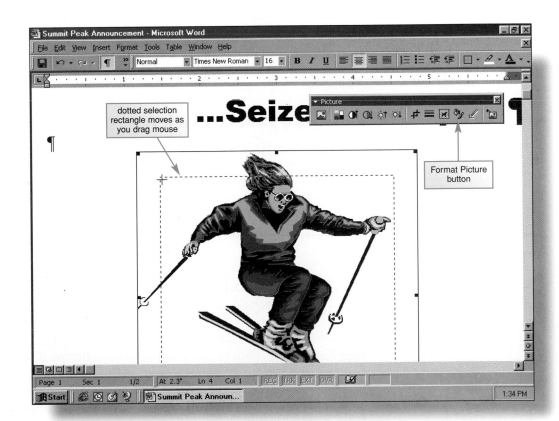

FIGURE 1-62

3 Release the mouse button. Press CTRL+HOME.

Word resizes the graphic (Figure 1-63). When you click outside of a graphic or press a key to scroll through a document, Word deselects the graphic. The Picture toolbar disappears from the screen when you deselect the graphic.

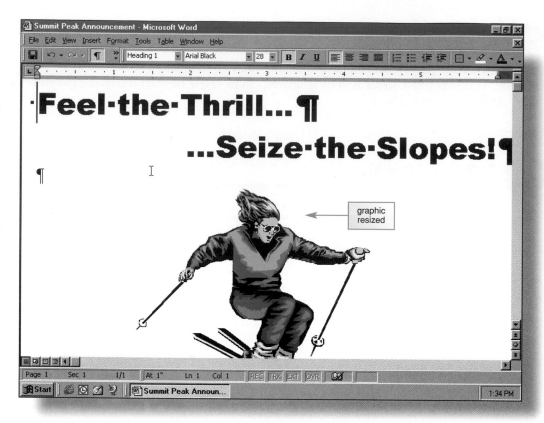

FIGURE 1-63

Other Ways

1. Click Format Picture button on Picture toolbar, click Size tab, enter desired height and width, click OK button
2. On Format menu click Picture, click Size tab, enter desired height and width, click OK button

Instead of resizing a selected graphic with the mouse, you also can use the Format Picture dialog box to resize a graphic by clicking the Format Picture button (Figure 1-62 on the previous page) on the Picture toolbar and then clicking the Size tab. Using the Size sheet, you enter exact height and width measurements. If you have a precise measurement for a graphic, use the Format Picture dialog box; otherwise, drag the sizing handles to resize a graphic.

Restoring a Resized Graphic to Its Original Size

Sometimes you might resize a graphic and realize it is the wrong size. In these cases, you may want to return the graphic to its original size and start again. You could drag the sizing handle until the graphic resembles its original size. To restore a resized graphic to its exact original size, click the graphic to select it and then click the Format Picture button on the Picture toolbar to display the Format Picture dialog box. Click the Size tab and then click the Reset button. Finally, click the OK button.

Saving an Existing Document with the Same File Name

The announcement for Project 1 now is complete. To transfer the modified document with formatting changes and graphic to your floppy disk in drive A, you must save the document again. When you saved the document the first time, you assigned a file name to it (Summit Peak Announcement). If you use the following procedure, Word automatically assigns the same file name to the document each time you subsequently save it.

To Save an Existing Document with the Same File Name

1 **Double-click the move handle on the Standard toolbar to display the entire toolbar. Click the Save button on the Standard toolbar.**

Word saves the document on a floppy disk inserted in drive A using the currently assigned file name, Summit Peak Announcement (Figure 1-64).

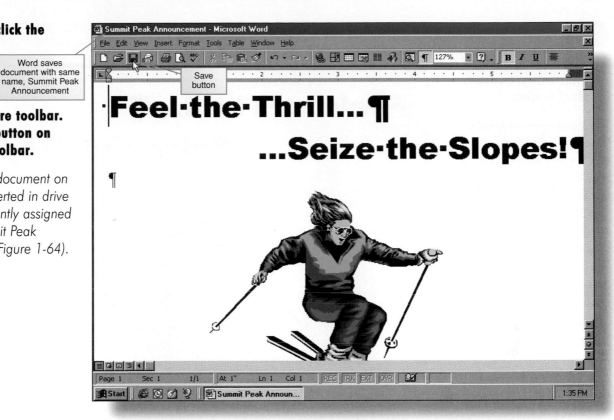

Word saves document with same name, Summit Peak Announcement

Save button

FIGURE 1-64

While Word is saving the document, the Background Save Status icon displays at the right edge of the status bar. When the save is complete, the document remains in memory and on the screen.

If, for some reason, you want to save an existing document with a different file name, click Save As on the File menu to display the Save As dialog box. Then, fill in the Save As dialog box as discussed in Steps 2 through 5 on pages WD 1.27 and WD 1.28.

Printing a Document

The next step is to print the document you created. A printed version of the document is called a **hard copy** or **printout**. Perform the steps on the next page to print the announcement created in Project 1.

Other Ways

1. On File menu click Save
2. Press CTRL+S

More About

Save As

In the Save As dialog box, you can create a new Windows folder by clicking the Create New Folder button. You also can delete or rename files by selecting the file and then clicking the Tools button arrow in the Save As dialog box. To display the Save As dialog box, click File on the menu bar and then click Save As.

Steps **To Print a Document**

1 **Ready the printer according to the printer instructions. Click the Print button on the Standard toolbar.**

The mouse pointer briefly changes to an hourglass shape as Word prepares to print the document. While the document is printing, a printer icon displays in the tray status area on the taskbar (Figure 1-65).

2 **When the printer stops, retrieve the printout (see Figure 1-1 on page WD1.7).**

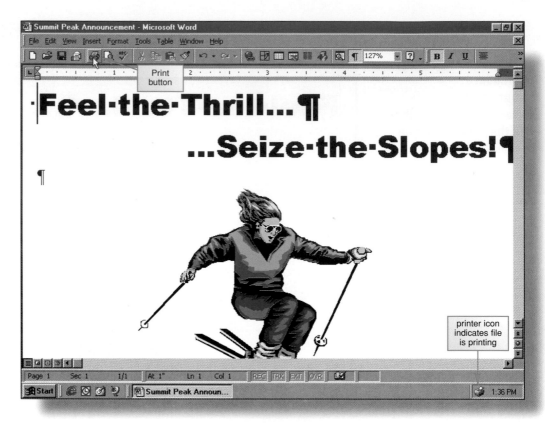

FIGURE 1-65

More About **2000**

Print Preview

To view a document before you print it, click the Print Preview button on the Standard toolbar. To return to the document window, click the Close Preview button on the Print Preview toolbar.

When you use the Print button to print a document, Word prints the entire document automatically. You then may distribute the hard copy or keep it as a permanent record of the document.

If you wanted to print multiple copies of the document, click File on the menu bar and then click Print to display the Print dialog box. This dialog box has several printing options, including specifying the number of copies to print.

If you wanted to cancel your job that is printing or one you have waiting to be printed, double-click the printer icon on the taskbar (Figure 1-65). In the printer window, click the job to be canceled and then click Cancel Printing on the Document menu.

Quitting Word

After you create, save, and print the announcement, Project 1 is complete. To quit Word and return control to Windows, perform the following steps.

Steps **To Quit Word**

1 Point to the Close button in the upper-right corner of the title bar (Figure 1-66).

2 Click the Close button.

The Word window closes.

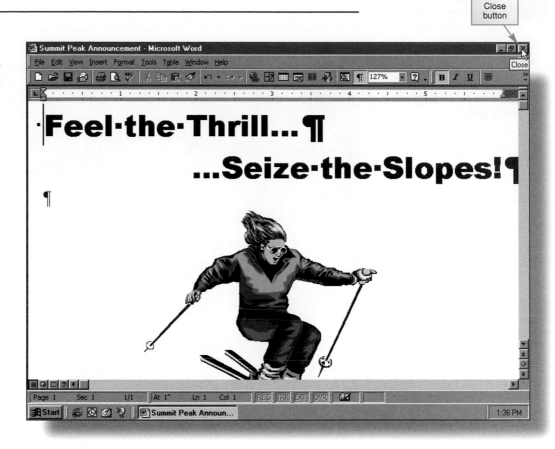

FIGURE 1-66

If you made changes to the document since the last save, Word displays dialog box asking if you want to save the changes. Clicking the Yes button saves the changes; clicking the No button ignores the changes; and clicking the Cancel button returns to the document. If you did not make any changes since you saved the document, this dialog box does not display.

You created and formatted the announcement, inserted clip art into it, printed it, and saved it. You might decide, however, to change the announcement at a later date. To do this, you must start Word and then retrieve your document from the floppy disk in drive A.

Opening a Document

Earlier, you saved the Word document created in Project 1 on a floppy disk using the file name Summit Peak Announcement. Once you have created and saved a document, you often will have reason to retrieve it from the disk. For example, you might want to revise the document or print it. The steps on the next page illustrate how to open the file Summit Peak Announcement.

 Other Ways

1. On File menu click Exit
2. Press ALT+F4

More About 2000

Opening Files

In Word, you can open a recently used file by clicking File on the menu bar and then clicking the file name on the File menu. To instruct Word to show the recently used documents on the File menu, click Tools on the menu bar, click Options, click the General tab, click Recently used file list, and then click the OK button.

Steps | To Open a Document

1 **Click the Start button on the taskbar and then point to Open Office Document (Figure 1-67).**

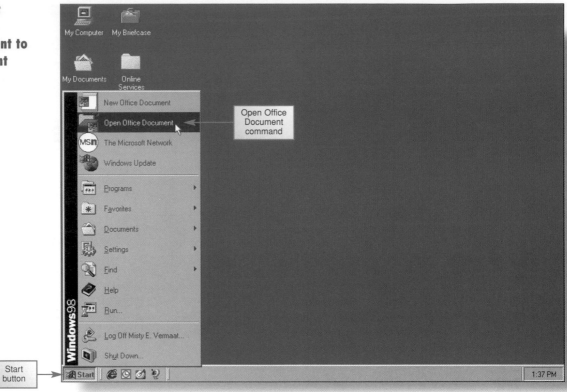

FIGURE 1-67

2 **Click Open Office Document. If necessary, click the Look in box arrow and then click 3½ Floppy (A:). If it is not selected already, click the file name Summit Peak Announcement. Point to the Open button.**

Office displays the Open Office Document dialog box (Figure 1-68). Office displays the files on the floppy disk in drive A.

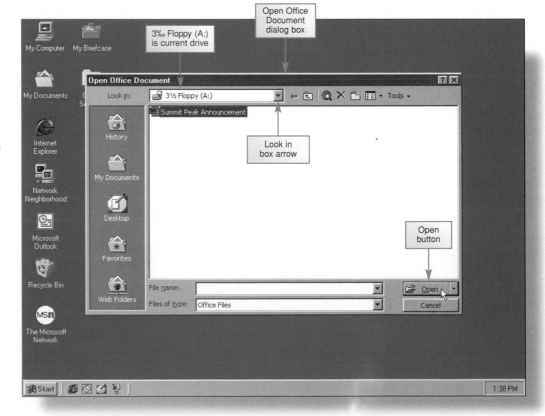

FIGURE 1-68

3 **Click the Open button.**

Office starts Word, and then Word opens the document, Summit Peak Announcement, from the floppy disk in drive A and displays the document on the screen (Figure 1-69).

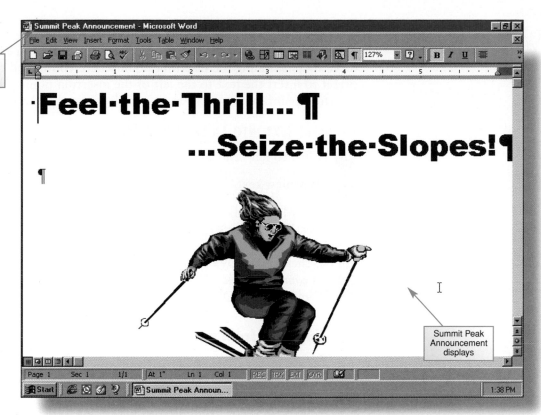

FIGURE 1-69

Correcting Errors

After creating a document, you often will find you must make changes to it. Changes can be required because the document contains an error or because of new circumstances.

Types of Changes Made to Documents

The types of changes made to documents normally fall into one of the three following categories: additions, deletions, or modifications.

ADDITIONS Additional words, sentences, or paragraphs may be required in a document. Additions occur when you omit text from a document and want to insert it later. For example, you may want to insert the word, winter, in front of vacation packages to differentiate winter packages from summer packages.

DELETIONS Sometimes, text in a document is incorrect or is no longer needed. For example, the resort might remove transportation from their package deals. In this case, you would delete the word, transportation, from the list.

MODIFICATIONS If an error is made in a document or changes take place that affect the document, you might have to revise the word(s) in the text. For example, the resort might purchase more land and have 6,500 acres of slopes and lakes; thus, you would change the number from 5,200 to 6,500.

Word provides several methods for correcting errors in a document. For each of the error correction techniques, you first must move the insertion point to the error.

Other **Ways**

1. In Microsoft Word, click Open button on Standard toolbar, select file name, click Open button in dialog box
2. In Microsoft Word, on File menu click Open, select file name, click Open button in dialog box
3. In Microsoft Word, press CTRL+O, select file name, press ENTER

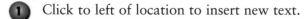

Inserting Text into an Existing Document

If you leave a word or phrase out of a sentence, you can include it in the sentence by positioning the insertion point where you intend to insert the text. Word is preset to insert the text to the left of the insertion point. The text to the right of the insertion point moves to the right and downward to accommodate the new text.

TO INSERT TEXT INTO AN EXISTING DOCUMENT

1 Click to left of location to insert new text.

2 Type new text.

In Word, the default typing mode is insert mode. In **insert mode**, as you type a character, Word inserts the character and moves all the characters to the right of the typed character one position to the right. You can change to overtype mode by double-clicking the **OVR status indicator** on the status bar (see Figure 1-4 on page WD 1.9). In **overtype mode**, Word replaces characters to the right of the insertion point. Double-clicking the OVR status indicator a second time returns you to insert mode.

Deleting Text from an Existing Document

It is not unusual to type incorrect characters or words in a document. You have learned that you can click the Undo button on the Standard toolbar to undo a command or action – this includes typing. Word also provides other methods of correcting typing errors. For example, you may want to delete certain letters or words.

TO DELETE AN INCORRECT CHARACTER IN A DOCUMENT

1 Click next to the incorrect character.

2 Press the BACKSPACE key to erase to the left of the insertion point; or press the DELETE key to erase to the right of the insertion point.

TO DELETE AN INCORRECT WORD OR PHRASE IN A DOCUMENT

1 Select the word or phrase you want to erase.

2 Right-click the selected word or phrase, and then click Cut on the shortcut menu; or click the Cut button on the Standard toolbar (Figure 1-7a on page WD 1.13); or press the DELETE key.

Closing the Entire Document

Sometimes, everything goes wrong. If this happens, you may want to close the document entirely and start over. You also may want to close a document when you are finished with it so you can begin your next document.

TO CLOSE THE ENTIRE DOCUMENT AND START OVER

1 Click File on the menu bar and then click Close.

2 If Word displays a dialog box, click the No button to ignore the changes since the last time you saved the document.

3 Click the New Blank Document button (see Figure 1-7a on page WD 1.13) on the Standard toolbar.

You also can close the document by clicking the Close button at the right edge of the menu bar.

Word Help System

At any time while you are using Word, you can get answers to questions by using the **Word Help system**. Used properly, this form of online assistance can increase your productivity and reduce your frustrations by minimizing the time you spend learning how to use Word.

The following section shows how to obtain answers to your questions using the Office Assistant. For additional information on using help, see Appendix A.

Using the Office Assistant

The **Office Assistant** answers your questions and suggests more efficient ways to complete a task. With the Office Assistant active, for example, you can type a question, word, or phrase in a text box and the Office Assistant provides immediate help on the subject. Also, as you create a document, the Office Assistant accumulates tips that suggest more efficient ways to do the tasks you completed while creating a document, such as formatting, printing, and saving. This tip feature is part of the **IntelliSense technology** that is built into Word, which understands what you are trying to do and suggests better ways to do it. When the light bulb displays above the Office Assistant, click it to see a tip.

The following steps show how to use the Office Assistant to obtain information on changing the size of a toolbar.

Steps To Obtain Help Using the Office Assistant

1 **If the Office Assistant is not on the screen, click Help on the menu bar and then click Show the Office Assistant. With the Office Assistant on the screen, click it. Type** change toolbar size **in the What would you like to do? text box. Point to the Search button (Figure 1-70).**

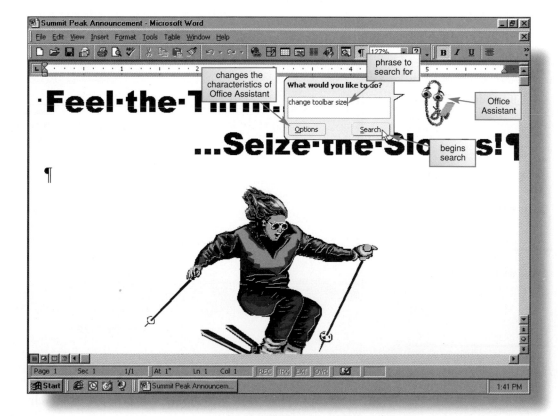

FIGURE 1-70

2 **Click the Search button. Point to Resize a toolbar in the list of topics.**

The Office Assistant displays a list of topics relating to the typed question, change toolbar size (Figure 1-71). The mouse pointer changes to a pointing hand.

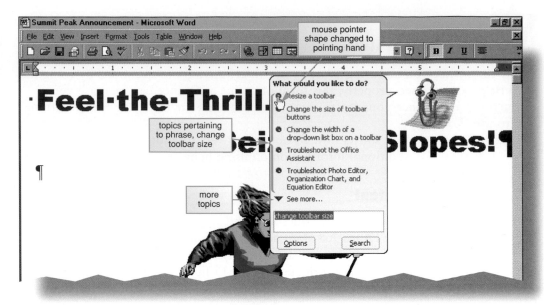

FIGURE 1-71

3 **Click Resize a toolbar. When Word opens the Word Help window, click its Maximize button. If necessary, drag the Office Assistant out of the way of the Help text.**

The Office Assistant opens a Word Help window that provides Help information on resizing toolbars (Figure 1-72).

4 **Click the Close button on the Word Help window title bar.**

The Word Help window closes and the Word document window again is active.

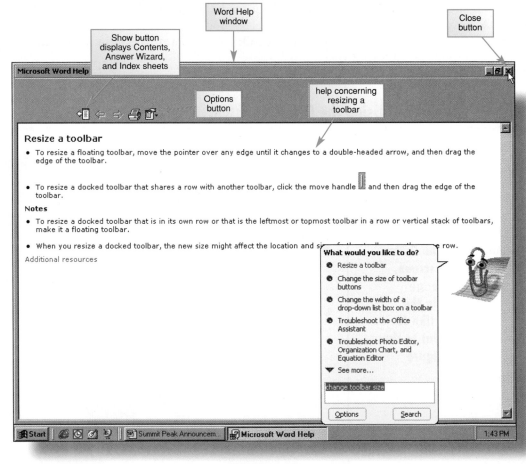

FIGURE 1-72

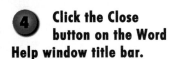

Other **Ways**

1. If the Office Assistant is on, click Microsoft Word Help button or click Microsoft Word Help on the Help menu

You can use the Office Assistant to search for Help on any topic concerning Word.

Table 1-3 summarizes the nine categories of help available to you. Because of the way the Word Help system works, please review the right-most column of Table 1-3 if you have difficulties activating the desired category of help.

Table 1-3	Word Help System		
TYPE	DESCRIPTION	HOW TO ACTIVATE	TURNING THE OFFICE ASSISTANT ON AND OFF
Answer Wizard	Similar to the Office Assistant in that it answers questions that you type in your own words.	Click the Microsoft Word Help button on the Standard toolbar. If necessary, maximize the Help window by double-clicking its title bar. Click the Answer Wizard tab.	If the Office Assistant displays, right-click it, click Options, click Use the Office Assistant to remove the check mark, click the OK button.
Contents sheet	Groups Help topics by general categories. Use when you know only the general category of the topic in question. Similar to a table of contents in a book.	Click the Microsoft Word Help button on the Standard toolbar. If necessary, maximize the Help window by double-clicking its title bar. Click the Contents tab.	If the Office Assistant displays, right-click it, click Options, click Use the Office Assistant to remove the check mark, click the OK button.
Detect and Repair	Automatically finds and fixes errors in the application.	Click Detect and Repair on the Help menu.	
Hardware and Software Information	Shows Product ID and allows access to system information and technical support information.	Click About Microsoft Word on the Help menu and then click the appropriate button.	
Index sheet	Similar to an index in a book; use when you know exactly what you want.	Click the Microsoft Word Help button on the Standard toolbar. If necessary, maximize the Help window by double-clicking its title bar. Click the Index tab.	If the Office Assistant displays, right-click it, click Options, click Use the Office Assistant to remove the check mark, click the OK button.
Office Assistant	Answers questions that you type in your own words, offers tips, and provides Help for a variety of Word features.	Click the Microsoft Word Help button on the Standard toolbar or double-click the Office Assistant icon. Some dialog boxes also include the Microsoft Word Help button.	If the Office Assistant does not display, click Show the Office Assistant on the Help menu.
Office on the Web	Used to access technical resources and download free product enhancements on the Web.	Click Office on the Web on the Help menu.	
Question Mark button and What's This? command	Used to identify unfamiliar items on the screen.	In a dialog box, click the Question Mark button and then click an item in the dialog box. Click What's This? on the Help menu, and then click an item on the screen.	
WordPerfect Help	Used to assist WordPerfect users who are learning Microsoft Word.	Click WordPerfect Help on the Help menu.	

The final step in this project is to quit Word.

TO QUIT WORD

 Click the Close button in the Word window.

The Word window closes.

Quick Reference

For a table that lists how to complete the tasks covered in this book using the mouse, menu, shortcut menu, and keyboard, visit the Shelly Cashman Series Office Web page (www.scsite.com/ off2000/qr.htm) and then click Microsoft Word 2000.

CASE PERSPECTIVE SUMMARY

Jackie is thrilled with the completed announcement. The characters in the headline and body title are large enough so students can read them from a distance and the graphic is quite eye-catching. She takes the announcement to the school's Promotions Department and receives approval to post it in several locations around campus, have it printed in the school newspaper, and mailed to each student's home. Members of the SGA assist Jackie with these activities.

Project Summary

Project 1 introduced you to starting Word and creating a document. Before entering any text in the document, you learned how to change the font size. You also learned how to save and print a document. You used Word's check spelling as you type feature. Once you saved the document, you learned how to format its paragraphs and characters. Then, you inserted and resized clip art. You learned how to move the insertion point so you could insert, delete, and modify text. Finally, you learned one way to use Word Help.

What You Should Know

Having completed this project, you now should be able to perform the following tasks:

- Bold Selected Text *(WD 1.33)*
- Center a Paragraph *(WD 1.35 and WD 1.40)*
- Center a Selected Graphic *(WD 1.46)*
- Change the Font of Selected Text *(WD 1.31)*
- Change the Font Size of Selected Text *(WD 1.32)*
- Check Spelling as You Type *(WD 1.22)*
- Close the Entire Document and Start Over *(WD 1.54)*
- Delete an Incorrect Character in a Document *(WD 1.54)*
- Delete an Incorrect Word or Phrase in a Document *(WD 1.54)*
- Display Formatting Marks *(WD 1.20)*
- Displays the Entire Standard Toolbar *(WD 1.15)*
- Enter Blank Lines into a Document *(WD 1.19)*
- Enter More Text *(WD 1.21)*
- Enter Text *(WD 1.18)*
- Enter Text that Scrolls the Document Window *(WD 1.25)*
- Format a Line of Text *(WD 1.37)*
- Increase the Default Font Size Before Typing *(WD 1.17)*
- Insert Clip Art into a Document *(WD 1.43)*
- Insert Text into an Existing Document *(WD 1.54)*
- Italicize Selected Text *(WD 1.39)*
- Obtain Help Using the Office Assistant *(WD 1.55)*
- Open a Document *(WD 1.52)*
- Print a Document *(WD 1.50)*
- Quit Word *(WD 1.51)*
- Resize a Graphic *(WD 1.47)*
- Right-Align a Paragraph *(WD 1.33)*
- Save a New Document *(WD 1.26)*
- Save an Existing Document with the Same File Name *(WD 1.49)*
- Scroll Through the Document *(WD 1.40)*
- Select a Graphic *(WD 1.46)*
- Select a Group of Words *(WD 1.41)*
- Select a Line *(WD 1.37)*
- Select a Word *(WD 1.38)*
- Select Multiple Paragraphs *(WD 1.30)*
- Start Word *(WD 1.8)*
- Underline Selected Text *(WD 1.42)*
- Undo an Action *(WD 1.36)*
- Wordwrap Text as You Type *(WD 1.21)*
- Zoom Page Width *(WD 1.15)*

More About 2000

Microsoft Certification

The Microsoft Office User Specialist (MOUS) Certification program provides an opportunity for you to obtain a valuable industry credential — proof that you have the Word 2000 skills required by employers. For more information, see Appendix D or visit the Shelly Cashman Series MOUS Web page at www.scsite.com/off2000/cert.htm.

Apply Your Knowledge

➕ Project Reinforcement at www.scsite.com/off2000/reinforce.htm

1 Checking Spelling of a Document

Instructions: Start Word. Open the document, Meeting Announcement, on the Data Disk. If you did not download the Data Disk, see the inside back cover for instructions for downloading the Data Disk or see your instructor.

As shown in Figure 1-73, the document is a meeting announcement that contains many spelling and grammar errors. You are to right-click each of the errors and then click the appropriate correction on the shortcut menu.

You have learned that Word flags spelling errors with a red wavy underline. A green wavy underline indicates that Word has detected a possible grammar error. *Hint:* If your screen does not display the grammar errors, use the Word Help System to determine how to enable the check grammar feature. Perform the following tasks:

1. Position the insertion point at the beginning of the document. Right-click the flagged word, Notise. Change the incorrect word, Notise, to Notice by clicking Notice on the shortcut menu.
2. Right-click the flagged word, Januery. Change the incorrect word, Januery, to January by clicking January on the shortcut menu.
3. Right-click the flagged word, be. Click Delete Repeated Word on the shortcut menu to remove the duplicate occurrence of the word, be.

spelling and grammar errors are flagged on printout to help you identify them

Meeting Notise
All Employees

NEW HEALTH INSURANCE PLAN

Effective Januery 1, Kramer Enterprises will be be switching to a new insurance providor for major medical coverage. At that time, all employees must begin submitting claims and directing all claim-related questions to ofr new provider, Health America.

Representative's from Health America will be visiting our office on Friday, December 1, to discuss our nesw insurance plan. Please plan to attend either the morning session at 9:00 a.m. or the afternoon session at 2:00 p.m. Both session will be in the lunchroom.

insurance cards will be distributed at these meetings!

FIGURE 1-73

4. Right-click the flagged word, providor. Change the incorrect word, providor, to provider by clicking provider on the shortcut menu.
5. Right-click the flagged word, ofr. Because the shortcut menu does not display the correct word, click outside the shortcut menu to remove it from the screen. Correct the misspelled word, ofr, to the correct word, our, by removing the letter f and replacing it with the letter u.
6. Right-click the flagged word, Representative's. Change the word, Representative's, to its correct plural by clicking the word, Representatives, on the shortcut menu.
7. Right-click the incorrect word, nesw. Change the incorrect word, nesw, to new by clicking new on the shortcut menu.
8. Right-click the flagged word, session. Change the incorrect word, session, to its plural by clicking sessions on the shortcut menu.
9. Right-click the flagged word, insurance. Capitalize the word, insurance, by clicking Insurance on the shortcut menu.
10. Click File menu on the menu bar and then click Save As. Save the document using Corrected Meeting Announcement as the file name.
11. Print the revised document.

In the Lab

1 Creating an Announcement with Clip Art

Problem: The Director of the Harbor Theatre Company at your school has requested that each student in your Marketing 102 class prepare an announcement for auditions of its upcoming play. The student that creates the winning announcement will receive five complimentary tickets to the play. You prepare the announcement shown in Figure 1-74. *Hint:* Remember, if you make a mistake while formatting the announcement, you can click the Undo button on the Standard toolbar to undo your mistake.

FIGURE 1-74

Instructions:

1. Change the font size from 10 to 18 by clicking the Font Size box arrow on the formatting toolbar and then clicking 18.

2. If necessary, click the Show/Hide ¶ button on Standard toolbar to display formatting marks.

3. Create the announcement shown in Figure 1-74. Enter the document first without clip art and unformatted; that is without any bold, underlined, italicized, right-aligned, or centered text. If Word flags any misspelled words as you type, check the spelling of these words and correct them.

4. Save the document on a floppy disk with Grease Announcement as the file name.

5. Select the two lines of the headline. Change their font to Broadway, or a similar font. Change their font size from 18 to 36.

6. Click somewhere in the second line of the headline. Right-align it.

7. Click somewhere in the body title line. Center it.

8. Select the body title line. Increase its font size from 18 to 26. Bold it.

9. In the first paragraph of the body copy, select the following phrase: acting, singing, and dancing auditions. Bold the phrase.

10. In the same paragraph, select the word, Grease. Italicize it.

11. In the second paragraph of the body copy, select the following phrase: Only Harbor College students. Underline the phrase.

12. Click somewhere in the last line of the announcement. Center it.

13. Insert the graphic of the drama masks between the headline and the body title line. Search for the text, drama, in the Clip Gallery to locate the graphic.

14. Click the graphic to select it. Center the selected graphic.

15. Save the announcement again with the same file name.

16. Print the announcement.

In the Lab

2 Creating an Announcement with Resized Clip Art

Problem: You are an assistant for the Marketing Manager at Taylor Business School. She has asked you to prepare an announcement for Fall Registration. The announcement must include clip art. You prepare the announcement shown in Figure 1-75. *Hint:* Remember, if you make a mistake while formatting the announcement, you can click the Undo button on the Standard toolbar to undo your mistake.

Instructions:

1. Change the font size from 10 to 18 by clicking the Font Size box arrow on the Formatting toolbar and then clicking 18.
2. If it is not already selected, click the Show/Hide ¶ button on the Standard toolbar to display formatting marks.
3. Create the announcement shown in Figure 1-75. Enter the document first without the clip art and unformatted; that is without any bold, underlined, italicized, right-aligned, or centered text. If Word flags any misspelled words as you type, check the spelling of these words and correct them.
4. Save the document on a floppy disk with Registration Announcement as the file name.
5. Select the two lines of the headline. Change their font to Arial, or a similar font. Change their font size from 20 to 36. Bold both lines.
6. Click somewhere in the second line of the headline. Right-align it.
7. Click somewhere in the body title line. Center it.
8. Select the body title line. Increase its font size from 18 to 28. Bold it.
9. Select the words, and much more, in the first paragraph of the body copy. Italicize the words.
10. Select the word, variety, in the second paragraph of the body copy. Underline it.
11. Click somewhere in the last line of the announcement. Center it.
12. Insert the graphic of the classroom between the headline and the body title line. Search for the text, classroom, in the Clip Gallery to locate the graphic.
13. Enlarge the graphic of the classroom. If you make the graphic too large, the announcement may flow onto two pages. If this occurs, reduce the size of the graphic so the announcement fits on a single page. *Hint*: Use Help to learn about **print preview**, which is a way to see the page before you print it. To exit print preview and return to the document window, click the Close button on the Print Preview toolbar.
14. Click the graphic to select it. Center the selected graphic.
15. Save the announcement again with the same file name.
16. Print the announcement.

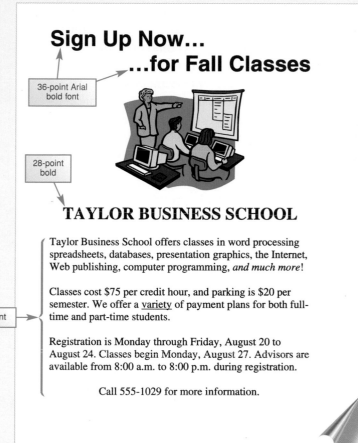

FIGURE 1-75

In the Lab

3 Creating an Announcement with Resized Clip Art and a Bulleted List

Problem: You are the secretary of The Computer Club at your school. One of your responsibilities is to announce the monthly meetings. For the February meeting, you prepare the announcement shown in Figure 1-76. *Hint:* Remember, if you make a mistake while formatting the announcement, you can click the Undo button on the Standard toolbar to undo your mistake.

Instructions:

1. Change the font size from 10 to 18.
2. If they are not already showing, display formatting marks.
3. Create the announcement shown in Figure 1-76. Enter the document first without the clip art and unformatted; that is without any bulleted, bold, underlined, italicized, right-aligned, or centered text. Check spelling as you type.
4. Save the document on a floppy disk with February Announcement as the file name.
5. Format the two lines of the headline to 28-point Arial Rounded MT Bold or a similar font.
6. Right-align the second line of the headline.
7. Center the body title line. Format the body title line to 22-point Courier New bold or a similar font.
8. Add bullets to the three paragraphs of body copy. A **bullet** is a symbol positioned at the beginning of a paragraph. In Word, the default bullet symbol is a small darkened circle. A list of paragraphs with bullets is called a **bulleted list**. *Hint:* Use Help to learn how to add bullets to a list of paragraphs.
9. Bold the date, Monday, February 19, in the first paragraph of the body copy.
10. Italicize the phrase, Word 2000, in the third paragraph of the body copy.
11. Center the last line of the announcement.
12. Insert the graphic of the computer between the headline and the body title line. Search for the text, academic computer, in the Clip Gallery to locate the graphic.
13. Enlarge the graphic of the computer. If you make the graphic too large, the announcement may flow onto two pages. If this occurs, reduce the size of the graphic so the announcement fits on a single page. *Hint:* Use Help to learn about **print preview**, which is a way to see the page before you print it. To exit print preview and return to the document window, click the Close button on the Print Preview toolbar.
14. Center the graphic.
15. Save the announcement again with the same file name.
16. Print the announcement.

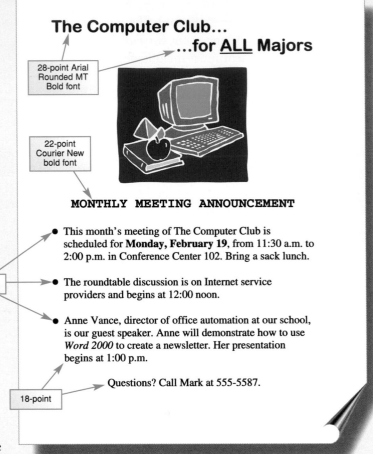

FIGURE 1-76

Cases and Places

The difficulty of these case studies varies:
▶ are the least difficult; ▶▶ are more difficult; and ▶▶▶ are the most difficult.

1 ▶ You have been assigned the task of preparing an announcement for Starport Airlines. The announcement is to contain a graphic of an airplane from the Clip Gallery. Use the following text: first line of headline – Fly With Us...; second line of headline – ... We Have Your Ticket; body title – Starport Airlines; first paragraph of body copy – For the month of October, we are offering flights to 25 cities nationwide for the unbelievable rate of $100 per person round trip.; second paragraph of body copy – Take advantage of these low, low rates and make your travel arrangements now for a vacation, a business trip, or a family reunion.; last line – For reservations, call 555-9898. Use the concepts and techniques presented in this project to create and format this announcement. Ask your instructor if you should bullet the list of paragraphs of the body copy.

2 ▶ You have been assigned the task of preparing an announcement for the Lake Shore Carnival. The announcement contains a graphic of a carnival from the Clip Gallery. Use the following text: first line of headline – It's Time...; second line of headline – ...for Our Carnival; body title – Lake Shore Carnival; first paragraph of body copy – Join us for fun, food, entertainment, crafts, contests, and rides at the Lake Shore Carnival on the weekend of July 21 and 22.; second paragraph of body copy – Admission is $10 per adult and $5 for children under 10 years old. Gates open at 8:00 a.m. each day and close at midnight.; last line – For information, call 555-9383. Use the concepts and techniques presented in this project to create and format this announcement. Ask your instructor if you should bullet the list of paragraphs of the body copy.

3 ▶▶ Your Uncle John, a graduate of Eagle High School, will be celebrating his twenty-fifth high school reunion this year. He has asked you to prepare an announcement that can be sent to each member of the graduating class. He asks that you include a graphic of the school's mascot, an eagle. The reunion will be held at Fisher Country Club and will feature live entertainment by The Jazzicians, a local band. The reunion will be held on Saturday, October 27. The doors open at 6:00 p.m. with dinner at 7:00 p.m., followed by entertainment from 8:00 p.m. until 11:00 p.m. Cost is $50 per person. Guests will have the opportunity to reminisce about old times, catch up on current projects, and share future plans. More information can be obtained by calling Sue Nordic at 555-9808. Use the concepts and techniques presented in this project to create the announcement. Ask your instructor if you should bullet the list of paragraphs of the body copy.

Cases and Places

4 ▶▶ Your parents own a campground called Quiet Oaks. With the new season just around the corner, they have asked you to prepare an announcement for their campground. Located at the intersection of I-293 and SR-35 in southern Louisiana, Quiet Oaks is a secluded campground situated in wooded, rolling hills. It has 75 paved pull-through sites and 46 gravel sites. All have city water and electric hook-ups. Facilities include restrooms, showers, dump, security, laundry, public telephone, and a data port. Recreation includes lake fishing, swimming pool, playground, horseshoes, and a game room. The campground is open from April 1 through October 31. Rates begin at $15 per night. Call 555-9393 for more information. Use the concepts and techniques presented in this project to create the announcement. Be sure to include an appropriate graphic from the Clip Gallery. Ask your instructor if you should bullet the list of paragraphs of the body copy.

5 ▶▶ You have a part-time job as the assistant to the Marketing Director at a new office supply store called Office World. The Director has asked you to prepare an announcement for the store's grand opening. Office World stocks thousands of office products including supplies, furniture, electronics, and computer software. Office World's low price guarantee states it will refund double a customer's money if the customer finds a comparable product for a lower price within ten days of purchase. Customers can purchase at the store, via fax or telephone, or on the Web at www.officeworld.com. Fax number is 555-2982 and telephone number is 555-2983. For purchases over $45.00, delivery is free. For a catalog, customers or potential customers can call 555-2900. Use the concepts and techniques presented in this project to create the announcement. Be sure to include an appropriate graphic from the Clip Gallery. Ask your instructor if you should bullet the list of paragraphs of the body copy.

6 ▶▶▶ Schools, churches, libraries, grocery stores, and other public places have bulletin boards for announcements and other postings. Often, these bulletin boards have so many announcements that some go unnoticed. At one of the above-mentioned organizations, find a posted announcement that you think might be overlooked. Copy the text from the announcement. Using this text, together with the techniques presented in this project, create an announcement that would be more likely to catch a reader's eye. Format the announcement effectively and include a bulleted list and suitable graphic from the Clip Gallery.

7 ▶▶▶ Advertisements are a company's way of announcing products or services to the public. You can find advertisements in printed media such as newspapers and magazines. Many companies also advertise on the World Wide Web. Find a printed advertisement or one on the Web that you feel lacks luster. Copy the text from the announcement. Using this text, together with the techniques presented in this project, create an announcement that would be more likely to catch a reader's eye. Format the announcement effectively and include a bulleted list and suitable graphic from the Clip Gallery.

Microsoft Word 2000

P R O J E C T

2

Creating a
Research Paper

You will have mastered the material in this project when you can:

- Describe the MLA documentation style for research papers
- Change the margin settings in a document
- Adjust line spacing in a document
- Use a header to number pages of a document
- Enter text using Click and Type
- Apply formatting using shortcut keys
- Indent paragraphs
- Use Word's AutoCorrect feature
- Add a footnote to a research paper
- Modify a style
- Insert a symbol automatically
- Insert a manual page break
- Create a hanging indent
- Create a hyperlink
- Sort selected paragraphs
- Go to a specific location in a document
- Find and replace text
- Move text
- Find a synonym for a word
- Count the words in a document
- Check spelling and grammar at once
- Display the Web site associated with a hyperlink
- E-mail a copy of a document

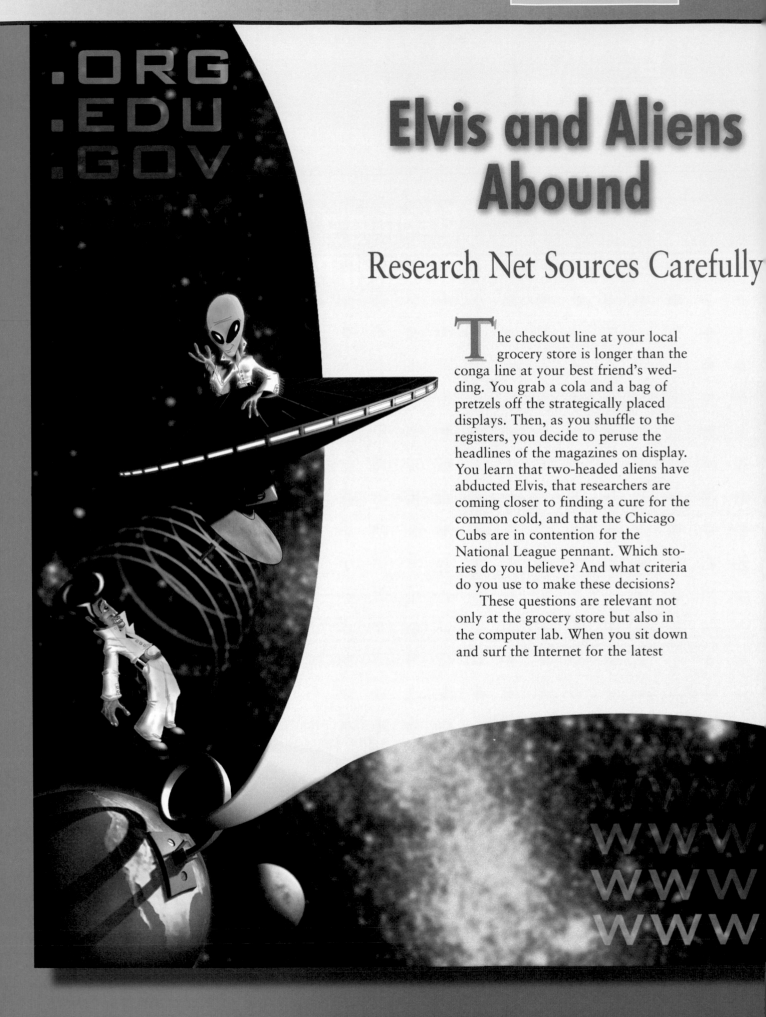

Elvis and Aliens Abound

Research Net Sources Carefully

The checkout line at your local grocery store is longer than the conga line at your best friend's wedding. You grab a cola and a bag of pretzels off the strategically placed displays. Then, as you shuffle to the registers, you decide to peruse the headlines of the magazines on display. You learn that two-headed aliens have abducted Elvis, that researchers are coming closer to finding a cure for the common cold, and that the Chicago Cubs are in contention for the National League pennant. Which stories do you believe? And what criteria do you use to make these decisions?

These questions are relevant not only at the grocery store but also in the computer lab. When you sit down and surf the Internet for the latest

news, celebrity sightings, sports scores, and reference sources, you make decisions on which sites to visit and which sites to avoid.

Not so long ago, students relied on books and magazines in the library for the bulk of their research material. These permanent sources were professionally evaluated and edited. Not so with the Internet. The Net is chock full of everything from reliable research to fictitious opinions. No one performs quality control checks to verify accuracy and reliability. Anyone can build a Web site and fill it with any content imaginable. And this content can be updated before your eyes.

In this project, you will create a research paper on the topic of Web publishing, which is the method of developing, maintaining, and posting Web pages. You will include a hyperlink that will permit you to navigate to a specific Internet site. Your Works Cited page will list the three sources used to obtain information for the paper. Two of these sources are books; one is an article available on the Shelly Cashman Series Web site

(www.scsite.com). How can you judge the reliability of these materials, particularly the article posted on the Web? Just remember the three S's: structure, source, and style.

Structure – Does the information seem objective or biased? Are authorities used as sources? When was the site created or updated? Is a contact person listed so you can verify information? Are working hyperlinks provided that refer you to additional sources?

Source – Examine the Web address to find out the site's sponsor. Is it a nonprofit organization (.org), a school (.edu), the government (.gov), or a commercial business (.com)? Is the purpose of the site to provide information or to make a profit?

Style – Does the site look organized and professional? Can you navigate easily with a minimum of mouse clicks? Does it contain an index and the capability of searching for specific information?

William Miller, a former president of the Association of College and Research Libraries, says that on the Web, "Much of what purports to be serious information is simply junk – not current, objective, or trustworthy." And by following the three S's, you will be able to decide that neither Elvis's abduction nor the Cubs's pennant seems likely.

Microsoft Word 2000

Creating a Research Paper

P R O J E C T

2

C A S E   P E R S P E C T I V E

Rick Williams is a full-time college student, majoring in Communications. Mr. Claremont, the instructor in his introductory computer class, has assigned a short research paper that must have a minimum of 425 words. The paper must discuss some aspect of computers and must be written according to the MLA documentation style, which specifies guidelines for report preparation. The paper must contain one footnote and three references — one of which must be obtained from the World Wide Web.

Rick's Internet service provider recently announced that all subscribers are entitled to 6 MB of free Web space for a personal Web page. Rick plans to publish his own Web page, so he decides to write the research paper on Web publishing. Rick intends to review computer magazines at the school's library, surf the Internet, contact his Internet service provider, and interview the Webmaster at his school for information on Web publishing. He also plans to use the Internet to obtain the guidelines for the MLA style of documentation. Because you are familiar with the Internet, Rick has asked you to assist him with the Web searches.

Introduction

In both academic and business environments, you will be asked to write reports. Business reports range from proposals to cost justifications to five-year plans to research findings. Academic reports focus mostly on research findings. Whether you are writing a business report or an academic report, you should follow a standard style when preparing it.

Many different styles of documentation exist for report preparation, depending on the nature of the report. Each style requires the same basic information; the differences among styles appear in the manner of presenting the information. For example, one documentation style may use the term *bibliography*, whereas another uses *references*, and yet a third prefers *works cited*. Two popular documentation styles for research papers are the **MLA** (**Modern Language Association of America**) and **APA** (**American Psychological Association**) styles. This project uses the MLA documentation style.

Project Two – Web Publishing Research Paper

Project 2 illustrates the creation of a short research paper describing Web publishing. As shown in Figure 2-1, the paper follows the MLA documentation style. The first two pages present the research paper and the third page lists the works cited alphabetically.

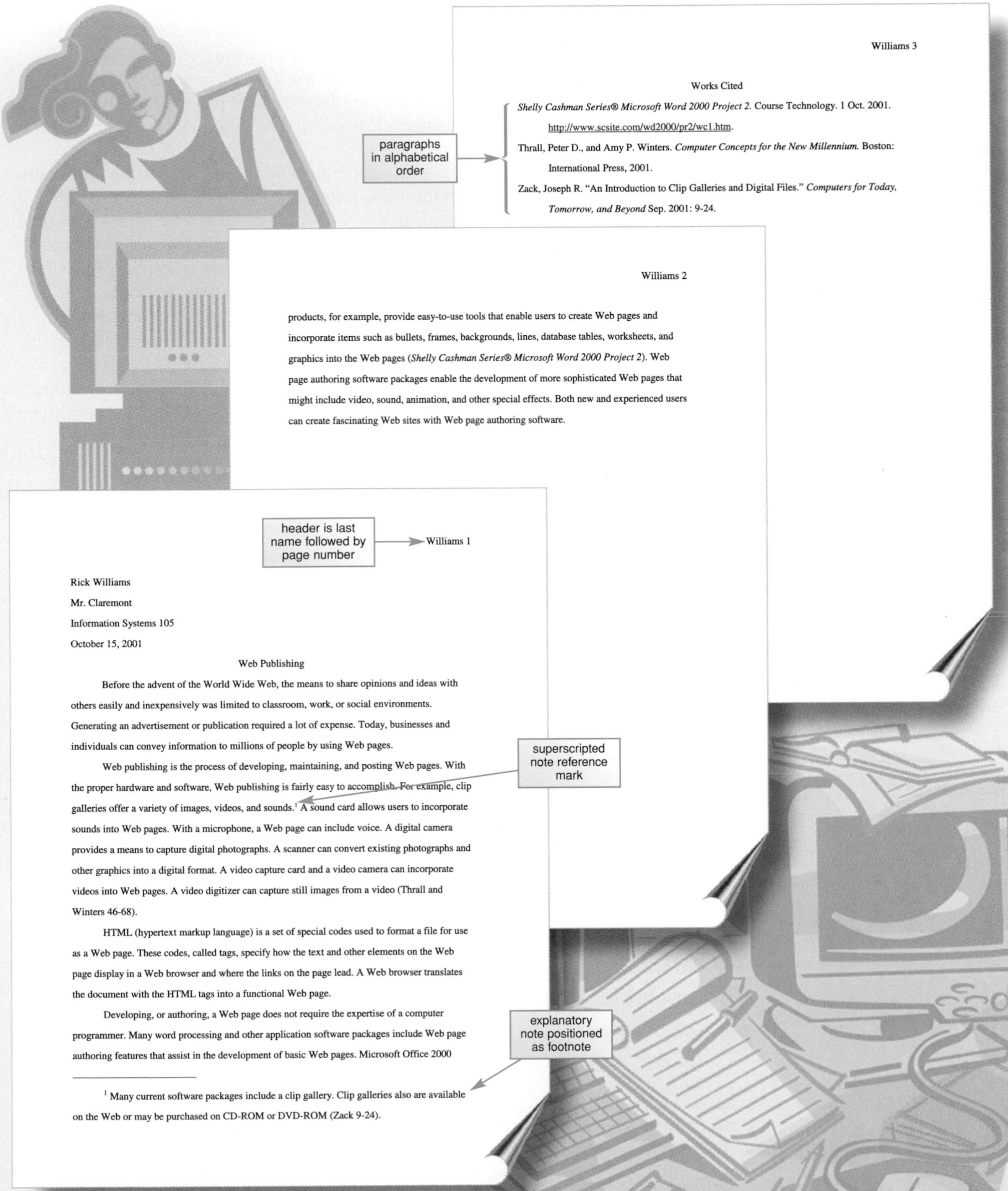

Williams 3

Works Cited

Shelly Cashman Series® Microsoft Word 2000 Project 2. Course Technology. 1 Oct. 2001.

http://www.scsite.com/wd2000/pr2/wc1.htm.

Thrall, Peter D., and Amy P. Winters. *Computer Concepts for the New Millennium.* Boston:

International Press, 2001.

Zack, Joseph R. "An Introduction to Clip Galleries and Digital Files." *Computers for Today,*

Tomorrow, and Beyond Sep. 2001: 9-24.

paragraphs in alphabetical order

Williams 2

products, for example, provide easy-to-use tools that enable users to create Web pages and

incorporate items such as bullets, frames, backgrounds, lines, database tables, worksheets, and

graphics into the Web pages (*Shelly Cashman Series® Microsoft Word 2000 Project 2*). Web

page authoring software packages enable the development of more sophisticated Web pages that

might include video, sound, animation, and other special effects. Both new and experienced users

can create fascinating Web sites with Web page authoring software.

header is last name followed by page number → Williams 1

Rick Williams

Mr. Claremont

Information Systems 105

October 15, 2001

Web Publishing

Before the advent of the World Wide Web, the means to share opinions and ideas with

others easily and inexpensively was limited to classroom, work, or social environments.

Generating an advertisement or publication required a lot of expense. Today, businesses and

individuals can convey information to millions of people by using Web pages.

Web publishing is the process of developing, maintaining, and posting Web pages. With

the proper hardware and software, Web publishing is fairly easy to accomplish. For example, clip

galleries offer a variety of images, videos, and sounds.[1] A sound card allows users to incorporate

sounds into Web pages. With a microphone, a Web page can include voice. A digital camera

provides a means to capture digital photographs. A scanner can convert existing photographs and

other graphics into a digital format. A video capture card and a video camera can incorporate

videos into Web pages. A video digitizer can capture still images from a video (Thrall and

Winters 46-68).

HTML (hypertext markup language) is a set of special codes used to format a file for use

as a Web page. These codes, called tags, specify how the text and other elements on the Web

page display in a Web browser and where the links on the page lead. A Web browser translates

the document with the HTML tags into a functional Web page.

Developing, or authoring, a Web page does not require the expertise of a computer

programmer. Many word processing and other application software packages include Web page

authoring features that assist in the development of basic Web pages. Microsoft Office 2000

superscripted note reference mark

explanatory note positioned as footnote

[1] Many current software packages include a clip gallery. Clip galleries also are available

on the Web or may be purchased on CD-ROM or DVD-ROM (Zack 9-24).

FIGURE 2-1

More **About**

MLA and APA

The MLA documentation style is the standard in the humanities, and the APA style is preferred in the social sciences. For more information from the MLA about its guidelines, visit the Word 2000 More About Web page (www.scsite.com/wd2000/more.htm) and then click MLA. For more information from the APA about its guidelines, visit the Word 2000 More About Web page (www.scsite.com/wd2000/more.htm) and then click APA.

More **About**

APA Style

In the APA style, double-space all pages of the paper with 1.5" top, bottom, left, and right margins. Indent the first word of each paragraph .5" from the left margin. In the upper-right margin of each page, place a running head that consists of the page number double-spaced below a summary of the paper title.

MLA Documentation Style

When writing papers, you should adhere to some style of documentation. The research paper in this project follows the guidelines presented by the MLA. To follow the MLA style, double-space text on all pages of the paper with one-inch top, bottom, left, and right margins. Indent the first word of each paragraph one-half inch from the left margin. At the right margin of each page, place a page number one-half inch from the top margin. On each page, precede the page number by your last name.

The MLA style does not require a title page; instead, place your name and course information in a block at the left margin beginning one inch from the top of the page. Center the title one double-space below your name and course information.

In the body of the paper, place author references in parentheses with the page number(s) where the referenced information is located. The MLA style uses these in-text **parenthetical citations** instead of footnoting each source at the bottom of the page or at the end of the paper. In the MLA style, footnotes are used only for explanatory notes. In the body of the paper, use **superscripts** (raised numbers) for **note reference marks**, which signal that an explanatory note exists.

According to the MLA style, explanatory notes are optional. **Explanatory notes** are used to elaborate on points discussed in the body of the paper. Explanatory notes may be placed either at the bottom of the page as footnotes or at the end of the paper as endnotes. Double-space the explanatory notes. Superscript each note reference mark, and indent it one-half inch from the left margin. Place one space following the note reference mark before beginning the note text. At the end of the note text, you may list bibliographic information for further reference.

The MLA style uses the term **works cited** for the bibliographical references. The works cited page alphabetically lists works that are referenced directly in the paper by each author's last name, or, if the author's name is not available, by the title of the work. Place the works cited on a separate numbered page. Center the title, Works Cited, one inch from the top margin. Double-space all lines. Begin the first line of each entry at the left margin; indent subsequent lines of the same entry one-half inch from the left margin.

Starting Word

Follow these steps to start Word or ask your instructor how to start Word for your system.

TO START WORD

1 Click the Start button on the taskbar.

2 Click New Office Document on the Start menu. If necessary, click the General tab when the New Office Document dialog box first displays.

3 Double-click the Blank Document icon in the General sheet.

4 If the Word window is not maximized, double-click its title bar to maximize it. If the Office Assistant displays, right-click it and then click Hide on the shortcut menu.

Office starts Word. After a few moments, an empty document titled Document1 displays in the Word window (Figure 2-2 on page WD 2.8). If your screen differs from Figure 2-2, click View on the menu bar and then click Normal.

Resetting Menus and Toolbars

To set the menus and toolbars so they appear exactly as shown in this book, you should reset your menus and toolbars as outlined in Appendix C or follow these steps.

TO RESET MENUS AND TOOLBARS

1 Click View on the menu bar and then point to Toolbars. Click Customize on the Toolbars submenu.

2 When the Customize dialog box displays, click the Options tab, make sure the top three check boxes have check marks and then click the Reset my usage data button. When the Microsoft Word dialog box displays, click the Yes button.

3 Click the Toolbars tab. Click Standard in the Toolbars list and then click the Reset button. When the Reset Toolbar dialog box displays, click the OK button.

4 Click Formatting in the Toolbars list and then click the Reset button. When the Reset Toolbar dialog box displays, click the OK button. Click the Close button.

Word resets the menus and toolbars.

Displaying Formatting Marks

As discussed Project 1, it is helpful to display **formatting marks** that indicate where in the document you pressed the ENTER key, SPACEBAR, and other keys. Follow this step to display formatting marks.

TO DISPLAY FORMATTING MARKS

1 Double-click the move handle on the Standard toolbar to display the entire toolbar. If the Show/Hide ¶ button on the Standard toolbar is not already recessed, click it.

Word displays formatting marks in the document window, and the Show/Hide ¶ button on the Standard toolbar is recessed (Figure 2-2 on the next page).

hanging the Margins

Word is preset to use standard 8.5-by-11-inch paper, with 1.25-inch left and right margins and 1-inch top and bottom margins. These margin settings affect every page in the document. Often, you may want to change these default margin settings. You have learned that the MLA documentation style requires one-inch top, bottom, left, and right margins throughout the paper.

The steps on the next page illustrate how to change the margin settings for a document when your screen is in normal view. To verify your screen is in normal view, click View on the menu bar and then click Normal.

Writing Papers

The World Wide Web contains a host of information, tips, and suggestions on writing research papers. College professors and fellow students develop many of these Web pages. For a list of Web links to sites on writing research papers, visit the Word 2000 More About Web page (www.scsite.com/wd2000/more.htm) and then click Links to Sites on Writing Research Papers.

Changing Margins

In print layout view, you can change margins using the horizontal and vertical rulers. Current margin settings are shaded in gray. The margin boundary is located where the gray meets the white. To change a margin, drag the margin boundary. Hold down the ALT key while dragging the margin boundary to display the margin settings.

Steps To Change the Margin Settings

1 Click File on the menu bar and then point to Page Setup (Figure 2-2).

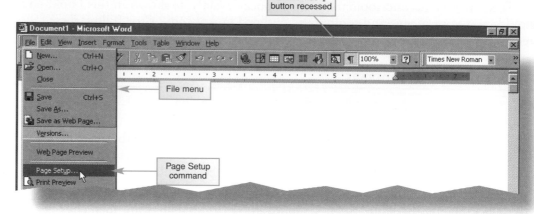

FIGURE 2-2

2 Click Page Setup. If necessary, click the Margins tab when the Page Setup dialog box first displays.

Word displays the Page Setup dialog box (Figure 2-3). Word lists the current margin settings in the text boxes.

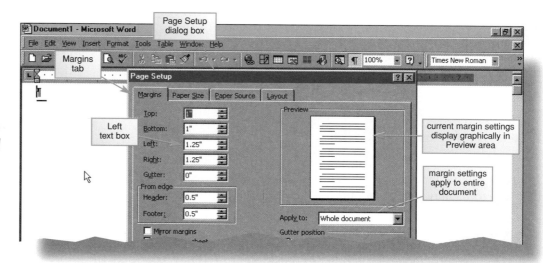

FIGURE 2-3

3 Drag through the text in the Left text box to highlight 1.25". Type 1 and then press the TAB key. Type 1 and then point to the OK button.

The new left and right margin settings are 1 inch (Figure 2-4).

4 Click the OK button.

Word changes the left and right margins.

 Other Ways

1. In print layout view, drag margin boundary(s) on ruler

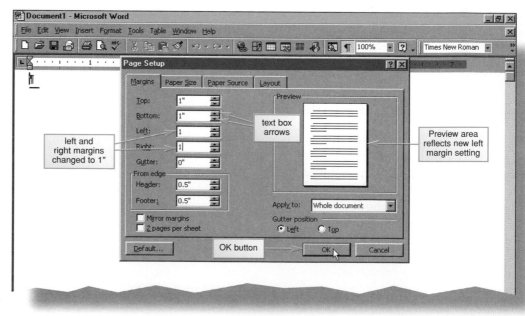

FIGURE 2-4

The new margin settings take effect in the document immediately, and Word uses these margins for the entire document.

When you change the margin settings in the text boxes in the Page Setup dialog box, the Preview area (Figure 2-4) does not adjust to reflect a changed margin setting until the insertion point leaves the respective text box. That is, you must press the TAB or ENTER key or click in another text box if you want to view the changes in the Preview area.

Zooming Page Width

As you learned in Project 1, when you **zoom page width**, Word displays text on the screen as large as possible without extending the right margin beyond the right edge of the document window. Perform the following steps to zoom page width.

TO ZOOM PAGE WIDTH

1 Click the Zoom box arrow on the Standard toolbar.

2 Click Page Width in the Zoom list.

Word extends the right margin to the right edge of the document window (Figure 2-5). Word computes the zoom percentage based on a variety of settings. Your percentage may be different depending on your system configuration.

Adjusting Line Spacing |

Line spacing is the amount of vertical space between lines of text in a document. Word, by default, single-spaces between lines of text and automatically adjusts line height to accommodate various font sizes and graphics. The MLA documentation style requires that you **double-space** the entire paper; that is, one blank line should display between each line of text. Thus, you must adjust the line spacing from single to double as described in the following steps.

More About

Line Spacing

Sometimes, the top of characters or a graphic is chopped off. This occurs when the line spacing is set to Exactly. To remedy the problem, change the line spacing to Single, 1.5 lines, Double, or At least in the Paragraph dialog box, all of which accommodate the largest font or graphic.

 **To Double-Space a Document**

1 **Right-click the paragraph mark above the end mark in the document window. Point to Paragraph on the shortcut menu (Figure 2-5).**

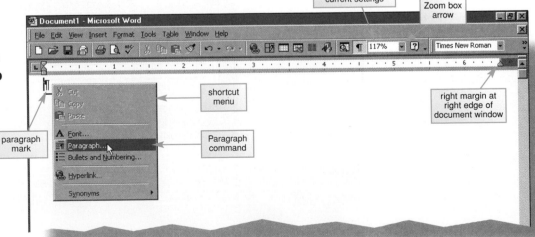

FIGURE 2-5

2 **Click Paragraph. If necessary, click the Indents and Spacing tab when the Paragraph dialog box first displays. Click the Line spacing box arrow and then point to Double.**

Word displays the Paragraph dialog box, which lists the current settings in the text boxes and displays them graphically in the Preview area (Figure 2-6). A list of available line spacing options displays.

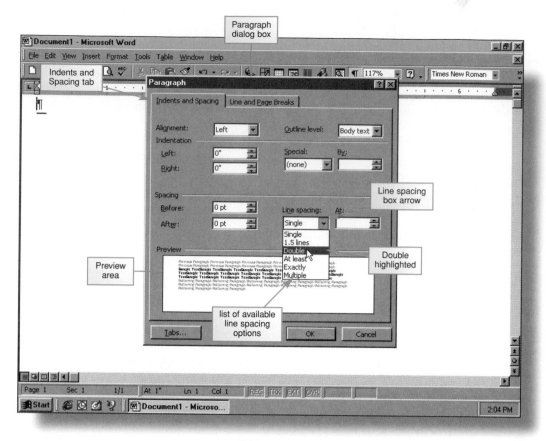

FIGURE 2-6

3 **Click Double. Point to the OK button.**

Word displays Double in the Line spacing box and graphically portrays the new line spacing in the Preview area (Figure 2-7).

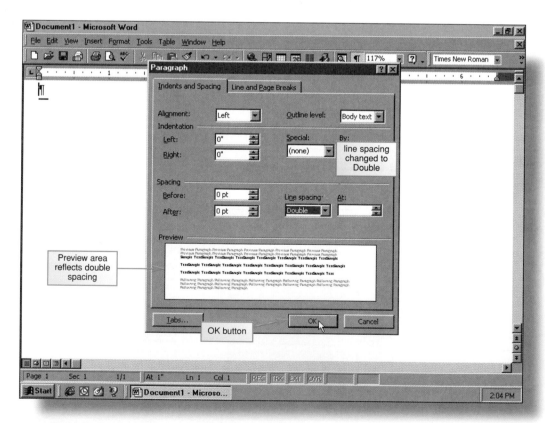

FIGURE 2-7

Click the OK button.

Word changes the line spacing to double in the current document (Figure 2-8).

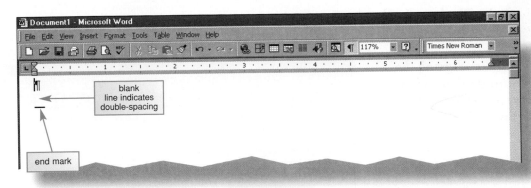

FIGURE 2-8

Notice that when line spacing is double (Figure 2-8), the end mark is positioned one blank line below the insertion point.

The Line spacing list (Figure 2-6) contains a variety of settings for the line spacing. The default, Single, and the options 1.5 lines and Double instruct Word to adjust line spacing automatically to accommodate the largest font or graphic on a line. The next two options, At least and Exactly, enable you to specify a line spacing not provided in the first three options. The difference is that the At least option instructs Word to increase the designation if necessary, whereas the Exactly option does not allow Word to increase the specification to accommodate larger fonts or graphics. With the last option, Multiple, you enter a value, which represents a percentage by which Word should increase or decrease the line spacing. For example, with the number 1 representing single-spacing, a multiple of 1.3 increases the line spacing by 30 percent and a multiple of .8 decreases the line spacing by 20 percent.

 **Other Ways**

1. On Format menu click Paragraph, click Indents and Spacing tab, click Line spacing box arrow, click Double, click OK button

2. Press CTRL+2

More About 2000

Data and Statistics

When researching for a paper, you may need to access data, graphs of data, or perform statistical computations on data. For more information on statistical formulas and available data and graphs, visit the Word 2000 More About Web page (www.scsite.com/wd2000/more.htm) and then click Data and Statistics.

Using a Header to Number Pages

In Word, you can number pages easily by clicking Insert on the menu bar and then clicking Page Numbers. Using the Page Numbers command, you can specify the location (top or bottom of page) and alignment (right, left, or centered) of the page numbers. You cannot, however, place your name as required by the MLA style in front of the page number with the Page Numbers command. To place your name in front of the page number, you must create a header that contains the page number.

Headers and Footers

A **header** is text you want printed at the top of each page in the document. A **footer** is text you want printed at the bottom of every page. In Word, headers are printed in the top margin one-half inch from the top of every page, and footers are printed in the bottom margin one-half inch from the bottom of each page, which meets the MLA style. Headers and footers can include text and graphics, as well as the page number, total number of pages, current date, and current time.

In this project, you are to precede the page number with your last name placed one-half inch from the top of each page. Your name and the page number should print right-aligned; that is, at the right margin.

To create the header, first you display the header area in the document window and then you can enter the header text into the header area. Use the procedures on the following pages to create the header with page numbers according to the MLA documentation style.

To Display the Header Area

1 **Click View on the menu bar and then point to Header and Footer (Figure 2-9).**

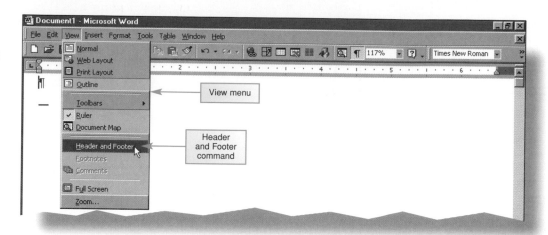

FIGURE 2-9

2 **Click Header and Footer.**

Word switches from normal view to print layout view and displays the Header and Footer toolbar (Figure 2-10). You type header text in the header area.

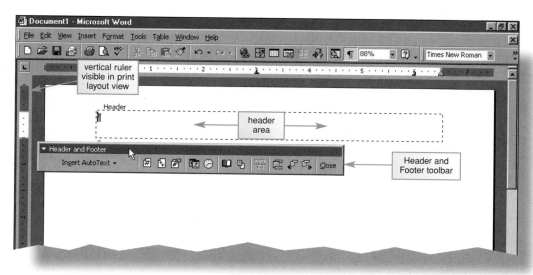

FIGURE 2-10

Print Layout View

You also can switch to print layout view by clicking the Print Layout View button on the horizontal scroll bar. Print layout view shows the positioning of headers, footers, and footnotes. To move forward or backward an entire page, click the double arrows on the bottom of the vertical scroll bar.

The Header and Footer toolbar initially floats in the document window. To move a floating toolbar, drag its title bar. You can **dock**, or attach, a floating toolbar below the Standard and Formatting toolbars by double-clicking the floating toolbar's title bar. To move a docked toolbar, drag its move handle. Recall that the move handle is the vertical bar to the left of the first button on a toolbar. If you drag a floating toolbar to an edge of the window, the toolbar snaps to the edge of the window. If you drag a docked toolbar to the middle of the window, the toolbar floats in the Word window. If you double-click between two buttons or boxes on a docked toolbar, it floats in its original floating position.

The header area does not display on the screen when the document window is in normal view because it tends to clutter the screen. To display the header in the document window with the rest of the text, you must display the document in print preview, which is discussed in a later project, or switch to print layout view. When you click the Header and Footer command on the View menu, Word automatically switches to **print layout view**, which displays the document exactly as it will print.

Entering Text using Click and Type

When in print layout view, you can use **Click and Type** to format and enter text, graphics, and other items. To use Click and Type, you double-click a blank area of the document window. Word automatically formats the item you enter according to the location where you double-click. Perform the following steps to use Click and Type to right-align and then enter the last name into the header area.

More *About*

Click and Type

Click and Type is not available in normal view, in a bulleted or numbered list, or in a document formatted into multiple columns.

 To Click and Type

---

1 Point to right edge of the header area so a right-align icon displays next to the I-beam.

As you move the *Click and Type pointer* around the window, the icon changes to represent formatting that will be applied if you double-click at that location (Figure 2-11).

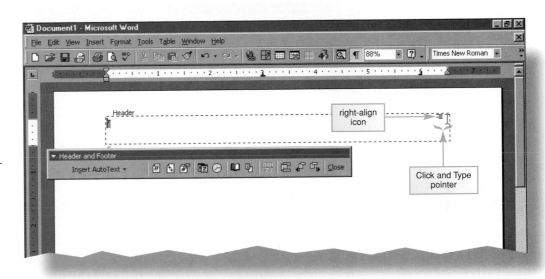

FIGURE 2-11

2 Double-click. Type Williams and then press the SPACEBAR.

Word displays the last name, Williams, right-aligned in the header area (Figure 2-12).

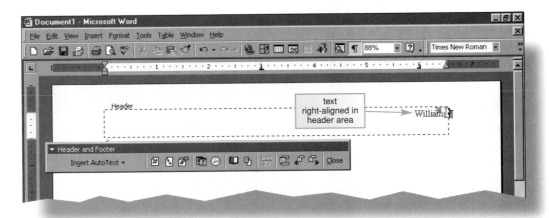

FIGURE 2-12

The next step is to enter the page number into the header area and then format it.

Entering a Page Number into the Header

Word formats the text in the header area using the current font size. Perform the steps on the next page to enter a page number into the header area and then, if necessary, format the entire line of text to 12 point.

To Enter and Format a Page Number

1 **Click the Insert Page Number button on the Header and Footer toolbar.**

Word displays the page number 1 in the header area (Figure 2-13).

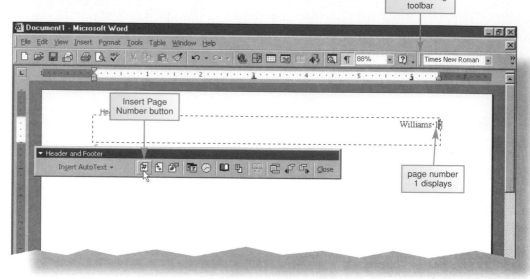

FIGURE 2-13

2 **Select the text, Williams 1, by dragging through it. Double-click the move handle on the Formatting toolbar to display the entire toolbar. If necessary, click the Font Size box arrow on the Formatting toolbar and then click 12 (Figure 2-14).**

3 **Click the Close Header and Footer button on the Header and Footer toolbar.**

Word closes the Header and Footer toolbar and returns the screen to normal view (see Figure 2-15 on page WD 2.16).

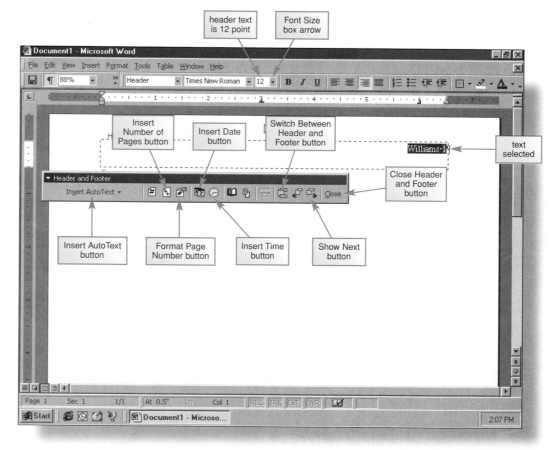

FIGURE 2-14

Other Ways

1. On Insert menu click Page Numbers, click OK button

Just as the Insert Page Number button on the Header and Footer toolbar inserts the page number into the document, three other buttons on the Header and Footer toolbar (Figure 2-14) insert items into the document. The Insert Number of Pages button inserts the total number of pages in the document; the Insert Date button inserts the current date into the document; and the Insert Time button inserts the current time.

To edit an existing header, you can follow the same procedure that you use to create a new header. That is, click View on the menu bar and then click Header and Footer to display the header area; or switch to print layout view by clicking the Print Layout View button on the horizontal scroll bar and then double-click the dimmed header. If you have multiple headers, click the Show Next button on the Header and Footer toolbar (Figure 2-14) until the appropriate header displays in the header area. Edit the header as you would any Word text and then click the Close Header and Footer button on the Header and Footer toolbar.

To create a footer, click View on the menu bar, click Header and Footer, click the Switch Between Header and Footer button on the Header and Footer toolbar, and then follow the same procedure as you would to create a header.

Typing the Body of the Research Paper

The body of the research paper encompasses the first two pages in Figure 2-1 on page WD 2.5. The steps on the following pages illustrate how to enter the body of the research paper.

Changing the Default Font Size

You learned in Project 1 that depending on how Word 2000 was installed on your computer, your default font size might be either 10 or 12. A font size of 10 point is difficult for some people to read. In this project, all characters in all paragraphs should be a font size of 12. If your default font size is 10, perform the following steps to change it to 12.

TO CHANGE THE DEFAULT FONT SIZE

① If necessary, click the Font Size box arrow on the Formatting toolbar.

② Click 12.

Word changes the font size to 12 (Figure 2-15 on the next page).

Entering Name and Course Information

You have learned that the MLA style does not require a separate title page for research papers. Instead, place your name and course information in a block at the top of the page at the left margin. Thus, follow the step on the next page to begin entering the body of the research paper.

More About

Writing Papers

When preparing to write a paper, many students take notes to keep track of information. One method is to summarize, or condense, the information. Another is to paraphrase, or rewrite the information in your own words. A third method is to quote, or record, the exact words of the original. Be sure to use quotation marks when directly quoting a source.

More About

APA Guidelines

APA guidelines require a title page as a separate page of a research paper, instead of placing name and course information on the paper's first page. The running head (a brief summary of the title and the page number) also is on the title page, along with the page number 1.

To Enter Name and Course Information

1 **Type** Rick Williams **and then press the ENTER key. Type** Mr. Claremont **and then press the ENTER key. Type** Information Systems 105 **and then press the ENTER key. Type** October 15, 2001 **and then press the ENTER key.**

The student name displays on line 1, the professor name on line 2, the course name on line 3, and the paper due date on line 4 (Figure 2-15).

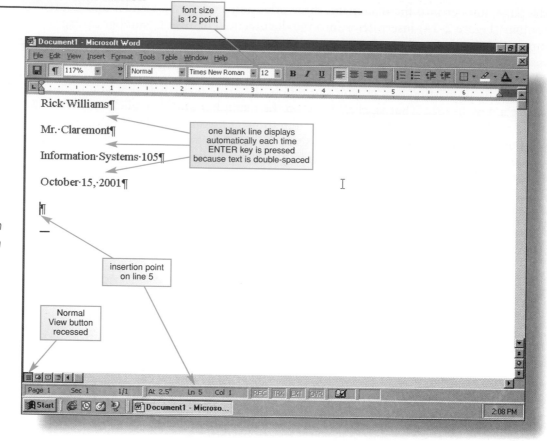

FIGURE 2-15

Notice in Figure 2-15 that the insertion point currently is on line 5. Each time you press the ENTER key, Word advances two lines on the screen, but increments the line counter on the status bar by only one because earlier you set line spacing to double.

If you watch the screen as you type, you may have noticed that as you typed the first few characters in the month, Octo, Word displayed the **AutoComplete tip**, October, above the characters. To save typing, you could press the ENTER key while the AutoComplete tip displays, which instructs Word to place the text of the AutoComplete tip at the location of your typing.

Applying Formatting Using Shortcut Keys

The next step is to enter the title of the research paper centered between the page margins. As you type text, you may want to format paragraphs and characters as you type them, instead of entering them and then formatting them later. In Project 1, you typed the characters in the document and then selected the ones to be formatted and applied the desired formatting using toolbar buttons. When your fingers are already on the keyboard, it sometimes is more efficient to use **shortcut keys**, or key z board key combinations, to format text as you type it. Perform the following steps to center a paragraph with the CTRL+E keys and then left-align a paragraph with the CTRL+L keys. (Recall from Project 1 that a notation such as CTRL+E means to press the letter E while holding the CTRL key.)

To Use Shortcut Keys to Format Text

1 **Press the CTRL+E keys. Type** Web Publishing **and then press the ENTER key.**

Word centers the title between the left and right margins (Figure 2-16). The paragraph mark and insertion point are centered because the formatting specified in the previous paragraph is carried forward to the next paragraph.

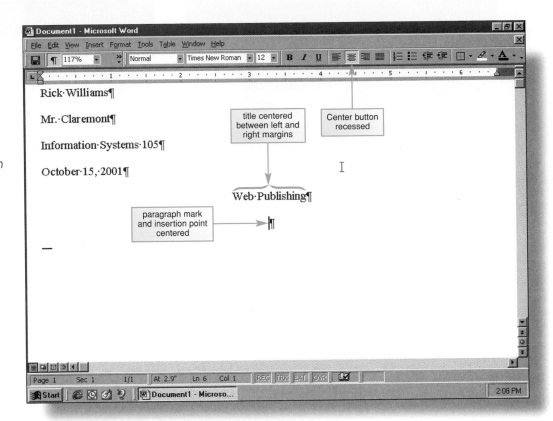

FIGURE 2-16

2 **Press the CTRL+L keys.**

Word positions the paragraph mark and the insertion point at the left margin (Figure 2-17). The next text you type will be left-aligned.

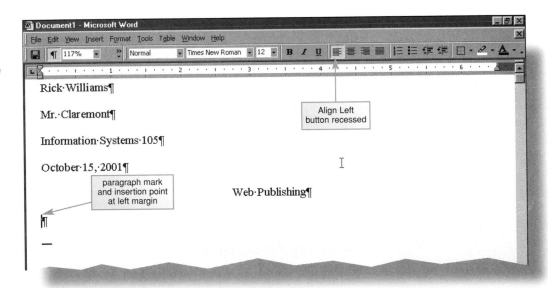

FIGURE 2-17

Word has many shortcut keys for your convenience while typing. Table 2-1 on the next page lists the common shortcut keys for formatting characters, and Table 2-2 on the next page lists common shortcut keys for formatting paragraphs.

Table 2-1 Shortcut Keys for Formatting Characters	
CHARACTER FORMATTING TASK	**SHORTCUT KEYS**
All capital letters	CTRL+SHIFT+A
Bold	CTRL+B
Case of letters	SHIFT+F3
Decrease font size	CTRL+SHIFT+<
Decrease font size 1 point	CTRL+[
Double-underline	CTRL+SHIFT+D
Increase font size	CTRL+SHIFT+>
Increase font size 1 point	CTRL+]
Italic	CTRL+I
Remove character formatting (plain text)	CTRL+SPACEBAR
Small uppercase letters	CTRL+SHIFT+K
Subscript	CTRL+=
Superscript	CTRL+SHIFT+PLUS SIGN
Underline	CTRL+U
Underline words, not spaces	CTRL+SHIFT+W

Table 2-2 Shortcut Keys for Formatting Paragraphs	
PARAGRAPH FORMATTING TASK	**SHORTCUT KEYS**
1.5 line spacing	CTRL+5
Add/remove one line above	CTRL+0
Center paragraph	CTRL+E
Decrease paragraph indent	CTRL+SHIFT+M
Double-space lines	CTRL+2
Hanging indent	CTRL+T
Increase paragraph indent	CTRL+M
Justify paragraph	CTRL+J
Left-align paragraph	CTRL+L
Remove hanging indent	CTRL+SHIFT+T
Remove paragraph formatting	CTRL+Q
Right-align paragraph	CTRL+R
Single-space lines	CTRL+1

Saving the Research Paper

You should save your research paper. For a detailed example of the procedure summarized below, refer to pages WD 1.26 through WD 1.28 in Project 1.

TO SAVE A DOCUMENT

1 Insert your floppy disk into drive A.

2 Double-click the move handle on the Standard toolbar to display the entire toolbar. Click the Save button on the Standard toolbar.

3 Type the file name Web Publishing Paper in the File name text box.

4 Click the Save in box arrow and then click 3½ Floppy (A:).

5 Click the Save button in the Save As dialog box.

Word saves your document with the name Web Publishing Paper (Figure 2-18).

Indenting Paragraphs

According to the MLA style, the first line of each paragraph in the research paper is to be indented one-half inch from the left margin. This procedure, called **first-line indent**, can be accomplished using the horizontal ruler. The **First Line Indent marker** is the top triangle at the 0" mark on the ruler (Figure 2-18). The small square at the 0" mark is the **Left Indent marker**. The Left Indent marker is used to change the entire left margin, whereas the First Line Indent marker affects only the first line of the paragraph. Perform the following steps to first-line indent the paragraphs in the research paper.

More About

First-Line Indent

You may be tempted to use the TAB key to indent the first line of each paragraph in your research paper. Using the TAB key for this task is inefficient because you must press it each time you begin a new paragraph. First-line indent is a paragraph format; thus, it is carried forward automatically each time you press the ENTER key.

Steps **To First-Line Indent Paragraphs**

1 With the insertion point on the paragraph mark in line 6, point to the First Line Indent marker on the ruler (Figure 2-18).

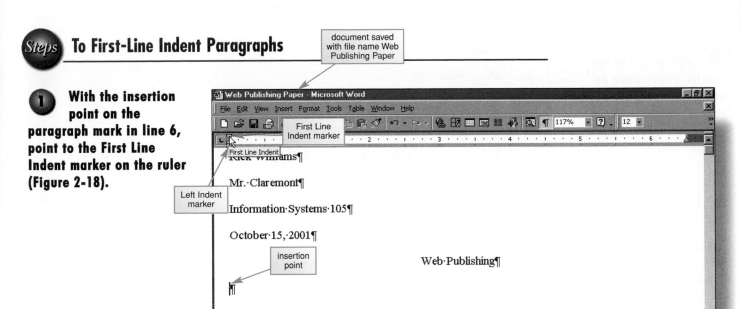

FIGURE 2-18

2 Drag the First Line Indent marker to the .5" mark on the ruler.

As you drag the mouse, a vertical dotted line displays in the document window, indicating the proposed location of the first line of the paragraph (Figure 2-19).

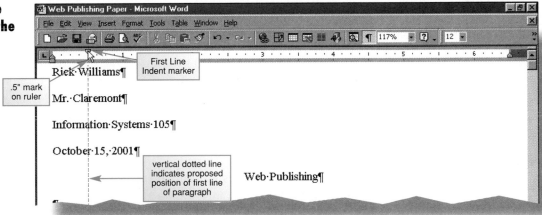

FIGURE 2-19

3 Release the mouse button.

The First Line Indent marker displays at the .5" mark on the ruler, or one-half inch from the left margin (Figure 2-20). The paragraph mark containing the insertion point in the document window also moves one-half inch to the right.

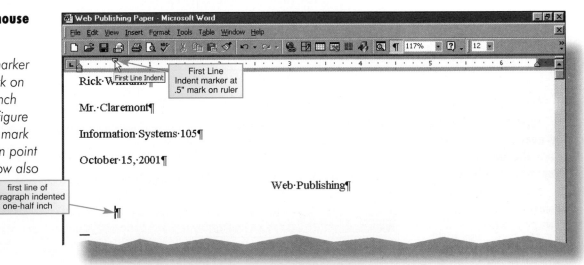

FIGURE 2-20

4 **Type the first paragraph of the research paper body as shown in Figure 2-21. Press the ENTER key. Type** Web publishing is the process of developing, maintaining, and posting Web pages.

Word automatically indents the first line of the second paragraph by one-half inch (Figure 2-21).

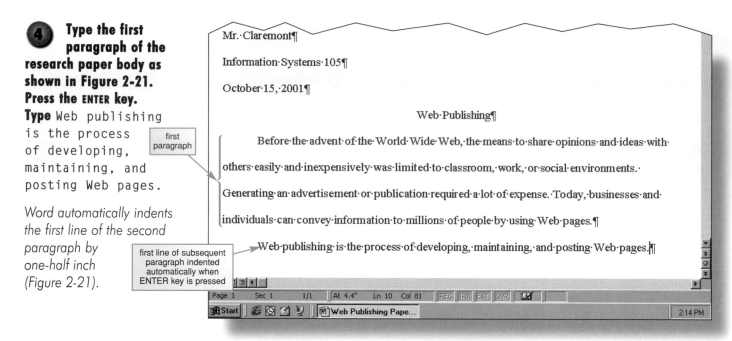

Mr.·Claremont¶

Information·Systems·105¶

October·15,·2001¶

Web·Publishing¶

Before·the·advent·of·the·World·Wide·Web,·the·means·to·share·opinions·and·ideas·with·

others·easily·and·inexpensively·was·limited·to·classroom,·work,·or·social·environments.·

Generating·an·advertisement·or·publication·required·a·lot·of·expense.·Today,·businesses·and·

individuals·can·convey·information·to·millions·of·people·by·using·Web·pages.¶

Web·publishing·is·the·process·of·developing,·maintaining,·and·posting·Web·pages.¶

first paragraph

first line of subsequent paragraph indented automatically when ENTER key is pressed

Page 1   Sec 1   1/1   At 4.4"   Ln 10   Col 81   REC TRK EXT OVR

Start   Web Publishing Pape...   2:14 PM

FIGURE 2-21

Recall that each time you press the ENTER key, the paragraph formatting in the previous paragraph is carried forward to the next paragraph. Thus, once you set the first-line indent, its format is carried automatically to each subsequent paragraph you type.

Using Word's AutoCorrect Feature

Because you may make typing, spelling, capitalization, or grammar errors as you type, Word provides an **AutoCorrect** feature that automatically corrects these errors as you type them into the document. For example, if you type the text, ahve, Word automatically changes it to the word, have, for you when you press the SPACEBAR or a punctuation mark key. Word has predefined many commonly misspelled words, which it automatically corrects for you. Perform the following steps to use the AutoCorrect as you type feature.

Steps **To AutoCorrect As You Type**

1 **Press the SPACEBAR. Type the beginning of the next sentence and misspell the word, accomplish, as follows:** With the proper hardware and software, Web publishing is fairly easy to acomplish **as shown in Figure 2-22.**

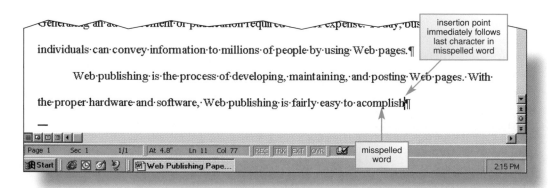

Generating·an·ad...ment·or·pu...ation·required·...·expense.·...day,·bus...

individuals·can·convey·information·to·millions·of·people·by·using·Web·pages.¶

Web·publishing·is·the·process·of·developing,·maintaining,·and·posting·Web·pages.·With·

the·proper·hardware·and·software,·Web·publishing·is·fairly·easy·to·acomplish¶

insertion point immediately follows last character in misspelled word

misspelled word

Page 1   Sec 1   1/1   At 4.8"   Ln 11   Col 77   REC TRK EXT OVR

Start   Web Publishing Pape...   2:15 PM

FIGURE 2-22

Press the PERIOD key.

As soon as you press the PERIOD key, Word's AutoCorrect feature detects the misspelling and corrects the misspelled word (Figure 2-23).

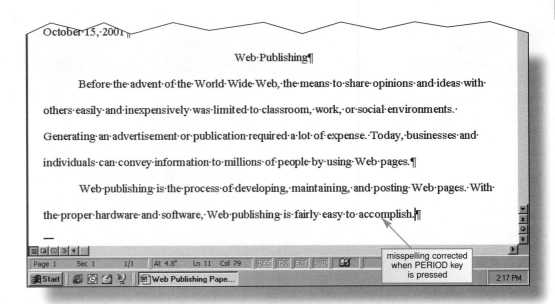

FIGURE 2-23

Word has a list of predefined typing, spelling, capitalization, and grammar errors that AutoCorrect can detect and correct. In addition to the predefined list, you can create your own AutoCorrect entries to add to the list. For example, if you often misspell the word, camera, as canera, you should create an AutoCorrect entry for it as shown in these steps.

 To Create an AutoCorrect Entry

 Click Tools on the menu bar and then point to AutoCorrect (Figure 2-24).

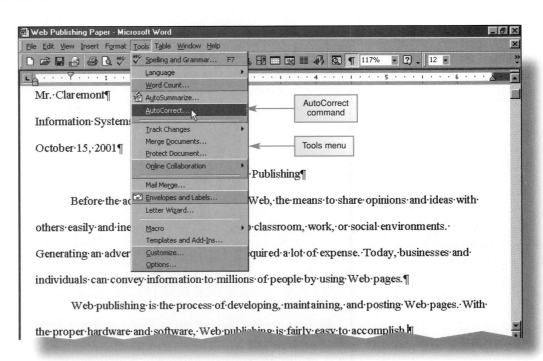

FIGURE 2-24

2 **Click AutoCorrect. When the AutoCorrect dialog box displays, type** canera **in the Replace text box. Press the TAB key and then type** camera **in the With text box.**

Word displays the AutoCorrect dialog box. The Replace text box contains the misspelled word, and the With text box contains its correct spelling (Figure 2-25).

3 **Click the Add button. (If your dialog box displays a Replace button instead, click it and then click the Yes button in the Microsoft Word dialog box.) Click the OK button.**

Word adds the entry alphabetically to the list of words to correct automatically as you type.

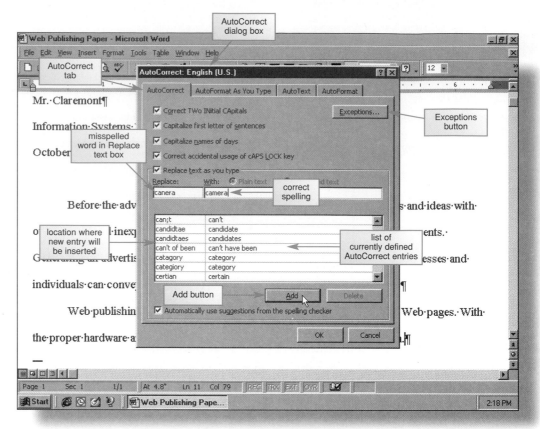

FIGURE 2-25

AutoCorrect

If you have installed the Microsoft Office 2000 Proofing Tools and have enabled editing for another language, Word automatically can detect the language you are using to create the document - as you type. These Proofing Tools provide fonts and templates, check spelling and grammar, and include AutoCorrect lists.

In addition to creating AutoCorrect entries for words you commonly misspell, you can create entries for abbreviations, codes, and so on. For example, you could create an AutoCorrect entry for asap, indicating that Word should replace this text with the phrase, as soon as possible.

If, for some reason, you do not want Word to correct automatically as you type, you can turn off the replace as you type feature by clicking Tools on the menu bar, clicking AutoCorrect, clicking the AutoCorrect tab (Figure 2-25), clicking the Replace text as you type check box to remove the check mark, and then clicking the OK button.

The AutoCorrect sheet (Figure 2-25) also contains four other check boxes that correct capitalization errors if the check boxes are selected. If you type two capital letters in a row such as TH, Word makes the second letter lowercase, Th. If you begin a sentence with a lowercase letter, Word capitalizes the first letter of the sentence. If you type the name of a day in lowercase such as tuesday, Word capitalizes the first letter of the day, Tuesday. Finally, if you leave the CAPS LOCK key on and begin a new sentence such as aFTER, Word corrects the typing, After, and turns off the CAPS LOCK key.

Sometimes you do not want Word to AutoCorrect a particular word or phrase. For example, you may use the code WD. in your documents. Because Word automatically capitalizes the first letter of a sentence, the character you enter following the period will be capitalized (in the previous sentence, it would capitalize the letter i in the word, in). To allow the code WD. to be entered into a document and still leave the AutoCorrect feature turned on, you need to set an exception. To set an exception to an AutoCorrect rule, click Tools on the menu bar, click AutoCorrect, click the AutoCorrect tab, click the Exceptions button in the AutoCorrect sheet (Figure 2-25), click the appropriate tab in the AutoCorrect Exceptions dialog box, type the exception entry in the text box, click the Add button, click the Close button in the AutoCorrect Exceptions dialog box, and then click the Close button in the AutoCorrect dialog box.

Adding Footnotes

You have learned that explanatory notes are optional in the MLA documentation style. They are used primarily to elaborate on points discussed in the body of the paper. The style specifies that a superscript (raised number) be used for a note reference mark to signal that an explanatory note exists either at the bottom of the page as a **footnote** or at the end of the document as an **endnote**.

Word, by default, places notes at the bottom of each page. In Word, **note text** can be any length and format. Word automatically numbers notes sequentially for you by placing a **note reference mark** in the body of the document and also in front of the note text. If you insert, rearrange, or remove notes, any subsequent note text and reference marks are renumbered according to their new sequence in the document. Perform the following steps to add a footnote to the research paper.

More About

MLA and APA

Both the MLA and APA guidelines suggest the use of in-text parenthetical citations, as opposed to footnoting each source of material in a paper. These parenthetical acknowledgments guide the reader to the end of the paper for complete information on the source.

  To Add a Footnote

Press the SPACEBAR and then type For example, clip galleries offer a variety of images, videos, and sounds. **Click Insert on the menu bar and then point to Footnote.**

The insertion point is positioned immediately after the period following the end of the sentence (Figure 2-26).

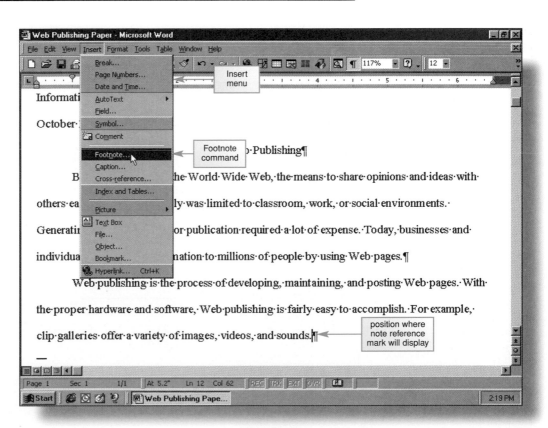

FIGURE 2-26

2 **Click Footnote. When the Footnote and Endnote dialog box displays, point to the OK button.**

Word displays the Footnote and Endnote dialog box (Figure 2-27).

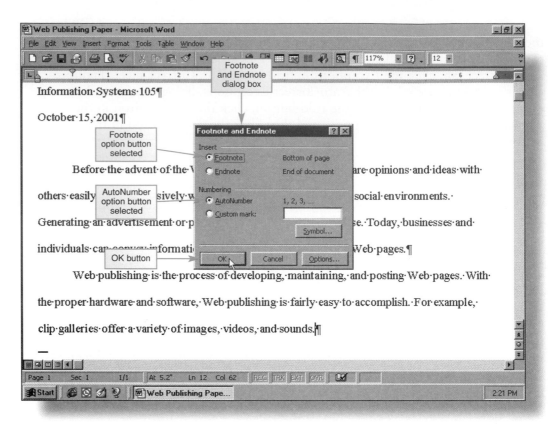

FIGURE 2-27

3 **Click the OK button.**

*Word opens a **note pane** in the lower portion of the Word window with the note reference mark (a superscripted 1) positioned at the left margin of the note pane (Figure 2-28). The note reference mark also displays in the document window at the location of the insertion point. Note reference marks are, by default, superscripted; that is, raised above other letters.*

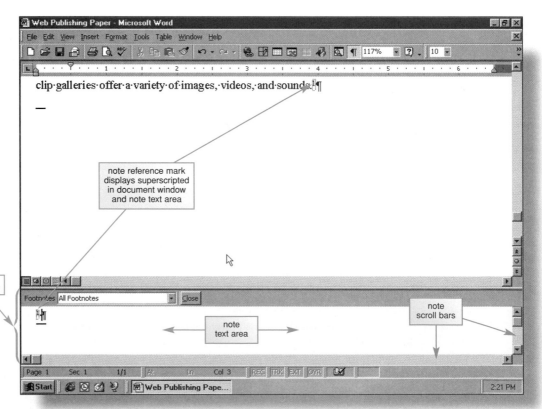

FIGURE 2-28

4 **Type** Many current software packages include a clip gallery. Clip galleries also are available on the Web or may be purchased on CD-ROM or DVD-ROM (Zack 9-24).

Word enters the note text in the note pane (Figure 2-29).

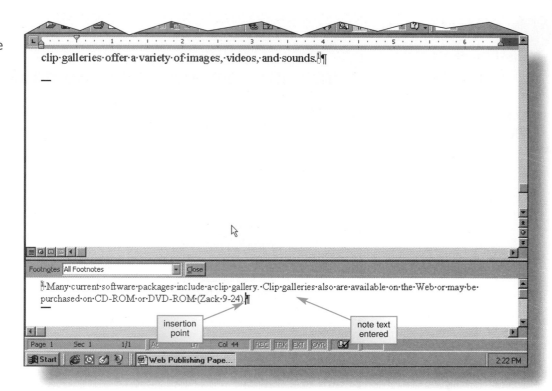

FIGURE 2-29

The footnote is not formatted according to the MLA style. Thus, the next step is to modify the style of the footnote.

Modifying a Style

A **style** is a customized format that you can apply to text. The formats defined by a style include character formatting such as the font and font size, and paragraph formatting such as line spacing and text alignment. Word has many built-in, or predefined, styles that you may use to format text. You can modify the formatting associated with these styles, or you can define new styles.

The base style for new Word documents is called the **Normal style**, which for a new installation of Word 2000 more than likely uses 12-point Times New Roman font for characters and single-spaced, left-aligned paragraphs. Recall from Project 1 that when you upgrade to Word 2000 from a previous version of Word, the default point size more than likely is 10 instead of 12.

In Figure 2-29, the insertion point is in the note text area, which is formatted using the Footnote Text style. The Footnote Text style is based on the Normal style. Thus, the text of the footnote you entered is single-spaced and left-aligned.

You could change the paragraph formatting of the footnote text to first-line indent and double-spacing as you did for the text in the document window. If you use this technique, however, you will have to change the format of the footnote text for each footnote you enter into the document. A more efficient technique is to modify the format of the Footnote Text style so paragraphs based on this style are double-spaced with a first-line indent format. Thus, by changing the formatting associated with the Footnote Text style, every footnote you enter will use the formats defined in this style. Perform the steps on the next page to modify the Footnote Text style.

Styles

The Style box on the Formatting toolbar displays the name of the style associated with the location of the insertion point. Click the Style box arrow on the Formatting toolbar to view the list of styles associated with the current document. To apply a style, select the text to format, click the Style box arrow, and then click the desired style name in the list.

To Modify a Style

1 **Click Format on the menu bar and then point to Style (Figure 2-30).**

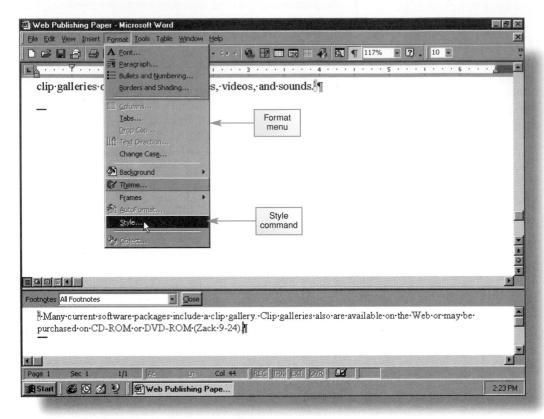

FIGURE 2-30

2 **Click Style. When the Style dialog box displays, click Footnote Text in the Styles list, if necessary, and then point to the Modify button.**

Word displays the Style dialog box (Figure 2-31). Footnote Text is highlighted in the Styles list. The Description area shows the formatting associated with the selected style.

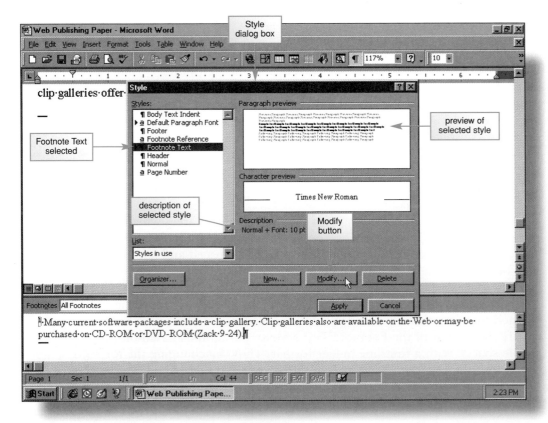

FIGURE 2-31

3 **Click the Modify button. When the Modify Style dialog box displays, click the Format button and then point to Paragraph.**

Word displays the Modify Style dialog box (Figure 2-32). A list of formatting commands displays above or below the Format button.

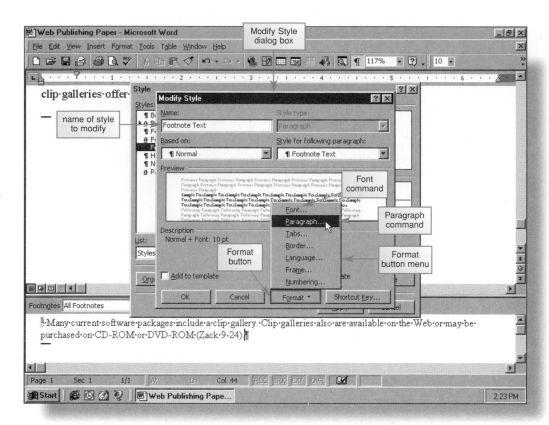

FIGURE 2-32

4 **Click Paragraph. When the Paragraph dialog box displays, click the Line spacing box arrow and then click Double. Click the Special box arrow and then point to First line.**

Word displays the Paragraph dialog box (Figure 2-33). The Preview area reflects the current settings in the Paragraph dialog box.

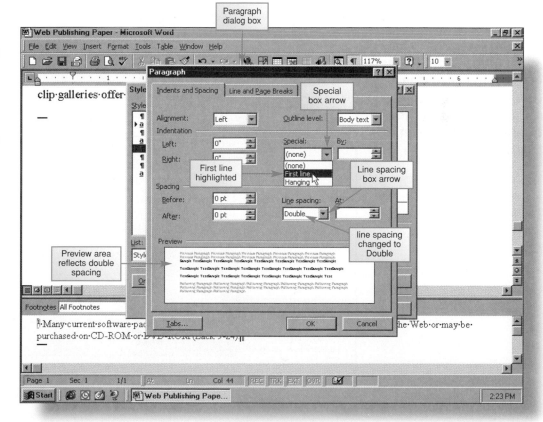

FIGURE 2-33

5 Click First line. Point to the OK button.

Word displays First line in the Special box and Double in the Line spacing box (Figure 2-34). Notice the default first-line indent is .5".

6 Click the OK button.

Word removes the Paragraph dialog box, and the Modify Style dialog box (see Figure 2-32 on the previous page) is visible again.

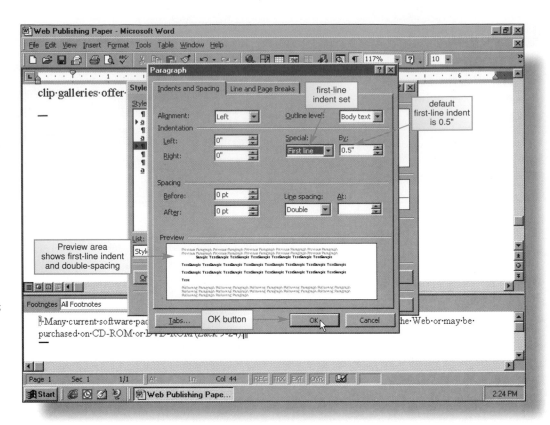

FIGURE 2-34

7 In the Modify Style dialog box, click the Format button and then click Font. When the Font dialog box displays, click 12 in the Size list. Point to the OK button.

Word displays the Font dialog box (Figure 2-35). Depending on your installation of Word 2000, the Size box already may display 12.

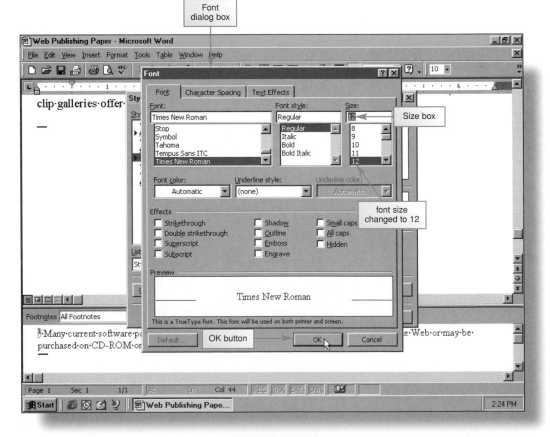

FIGURE 2-35

8 Click the OK button. When the Modify Style dialog box is visible again, point to the OK button.

Word removes the Font dialog box, and the Modify Style dialog box is visible again (Figure 2-36). Word modifies the Footnote Text style to a 12-point font with double-spaced and first-line indented paragraphs.

9 Click the OK button. When the Style dialog box is visible again, click the Apply button. Click the note pane up scroll arrow to display the entire footnote.

Word indents the first line of the note by one-half inch and sets the line spacing for the note to double (Figure 2-37 below).

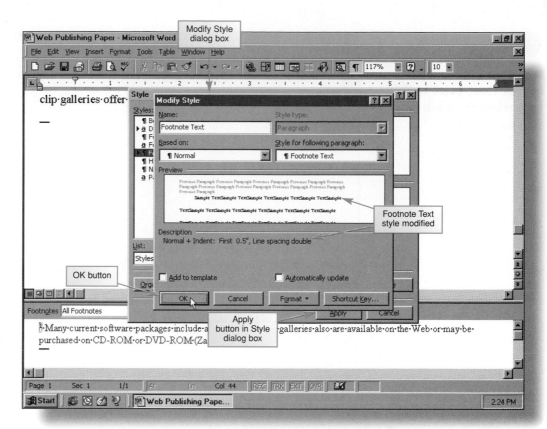

FIGURE 2-36

Any future footnotes entered into the document will use a 12-point font with first-line indented and double-spaced paragraphs. The footnote is complete. The next step is to close the note pane.

 To Close the Note Pane

1 Point to the Close button in the note pane (Figure 2-37).

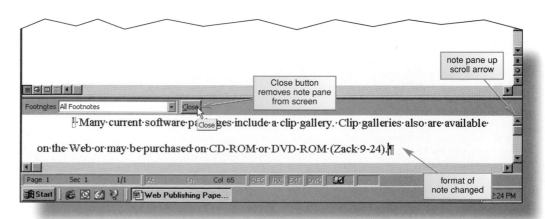

FIGURE 2-37

Microsoft **Word 2000**

2 **Click the Close button. If you want to see the note text in normal view, point to the note reference mark in the document window.**

Word closes the note pane (Figure 2-38).

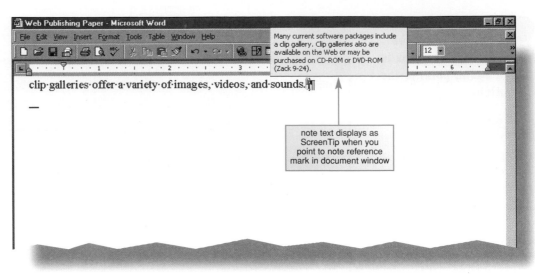

note text displays as ScreenTip when you point to note reference mark in document window

FIGURE 2-38

When Word closes the note pane and returns to the document window, the note text disappears from the screen. Although the note text still exists, it usually is not visible as a footnote in normal view. If, however, you point to the note reference mark, the note text displays above the note reference mark as a **ScreenTip** (Figure 2-38).

To delete a note, you select the note reference mark in the document window (not in the note pane) by dragging through the note reference mark and then clicking the Cut button on the Standard toolbar. Another way to delete a note is to click to the right of the note reference mark in the document window and then press BACKSPACE key twice, or click to the left of the note reference mark in the document window and then press the DELETE key twice. To move a note to a different location in a document, you select the note reference mark in the document window (not in the note pane), click the Cut button on the Standard toolbar, click the location where you want to move the note, and then click the Paste button on the Standard toolbar. When you move or delete notes, Word automatically renumbers any remaining notes in the correct sequence.

You edit note text using the note pane at the bottom of the Word window. To display the note text in a note pane, double-click the note reference mark in the document window or click View on the menu bar and then click Footnotes. Edit the note as you would any Word text and then click the Close button in the note pane. If you want to verify that the note text is positioned correctly on the page, you must switch to print layout view or display the document in print preview. These views are discussed later.

The next step is to enter more text into the body of the research paper. Follow these steps to enter more text.

Notes

To convert current footnotes to endnotes, click Insert on the menu bar and then click Footnote. Click the Options button in the Footnote and Endnote dialog box. Click the Convert button in the Note Options dialog box. Click Convert all footnotes to endnotes and then click the OK button in each of the dialog boxes.

TO ENTER MORE TEXT

1 Press the SPACEBAR. Type the remainder of the second paragraph of the paper as shown in Figure 2-39.

2 Press the ENTER key. Type the third paragraph of the paper as shown in Figure 2-39.

The second and third paragraphs are entered (Figure 2-39).

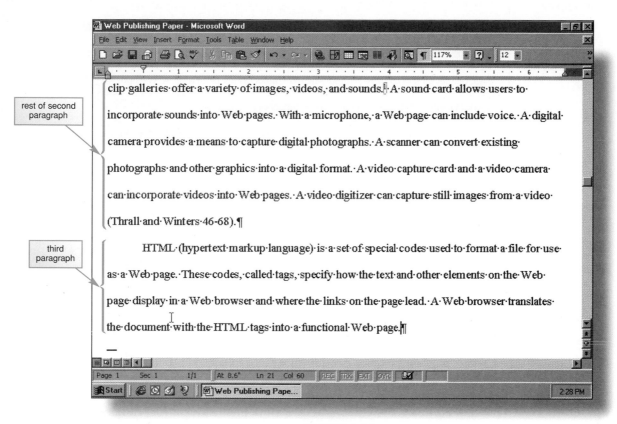

rest of second paragraph

third paragraph

FIGURE 2-39

Automatic Page Breaks

As you type documents that exceed one page, Word automatically inserts page breaks, called **automatic page breaks** or **soft page breaks**, when it determines the text has filled one page according to paper size, margin settings, line spacing, and other settings. If you add text, delete text, or modify text on a page, Word recomputes the position of automatic page breaks and adjusts them accordingly. Word performs page recomputation between the keystrokes; that is, in between the pauses in your typing. Thus, Word refers to the automatic page break task as **background repagination**. In normal view, automatic page breaks display on the Word screen as a single dotted horizontal line. Word's automatic page break feature is illustrated in the step on the next page.

More About

APA and MLA Documentation Styles

The World Wide Web contains a host of information on the APA and MLA documentation styles. College professors and fellow students develop many of these Web pages. For a list of Web links to sites on the APA and MLA styles, visit the Word 2000 More About Web page (www.scsite.com/wd2000/more.htm) and then click Links to Sites on the APA and MLA Styles.

Microsoft **Word 2000**

Steps To Page Break Automatically

1 Press the ENTER key and then type the first two sentences of the fourth paragraph of the paper, as shown in Figure 2-40.

As you begin typing the paragraph, Word places an automatic page break between the third and fourth paragraphs in the paper (Figure 2-40). The status bar now displays Page 2 as the current page.

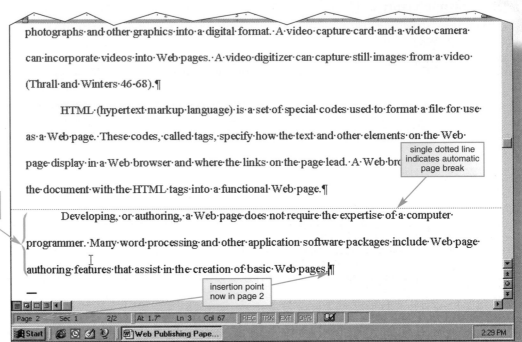

photographs and other graphics into a digital format. A video capture card and a video camera can incorporate videos into Web pages. A video digitizer can capture still images from a video (Thrall and Winters 46-68).¶

HTML (hypertext markup language) is a set of special codes used to format a file for use as a Web page. These codes, called tags, specify how the text and other elements on the Web page display in a Web browser and where the links on the page lead. A Web bro the document with the HTML tags into a functional Web page.¶

two sentences entered

single dotted line indicates automatic page break

Developing, or authoring, a Web page does not require the expertise of a computer programmer. Many word processing and other application software packages include Web page authoring features that assist in the creation of basic Web pages.¶

insertion point now in page 2

Page 2   Sec 1   2/2   At 1.7"   Ln 3   Col 67   REC TRK EXT OVR

Start   Web Publishing Pape...   2:29 PM

FIGURE 2-40

Your page break may occur at a different location, depending on your printer type.

The header, although not shown in normal view, contains the name Williams and the page number 2. If you wanted to view the header, click View on the menu bar and then click Header and Footer. Then, click the Close button on the Header and Footer toolbar to return to normal view.

Word, by default, prevents widows and orphans from occurring in a document. A **widow** is created when the last line of a paragraph displays by itself at the top of a page, and an **orphan** occurs when the first line of a paragraph displays by itself at the bottom of a page. You turn this setting on and off through the Paragraph dialog box. If, for some reason, you wanted to allow a widow or an orphan in a document, you would right-click the paragraph in question, click Paragraph on the shortcut menu, click the Line and Page Breaks tab in the Paragraph dialog box, click Widow/Orphan control to select or deselect the check box, and then click the OK button.

The Line and Page Breaks sheet in the Paragraph dialog box also contains two other check boxes that control how Word places automatic page breaks. If you did not want a page break to occur within a particular paragraph, you would right-click the paragraph you wanted to keep together, click Paragraph on the shortcut menu, click the Line and Page Breaks tab in the Paragraph dialog box, click Keep lines together to select the check box, and then click the OK button. If you did not want a page break to occur between two paragraphs, you would select the two paragraphs, right-click the selection, click Paragraph on the shortcut menu, click the Line and Page Breaks tab in the Paragraph dialog box, click Keep with next to select the check box, and then click the OK button.

Inserting Arrows, Faces, and Other Symbols Automatically

Earlier in this project, you learned that Word has predefined many commonly misspelled words, which it automatically corrects for you as you type. In addition to words, this built-in list of **AutoCorrect entries** also contains many commonly used symbols. For example, to insert a smiling face into a document, you type :) and Word automatically changes it to ☺. Table 2-3 lists the characters you type to insert arrows, faces, and other symbols into a Word document.

You also can enter the first four symbols in Table 2-3 by clicking Insert on the menu bar, clicking Symbol, clicking the Special Characters tab, clicking the desired symbol in the Character list, clicking the Insert button, and then clicking the Close button in the Symbol dialog box.

If you do not like a change that Word automatically makes in a document, undo the change by clicking the Undo button on the Standard toolbar; clicking Edit on the menu bar and then clicking Undo; or pressing CTRL+Z.

The next step in the research paper is to enter a sentence that uses the registered trademark symbol. Perform the following steps to insert automatically the registered trademark symbol into the research paper.

Table 2-3 Word's Automatic Symbols		
TO DISPLAY	**DESCRIPTION**	**TYPE**
©	copyright symbol	(c)
®	registered trademark symbol	(r)
™	trademark symbol	(tm)
…	ellipsis	...
☺	smiley face	:) or :-)
☺	indifferent face	:| or :-|
☹	frowning face	:(or :-(
→	thin right arrow	-->
←	thin left arrow	<--
→	thick right arrow	==>
←	thick left arrow	<==
↔	double arrow	<=>

 Steps To Insert a Symbol Automatically

1 **With the insertion point positioned as shown in Figure 2-40, press the SPACEBAR. Type** Microsoft Office 2000 products, for example, provide easy-to-use tools that enable users to create Web pages and include items such as bullets, frames, backgrounds, lines, database tables, worksheets, and graphics into the Web pages (**as the beginning of the sentence. Press CTRL+I to turn on italics. Type** Shelly Cashman Series(r **as shown in Figure 2-41.**

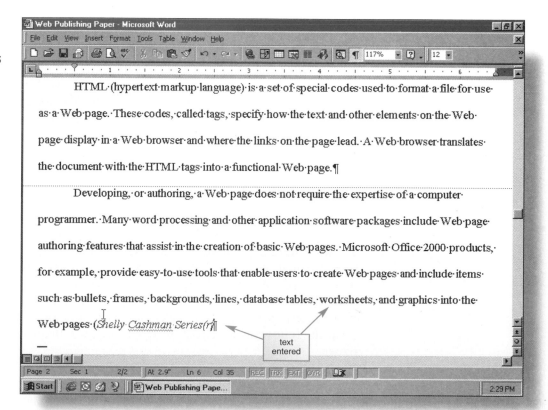

FIGURE 2-41

2 **Press the** RIGHT
PARENTHESIS **key.**

*Word automatically converts
the (r) to ®, the registered
trademark symbol.*

3 **Press the** SPACEBAR.
Type Microsoft
Word 2000 Project 2
and then press CTRL+I **to
turn off italics. Press the**
RIGHT PARENTHESIS **key and
then press the** PERIOD **key.
Press the** SPACEBAR. **Enter the
last two sentences of the
research paper as shown in
Figure 2-42.**

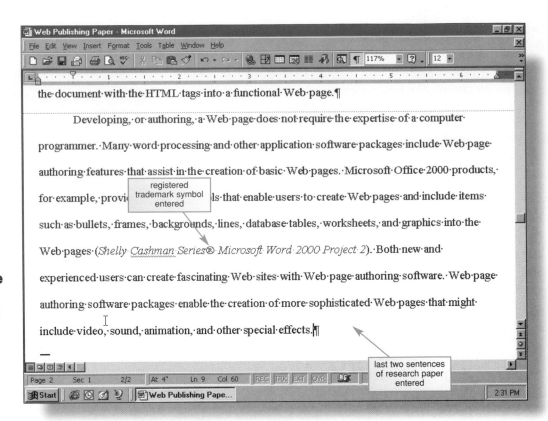

the document with the HTML tags into a functional Web page.¶

Developing, or authoring, a Web page does not require the expertise of a computer programmer. Many word processing and other application software packages include Web page authoring features that assist in the creation of basic Web pages. Microsoft Office 2000 products, for example, provide [registered trademark symbol entered] tools that enable users to create Web pages and include items such as bullets, frames, backgrounds, lines, database tables, worksheets, and graphics into the Web pages (*Shelly Cashman Series*® *Microsoft Word 2000 Project 2*). Both new and experienced users can create fascinating Web sites with Web page authoring software. Web page authoring software packages enable the creation of more sophisticated Web pages that might include video, sound, animation, and other special effects.¶

[last two sentences of research paper entered]

FIGURE 2-42

Creating an Alphabetical Works Cited Page

According to the MLA style, the **works cited page** is a bibliographical list of works you reference directly in your paper. The list is placed on a separate page with the title, Works Cited, centered one inch from the top margin. The works are to be alphabetized by the author's last name or, if the work has no author, by the work's title. The first line of each entry begins at the left margin; subsequent lines of the same entry are indented one-half inch from the left margin.

The first step in creating the works cited page is to force a page break so the works cited display on a separate page.

Manual Page Breaks

Because the works cited are to display on a separate numbered page, you must insert a manual page break following the body of the research paper. A **manual page break,** or **hard page break,** is one that you force into the document at a specific location. Manual page breaks display on the screen as a horizontal dotted line, separated by the words, Page Break. Word never moves or adjusts manual page breaks; however, Word does adjust any automatic page breaks that follow a manual page break. Word inserts manual page breaks just before the location of the insertion point. Perform the following step to insert a manual page break after the body of the research paper.

To Page Break Manually

1 **With the insertion point at the end of the research paper, press the ENTER key. Then, press the CTRL+ENTER keys.**

The shortcut keys, CTRL+ENTER, instruct Word to insert a manual page break immediately above the insertion point and position the insertion point immediately below the manual page break (Figure 2-43). The status bar indicates the insertion point is located on page 3.

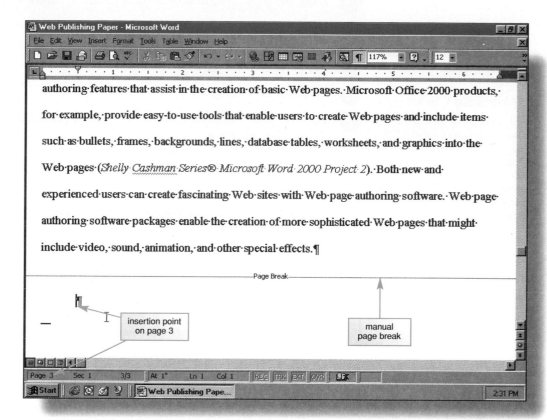

FIGURE 2-43

The manual page break displays as a horizontal dotted line with the words, Page Break, in the middle of the line. The header, although not shown in normal view, contains the name Williams and the page number 3. If you wanted to view the header, click View on the menu bar and then click Header and Footer. Then, click the Close button on the Header and Footer toolbar to return to normal view.

If, for some reason, you wanted to remove a manual page break from your document, you must first select it by double-clicking it. Then, press the DELETE key; or click the Cut button on the Standard toolbar; or right-click the selection and then click Cut on the shortcut menu.

Centering the Title of the Works Cited Page

The works cited title is to be centered between the margins. If you simply click the Center button on the Formatting toolbar, the title will not be centered properly; instead, it will be one-half inch to the right of the center point because earlier you set first-line indent at one-half inch. Thus, the first line of every paragraph is indented one-half inch. To properly center the title of the works cited page, you must move the First Line Indent marker back to the left margin before clicking the Center button as described in the steps on the next page.

 Other **Ways**

1. On Format menu click Insert, click Break, click OK button

 More **About**

Documentation Styles

The MLA documentation style uses the title *Works Cited* for the page containing bibliographical references, whereas the APA style uses the title *References*. APA guidelines for preparing the reference list entries differ significantly from the MLA style. Refer to an APA handbook for specifics.

TO CENTER THE TITLE OF THE WORKS CITED PAGE

1 Drag the First Line Indent marker to the 0" mark on the ruler.

2 Double-click the move handle on the Formatting toolbar to display the entire toolbar. Click the Center button on the Formatting toolbar.

3 Type Works Cited as the title.

4 Press the ENTER key.

5 Because your fingers are on the keyboard, press the CTRL+L keys to left-align the paragraph mark.

The title displays centered properly and the insertion point is left-aligned (Figure 2-44).

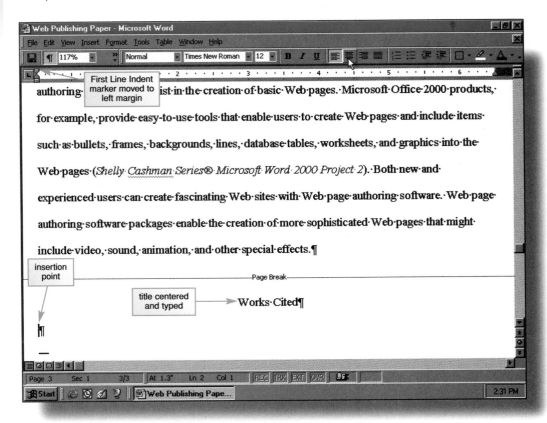

FIGURE 2-44

Formatting

Minimize strain on your wrist by switching between the mouse and keyboard as little as possible. If your fingers are already on the keyboard, use shortcut keys to format text; if your fingers are already on the mouse, use the mouse to format text.

Crediting Sources

When writing a research paper, you must acknowledge sources of information. Citing sources is a matter of ethics and honesty. Use caution when summarizing or paraphrasing a source. Be sure to avoid plagiarism, which includes using someone else's words or ideas and claiming them as your own.

Creating a Hanging Indent

On the works cited page, the first line of each entry begins at the left margin. Subsequent lines in the same paragraph are indented one-half inch from the left margin. In essence, the first line *hangs* to the left of the rest of the paragraph; thus, this type of paragraph formatting is called a **hanging indent**.

One method of creating a hanging indent is to use the horizontal ruler. The **Hanging Indent marker** is the bottom triangle at the 0" mark on the ruler (Figure 2-45). You have learned that the small square at the 0" mark is called the Left Indent marker. Perform the following steps to create a hanging indent.

To Create a Hanging Indent

1 **With the insertion point in the paragraph to format (see Figure 2-44), point to the Hanging Indent marker on the ruler (Figure 2-45).**

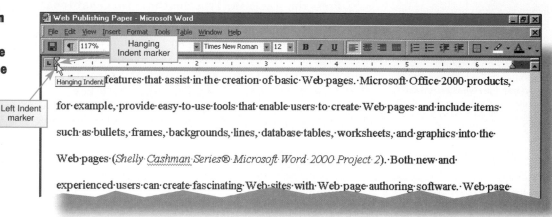

FIGURE 2-45

2 **Drag the Hanging Indent marker to the .5" mark on the ruler.**

The Hanging Indent marker and Left Indent marker display one-half inch from the left margin (Figure 2-46). When you drag the Hanging Indent marker, the Left Indent marker moves with it. The insertion point in the document window remains at the left margin because only subsequent lines in the paragraph are to be indented.

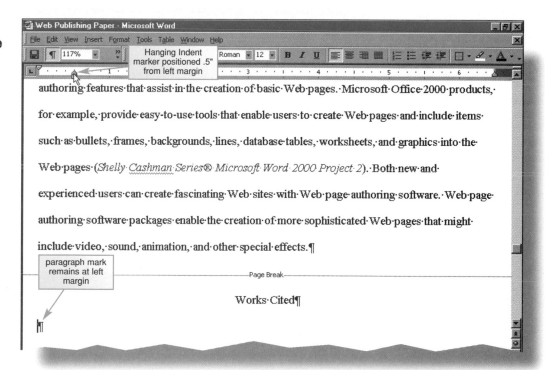

FIGURE 2-46

To drag both the First Line Indent and Hanging Indent markers at the same time, you drag the Left Indent marker on the ruler.

Enter the first two works in the works cited as explained in the steps on the next page.

Other Ways

1. Right-click paragraph, click Paragraph on shortcut menu, click Indents and Spacing tab, click Special box arrow, click Hanging, click OK button

2. On Format menu click Paragraph, click Indents and Spacing tab, click Special box arrow, click Hanging, click OK button

3. Press CTRL+T

TO ENTER WORK CITED PARAGRAPHS

1 Type Thrall, Peter D., and Amy P. Winters. Press the SPACEBAR. Press CTRL+I. Type Computer Concepts for the New Millennium. Press CTRL+I. Press the SPACEBAR. Type Boston: International Press, 2001. Press the ENTER key.

2 Type Zack, Joseph R. "An Introduction to Clip Galleries and Digital Files." Press the SPACEBAR. Press CTRL+I. Type Computers for Today, Tomorrow, and Beyond and then press CTRL+I. Press the SPACEBAR. Type Sep. 2001: 9-24. Press the ENTER key.

The first two works cited paragraphs are entered (Figure 2-47).

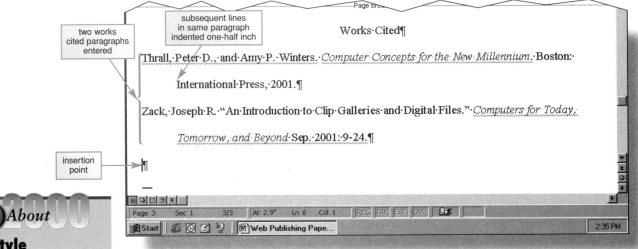

FIGURE 2-47

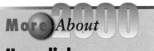
When Word wraps the text in each works cited paragraph, it automatically indents the second line of the paragraph by one-half inch. When you press the ENTER key at the end of the first paragraph of text, the insertion point returns automatically to the left margin for the next paragraph. Recall that each time you press the ENTER key, the paragraph formatting in the previous paragraph is carried forward to the next paragraph.

Creating a Hyperlink

In Word, you can create a hyperlink simply by typing the address of the file or Web page to which you want to jump and then pressing the SPACEBAR or the ENTER key. A **hyperlink** is a shortcut that allows a user to jump easily and quickly to another location in the same document or to other documents or Web pages. **Jumping** is the process of following a hyperlink to its destination. For example, by clicking a hyperlink in the document window, you jump to another document on your computer, on your network, or on the World Wide Web. When you close the hyperlink destination page or document, you return to the original location in your Word document.

In this project, one of the works cited is from a Web page on the Internet. When someone displays your research paper on the screen, you want him or her to be able to click the Web address in the work and jump to the associated Web site for more information. If you wish to create a hyperlink to a Web page from a Word document, you do not have to be connected to the Internet. Perform the following steps to create a hyperlink as you type.

To Create a Hyperlink as You Type

1 **Press CTRL+I. Type**
Shelly Cashman
Series(r) Microsoft
Word 2000 Project 2.
Press CTRL+I. Press the
SPACEBAR. Type Course
Technology. 1 Oct.
2001. http://
www.scsite.com/
wd2000/pr2/wc1.htm.

The insertion point immediately follows the Web address (Figure 2-48).

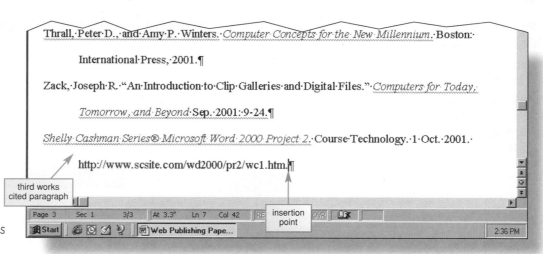

third works
cited paragraph

insertion
point

FIGURE 2-48

2 **Press the ENTER**
key.

As soon as you press the ENTER key after typing the Web address, Word formats it as a hyperlink (Figure 2-49). That is, the Web address is underlined and colored blue.

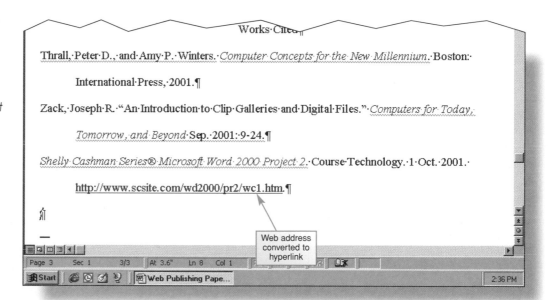

Web address
converted to
hyperlink

FIGURE 2-49

Later in this project, you will jump to the hyperlink destination.

Sorting Paragraphs

The MLA style requires that the works cited be listed in alphabetical order by author's last name. With Word, you can arrange paragraphs in alphabetic, numeric, or date order based on the first character in each paragraph. Ordering characters in this manner is called **sorting**. Arrange the works cited paragraphs in alphabetic order as illustrated in the steps on the next page.

Other **Ways**

1. Right-click text, click Hyperlink on shortcut menu, click Existing File or Web Page in the Link to list, type Web address in Type the file or Web page name text box, click OK button

2. Click text, click Insert Hyperlink button on Standard toolbar, click Existing File or Web Page in the Link to list, type Web address in Type the file or Web page name text box, click OK button

Steps **To Sort Paragraphs**

1 **Select all the works cited paragraphs by pointing to the left of the first paragraph and dragging down. Click Table on the menu bar and then point to Sort.**

Word displays the Table menu (Figure 2-50). All of the paragraphs to be sorted are selected.

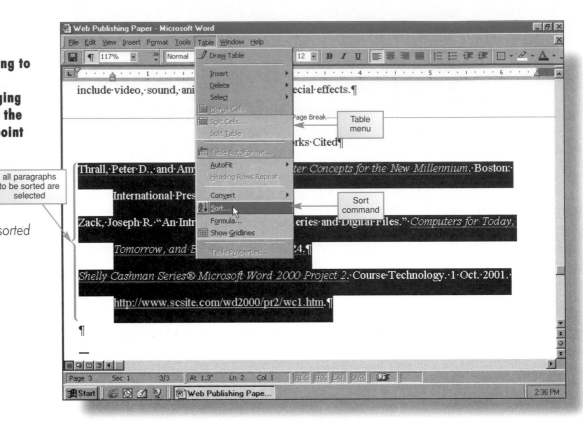

FIGURE 2-50

2 **Click Sort. Point to the OK button.**

Word displays the Sort Text dialog box (Figure 2-51). In the Sort by area, Ascending is selected. Ascending sorts in alphabetic, numeric, or earliest to latest date order.

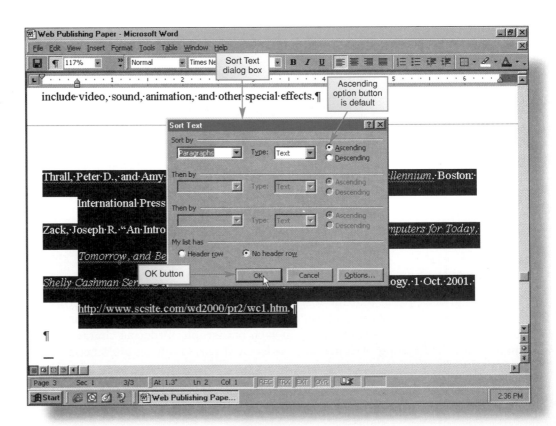

FIGURE 2-51

3 **Click the OK button. Click outside of the selection to remove the highlight.**

Word sorts the works cited paragraphs alphabetically (Figure 2-52).

paragraphs sorted alphabetically

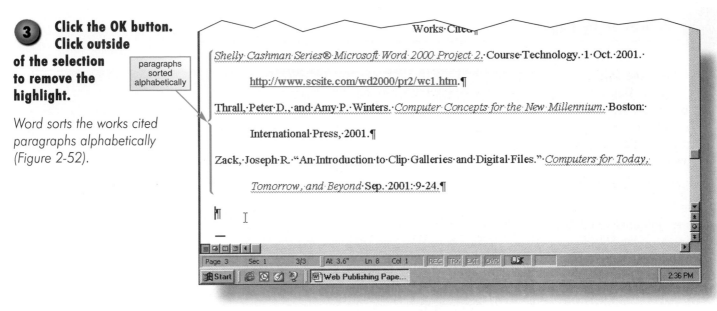

FIGURE 2-52

If you accidentally sort the wrong paragraphs, you can undo a sort by clicking the Undo button on the Standard toolbar.

In the Sort Text dialog box (Figure 2-51), the default sort order is Ascending. By default, Word orders in **ascending sort order**, which means from the beginning of the alphabet to the end of the alphabet, smallest number to the largest number, or earliest date to the most recent date. For example, if the first character of each paragraph to be sorted is a letter, Word sorts the selected paragraphs alphabetically.

You also can sort in descending order by clicking Descending in the Sort Text dialog box. **Descending sort order** means sorting from the end of the alphabet to the beginning of the alphabet, the largest number to the smallest number, or the most recent date to the earliest date.

Proofing and Revising the Research Paper

As discussed in Project 1, once you complete a document, you might find it necessary to make changes to it. Before submitting a paper to be graded, you should proofread it. While **proofreading**, you look for grammatical errors and spelling errors. You want to be sure the transitions between sentences flow smoothly and sentences themselves make sense. Very often, you may count the words in a paper to meet minimum word guidelines specified by an instructor. To assist you in this proofreading effort, Word provides several tools. These tools are discussed in the following pages.

Going to a Specific Location in a Document

Often, you would like to bring a certain page, footnote, or other object into view in the document window. To accomplish this, you could scroll through the document to find the desired page, footnote, or item. Instead of scrolling through the document, Word provides an easier method of going to a specific location via the **Select Browse Object menu**. Perform the steps on the next page to go to the top of page two in the research paper.

More About

Proofreading

When proofreading a paper, ask yourself these questions: Is the purpose clear? Does the title suggest the topic? Does the paper have an introduction, body, and conclusion? Is the thesis clear? Does each paragraph in the body relate to the thesis? Is the conclusion effective? Are all sources acknowledged?

To Browse by Page

1 **Click the Select Browse Object button on the vertical scroll bar. When the Select Browse Object menu displays, point to Browse by Page.**

Word displays the Select Browse Object menu (Figure 2-53). As you point to various commands on the Select Browse Object menu, Word displays the command name at the bottom of the menu.

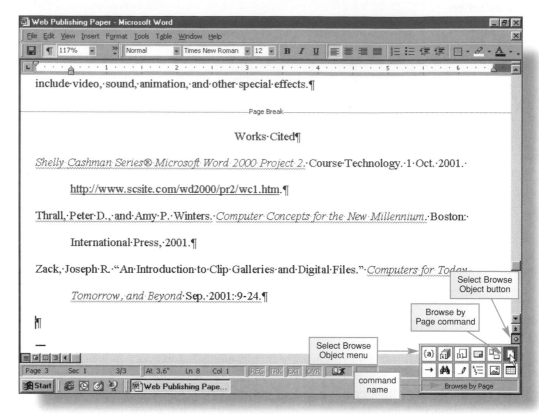

FIGURE 2-53

2 **Click Browse by Page. Point to the Previous Page button on the vertical scroll bar.**

Word closes the Select Browse Object menu and displays the top of page 3 at the top of the document window (Figure 2-54).

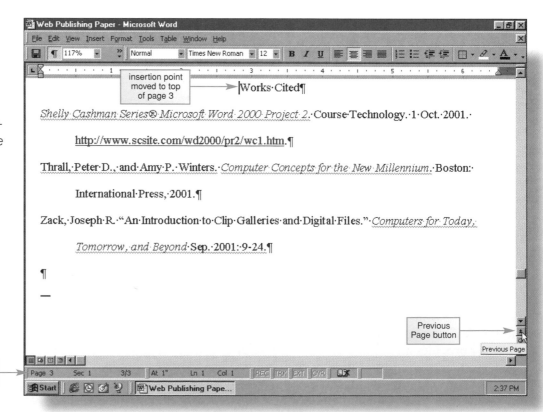

FIGURE 2-54

Click the Previous Page button.

Word places the top of page 2 (the previous page) at the top of the document window (Figure 2-55).

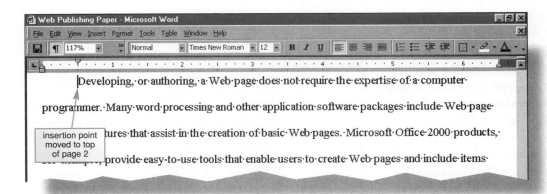

FIGURE 2-55

Other Ways

1. Double-click page indicator on status bar (Figure 2-54), click Page in Go to what list, type page number in Enter page number text box, click Go To button, click Close button

2. On Edit menu click Go To, and then proceed as described in 1 above starting with click Page in Go to what list

3. Press CTRL+G, and then proceed as described in 1 above starting with click Page in Go to what list

Depending on the command you click in the Select Browse Object menu, the function of the buttons above and below the Select Browse Object button on the vertical scroll bar changes. When you select Browse by Page, the buttons become Previous Page and Next Page buttons; when you select Browse by Footnote, the buttons become Previous Footnote and Next Footnote buttons, and so on.

Finding and Replacing Text

While proofreading the paper, you notice that it contains the word, creation, more than once in the document (see Figure 2-56 below); and you would rather use the word, development. Therefore, you wish to change all occurrences of the word, creation, to the word, development. To do this, you can use Word's find and replace feature, which automatically locates each occurrence of a specified word or phrase and then replaces it with specified text as shown in these steps.

 To Find and Replace Text

 Click the Select Browse Object button on the vertical scroll bar. Point to Find on the Select Browse Object menu (Figure 2-56).

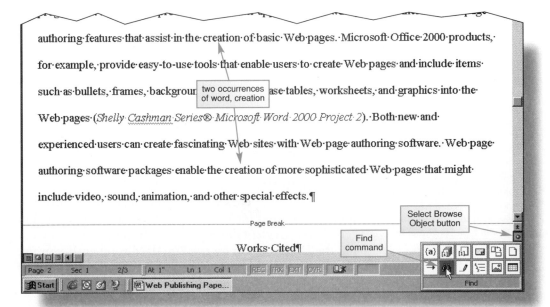

FIGURE 2-56

2 Click Find. When the Find and Replace dialog box displays, click the Replace tab. Type creation in the Find what text box. Press the TAB key. Type development in the Replace with text box. Point to the Replace All button.

Word displays the Find and Replace dialog box (Figure 2-57). The Replace All button replaces all occurrences of the Find what text with the Replace with text.

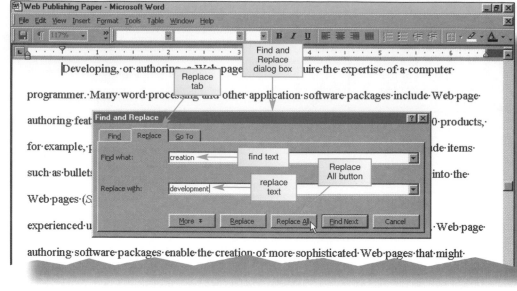

FIGURE 2-57

3 Click the Replace All button.

A Microsoft Word dialog box displays indicating the total number of replacements made (Figure 2-58).

4 Click the OK button. Click the Close button in the Find and Replace dialog box.

The word, development, displays in the document instead of the word, creation (see Figure 2-59).

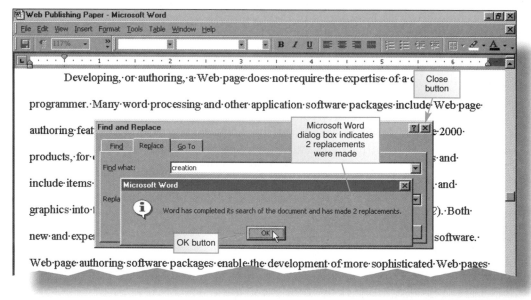

FIGURE 2-58

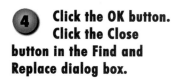

1. Double-click page indicator on status bar, click Replace tab, type Find what text, type Replace with text, click OK button, click Close button

2. On Edit menu click Replace, and then proceed as described in 1 above starting with type Find what text

3. Press CTRL+H, and then proceed as described in 1 above starting with type Find what text

In some cases, you may want to replace only certain occurrences of the text, not all of them. To instruct Word to confirm each change, click the Find Next button in the Find and Replace dialog box (Figure 2-57), instead of the Replace All button. When Word locates an occurrence of the text, it pauses and waits for you to click either the Replace button or the Find Next button. Clicking the Replace button changes the text; clicking the Find Next button instructs Word to disregard the replacement and look for the next occurrence of the Find what text.

If you accidentally replace the wrong text, you can undo a replacement by clicking the Undo button on the Standard toolbar. If you used the Replace All button, Word undoes all replacements. If you used the Replace button, Word undoes only the most recent replacement.

Finding Text

Sometimes, you may want to find only text, instead of find *and* replace text. To search for just a single occurrence of text, you would follow these steps.

TO FIND TEXT

1 Click the Select Browse Object button on the vertical scroll bar and then click Find on the Select Browse Object menu.

2 Type the text to locate in the Find what text box and then click the Find Next button. To edit the text, click the Close button in the Find and Replace dialog box; to find the next occurrence of the text, click the Find Next button.

Moving Text

While proofreading the research paper, you might realize that text in the last paragraph would flow better if the last two sentences were reversed. That is, you want to move the fourth sentence in the last paragraph to the end of the paragraph.

To move text, such as words, characters, sentences, or paragraphs, you first select the text to be moved and then use drag-and-drop editing or the cut-and-paste technique to move the selected text. With **drag-and-drop editing**, you drag the selected item to the new location and then insert, or drop, it there. **Cutting** involves removing the selected item from the document and then placing it on the **Office Clipboard**, which is a temporary storage area. **Pasting** is the process of copying an item from the Clipboard into the document at the location of the insertion point.

Use drag-and-drop editing to move an item a short distance. To drag-and-drop a sentence in the research paper, first select a sentence as shown below.

More About

Finding

To search for formatting or special characters, click the More button in the Find dialog box. To find formatting, click the Format button, select the formats you want to search for, then click the Find button. To find a special character, click the Special button, click the special character you desire, and then click the Find button.

More About

Cutting and Pasting

To move text a long distance (from one page to another page), the cut-and-paste technique is more efficient. When you paste text into a document, the contents of the Office Clipboard are not erased.

 To Select a Sentence

1 **Position the mouse pointer (an I-beam) in the sentence to be moved. Press and hold the CTRL key. While holding the CTRL key, click the sentence. Release the CTRL key.**

Word selects the entire sentence (Figure 2-59). Notice the space after the period is included in the selection.

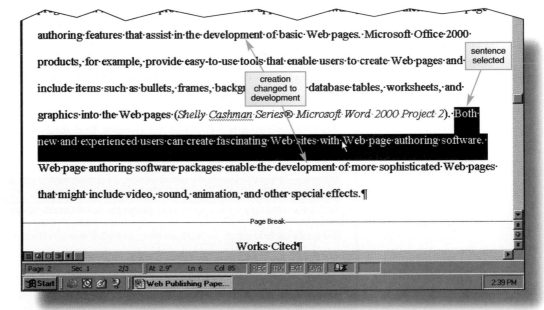

FIGURE 2-59

Other Ways

1. Drag through the sentence

Table 2-4 Techniques for Selecting Items with the Mouse

ITEM TO SELECT	MOUSE ACTION
Block of text	Click at beginning of selection, scroll to end of selection, position mouse pointer at end of selection, hold down SHIFT key and then click
Character(s)	Drag through character(s)
Document	Move mouse to left of text until mouse pointer changes to a right-pointing block arrow, then triple-click
Graphic	Click the graphic
Line	Move mouse to left of line until mouse pointer changes to a right-pointing block arrow, then click
Lines	Move mouse to left of first line until mouse pointer changes to a right-pointing block arrow, then drag up or down
Paragraph	Triple-click paragraph; or move mouse to left of paragraph until mouse pointer changes to a right-pointing block arrow, then double-click
Paragraphs	Move mouse to left of paragraph until mouse pointer changes to a right-pointing block arrow, double-click, then drag up or down
Sentence	Press and hold CTRL key, then click sentence
Word	Double-click the word
Words	Drag through words

Throughout Projects 1 and 2, you have selected text and then formatted it. Because selecting text is such a crucial function of Word, Table 2-4 summarizes the techniques used to select various items with the mouse.

With the sentence to be moved selected, you can use drag-and-drop editing to move it. You should be sure that drag-and-drop editing is enabled by clicking Tools on the menu bar, clicking Options, clicking the Edit tab, verifying a check mark is next to Drag and drop text editing, and then clicking the OK button. Follow these steps to move the selected sentence to the end of the paragraph.

 To Move Text

1 **With the mouse pointer in the selected text, press and hold the mouse button.**

*When you begin to drag the selected text, the insertion point changes to a **dotted insertion point** (Figure 2-60).*

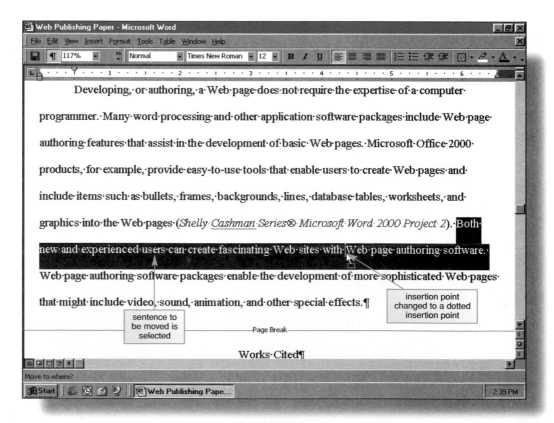

FIGURE 2-60

2 Drag the dotted insertion point to the location where the selected text is to be moved.

The dotted insertion point is at the end of the paragraph (Figure 2-61).

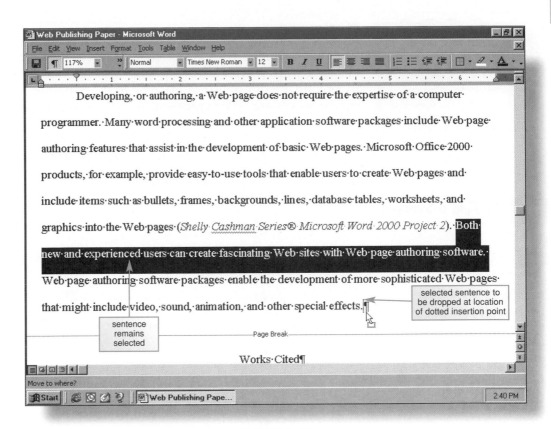

Developing, or authoring, a Web page does not require the expertise of a computer programmer. Many word processing and other application software packages include Web page authoring features that assist in the development of basic Web pages. Microsoft Office 2000 products, for example, provide easy-to-use tools that enable users to create Web pages and include items such as bullets, frames, backgrounds, lines, database tables, worksheets, and graphics into the Web pages (*Shelly Cashman Series® Microsoft Word 2000 Project 2*). Both new and experienced users can create fascinating Web sites with Web page authoring software. Web page authoring software packages enable the development of more sophisticated Web pages that might include video, sound, animation, and other special effects.

selected sentence to be dropped at location of dotted insertion point

sentence remains selected

Page Break

Works Cited¶

FIGURE 2-61

3 Release the mouse button. Click outside selection to remove the highlight.

Word moves the selected text to the location of the dotted insertion point (Figure 2-62).

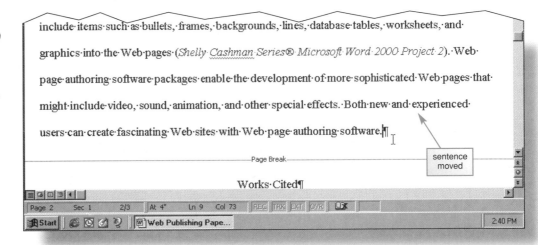

include items such as bullets, frames, backgrounds, lines, database tables, worksheets, and graphics into the Web pages (*Shelly Cashman Series® Microsoft Word 2000 Project 2*). Web page authoring software packages enable the development of more sophisticated Web pages that might include video, sound, animation, and other special effects. Both new and experienced users can create fascinating Web sites with Web page authoring software.¶

sentence moved

Page Break

Works Cited¶

FIGURE 2-62

You can click the Undo button on the Standard toolbar if you accidentally drag text to the wrong location.

You can use drag-and-drop editing to move any selected item. That is, you can select words, sentences, phrases, and graphics and then use drag-and-drop editing to move them.

If you hold the CTRL key while dragging the selected item, Word copies the item instead of moving it.

Other Ways

1. Click Cut button on Standard toolbar, click where text is to be pasted, click Paste button on Standard toolbar

2. On Edit menu click Cut, click where text is to be pasted, on Edit menu click Paste

3. Press CTRL+X, position insertion point where text is to be pasted, press CTRL+V

Synonyms

For access to an online the-saurus, visit the Word 2000 More About Web page (www.scsite.com/wd2000/more.htm) and then click Online Thesaurus.

Finding a Synonym

When writing, you may find that you used the same word in multiple locations or that a word you used was not quite appropriate. In these instances, you will want to look up a word similar in meaning to the duplicate or inappropriate word. These similar words are called **synonyms**. A book of synonyms is referred to as a **thesaurus**. Word provides synonyms and a thesaurus for your convenience. In this project, you would like a synonym for the word, include, in the middle of the last paragraph of the research paper. Perform the following steps to find an appropriate synonym.

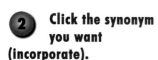 **To Find a Synonym**

1 **Right-click the word for which you want to look up a synonym (include). Point to Synonyms on the shortcut menu and then point to the appropriate synonym (incorporate) on the Synonyms submenu.**

Word displays a list of synonyms for the word con-taining the insertion point (Figure 2-63).

2 **Click the synonym you want (incorporate).**

Word replaces the word, include, in the document with the selected word, incorporate (Figure 2-64).

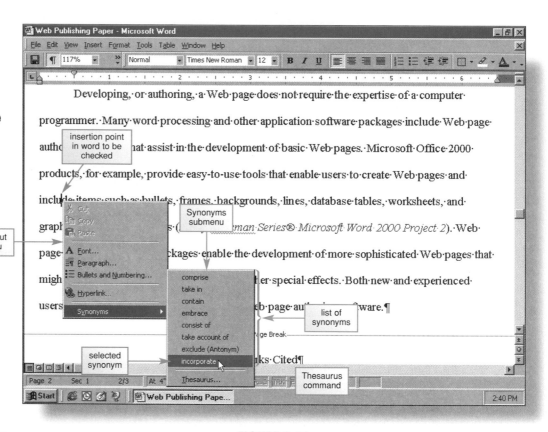

FIGURE 2-63

Other Ways

1. Click word, on Tools menu point to Language, on Language menu click Thesaurus, click appropriate meaning in Meanings list, click desired synonym in Replace with Synonym list, click Replace button

2. Click word, press SHIFT+F7, click appropriate meaning in Meanings list, click desired synonym in Replace with Synonym list, click Replace button

If the synonyms list does not display an appropriate word, you can display the Thesaurus dialog box by clicking Thesaurus on the Synonyms submenu (Figure 2-63). In the Thesaurus dialog box, you can look up synonyms for a different meaning of the word. You also can look up **antonyms**, or words with an opposite meaning.

Using Word Count

Often when you write papers, you are required to compose a paper with a mini-mum number of words. The requirement for the research paper in this project was a minimum of 425 words. Word provides a command that displays the number of words, as well as the number of pages, characters, paragraphs, and lines in your document. Perform the following steps to use word count.

Steps **To Count Words**

1 Click Tools on the menu bar and then point to Word Count (Figure 2-64).

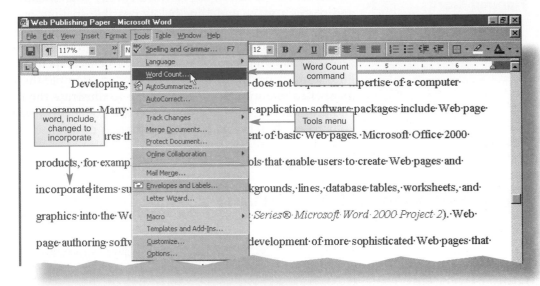

FIGURE 2-64

2 Click Word Count. When the Word Count dialog box displays, if necessary, click Include footnotes and endnotes to select the check box.

Word displays the Word Count dialog box (Figure 2-65).

3 Click the Close button in the Word Count dialog box.

Word returns you to the document.

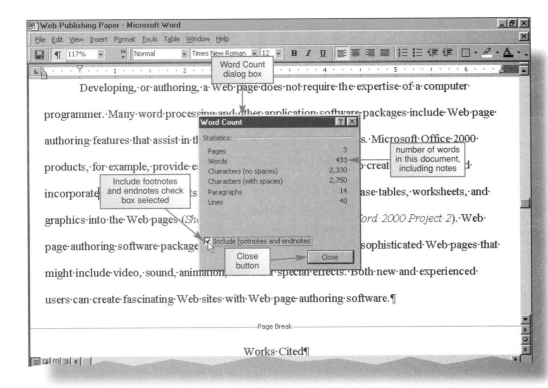

FIGURE 2-65

 Other **Ways**

1. On File menu click Properties, click Statistics tab, click OK button

The Word Count dialog box presents a variety of statistics about the current document, including number of pages, words, characters, paragraphs, and lines (Figure 2-65). You can choose to have note text included or not included in these statistics. If you want statistics on only a section of your document, select the section and then invoke the Word Count command.

Flagged Words

If you right-click a word, a shortcut menu displays. Recall that commands in a shortcut menu differ depending on the object that you right-click. If you right-click a word flagged with a red or green wavy underline, the shortcut menu displays spelling or grammar corrections for the flagged word.

Checking Spelling and Grammar at Once

As discussed in Project 1, Word checks your spelling and grammar as you type and places a wavy underline below possible spelling or grammar errors. You learned in Project 1 how to check these flagged words immediately. You also can wait and check the entire document for spelling and grammar errors at once.

The following steps illustrate how to check spelling and grammar in the Web Publishing Paper at once. In the following example the word, maintaining, has been misspelled intentionally as maintining to illustrate the use of Word's check spelling and grammar at once feature. If you are doing this project on a personal computer, your research paper may contain different misspelled words, depending on the accuracy of your typing.

Steps **To Check Spelling and Grammar At Once**

① **Press the CTRL+HOME keys to move the insertion point to the beginning of the document. Double-click the move handle on the Standard toolbar to display the entire toolbar. Point to the Spelling and Grammar button on the Standard toolbar.**

Word will begin the spelling and grammar check at the location of the insertion point, which is at the beginning of the document (Figure 2-66).

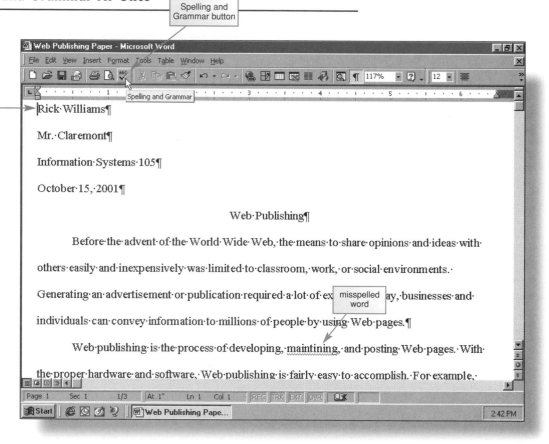

FIGURE 2-66

2 **Click the Spelling and Grammar button. When the Spelling and Grammar dialog box displays, click maintaining in the Suggestions list and then point to the Change button.**

Word displays the Spelling and Grammar dialog box (Figure 2-67). Word did not find the misspelled word, maintaining, in its dictionary. The Suggestions list displays suggested corrections for the flagged word.

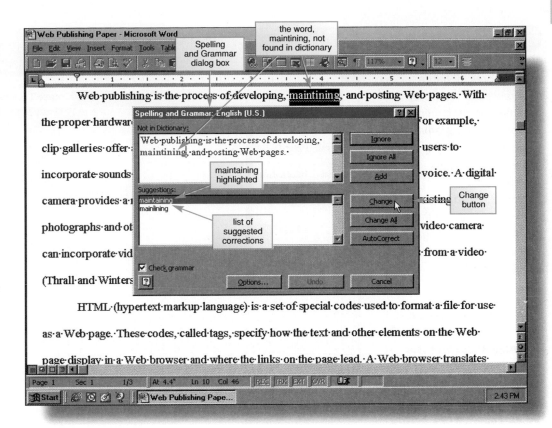

FIGURE 2-67

3 **Click the Change button.**

Word continues the spelling and grammar check until it finds the next error or reaches the end of the document (Figure 2-68). Word did not find Cashman in its dictionary because Cashman is a proper name. Cashman is spelled correctly.

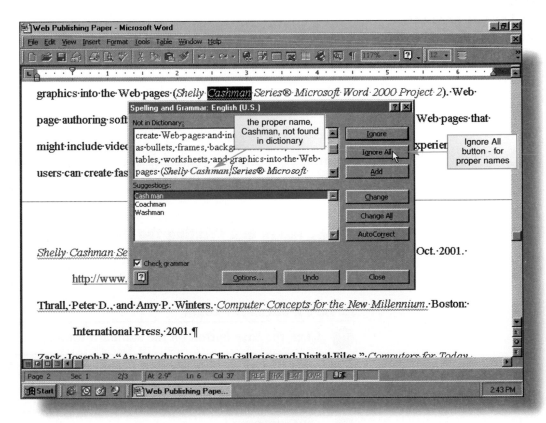

FIGURE 2-68

4 **Click the Ignore All button.**

Word ignores all future occurrences of the word, Cashman. Word continues the spelling and grammar check until it finds the next error or reaches the end of the document. Word flags a grammar error on the Works Cited page (Figure 2-69). The works cited is written correctly.

5 **Click the Ignore button. For each of the remaining grammar errors that Word flags on the Works Cited page, click the Ignore button. When the Microsoft Word dialog box displays indicating Word has completed the spelling and grammar check, click the OK button.**

Word returns to the document window.

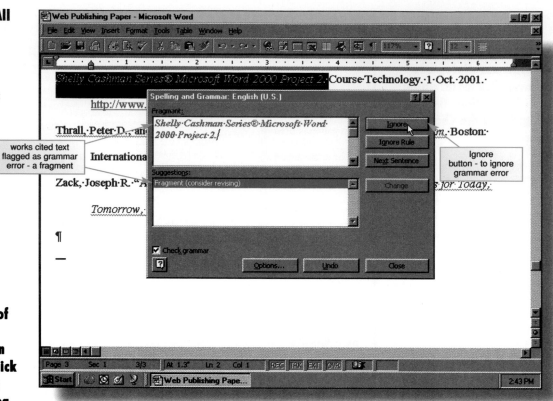

FIGURE 2-69

Your document no longer displays red and green wavy underlines below words and phrases. In addition, the red X on the Spelling and Grammar Status icon has returned to a red check mark.

Saving Again and Printing the Document

The document now is complete. You should save the research paper again and print it, as described in the following steps.

TO SAVE A DOCUMENT AGAIN

 Click the Save button on the Standard toolbar.

Word saves the research paper with the same file name, Web Publishing Paper.

TO PRINT A DOCUMENT

 Click the Print button on the Standard toolbar.

The completed research paper prints as shown in Figure 2-1 on page WD 2.5.

Navigating to a Hyperlink

Recall that one requirement of this research paper is that one of the works be a Web site and be formatted as a hyperlink. Perform the following steps to check your hyperlink.

 To Navigate to a Hyperlink

1 **Display the third page of the research paper in the document window and then point to the hyperlink.**

When you point to a hyperlink in a Word document, the mouse pointer shape changes to a pointing hand (Figure 2-70).

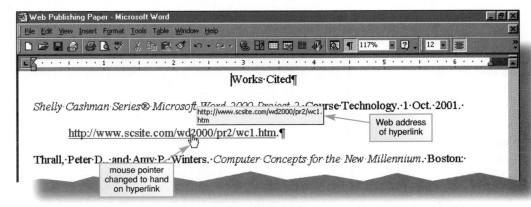

FIGURE 2-70

2 **Click the hyperlink.**

If you currently are not connected to the Web, Word connects you using your default browser. The www.scsite.com/wd2000/ pr2/wc1.htm Web page displays (Figure 2-71).

3 **Close the browser window. If necessary, click the Microsoft Word program button on the taskbar to redisplay the Word window. Press CTRL+HOME.**

The first page of the research paper displays in the Word window.

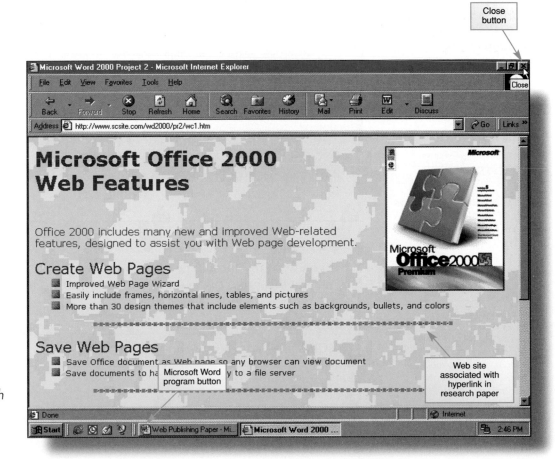

FIGURE 2-71

More About

E-mailing

To e-mail a document as an attachment, click File on the menu bar, point to Send To, and then click Mail Recipient (as Attachment).

E-mailing a Copy of the Research Paper

Your instructor, Mr. Claremont, has requested you e-mail him a copy of your research paper so he can verify your hyperlink. Perform the following step to e-mail the document from within Word.

Steps To E-mail a Document

1 **Click the E-mail button on the Standard toolbar. Fill in the To text box with Mr. Claremont's e-mail address and the Subject text box (Figure 2-72) and then click the Send a Copy button.**

Word displays certain buttons and boxes from your e-mail editor inside the Word window. The document is e-mailed to the recipient named in the To text box.

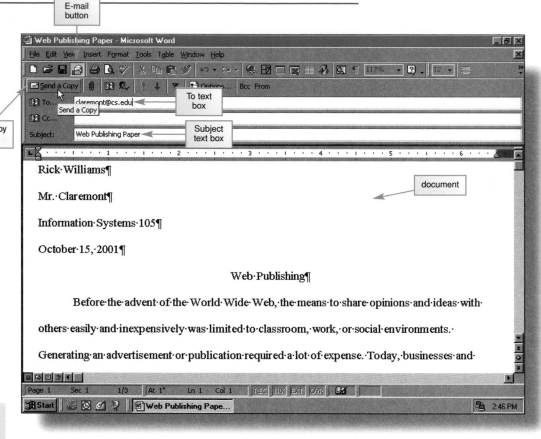

FIGURE 2-72

Other Ways

1. On File menu point to Send To, on Send To menu click Mail Recipient

More About

Quick Reference

For a table that lists how to complete the tasks covered in this book using the mouse, menu, shortcut menu, and keyboard, visit the Office 2000 Web page (www.scsite.com/off2000/qr.htm) and then click Microsoft Word 2000.

If you want to cancel the e-mail operation, click the E-mail button again. The final step in this project is to quit Word, as described in the following step.

TO QUIT WORD

1 Click the Close button in the Word window.

The Word window closes.

CASE PERSPECTIVE SUMMARY

Rick accomplished his goal – learning about the basics of Web publishing while completing Mr. Claremont's research paper assignment. Now he is ready to create a personal Web page and publish it to a Web server. Rick decides to use Word's Web Page Wizard to create his Web page. He also contacts his Internet service provider to set up his free 6 MB of Web space. After receiving his personal Web site address from his Internet service provider, Rick publishes his Web page for the world to see. (For more information on publishing Web pages to a Web server, see Appendix B.) He shows Mr. Claremont the Web page, who in turn shows Rick's classmates.

Project Summary

Project 2 introduced you to creating a research paper using the MLA documentation style. You learned how to change margin settings, adjust line spacing, create headers with page numbers, and indent paragraphs. You learned how to use Word's AutoCorrect feature. Then, you added a footnote in the research paper. You alphabetized the works cited page by sorting its paragraphs and included a hyperlink to a Web page in one of the works. You learned how to browse through a Word document, find and replace text, and move text. You looked up a synonym and saw how to display statistics about your document. Finally, you navigated to a hyperlink and e-mailed a copy of a document.

What You Should Know

Having completed this project, you now should be able to perform the following tasks:

- Add a Footnote *(WD 2.23)*
- AutoCorrect As You Type *(WD 2.20)*
- Browse by Page *(WD 2.42)*
- Center the Title of the Works Cited Page *(WD 2.36)*
- Change the Default Font Size *(WD 2.15)*
- Change the Margin Settings *(WD 2.8)*
- Check Spelling and Grammar at Once *(WD 2.50)*
- Click and Type *(WD 2.13)*
- Close the Note Pane *(WD 2.29)*
- Count Words *(WD 2.49)*
- Create a Hanging Indent *(WD 2.37)*
- Create a Hyperlink as You Type *(WD 2.39)*
- Create an AutoCorrect Entry *(WD 2.21)*
- Display Formatting Marks *(WD 2.7)*
- Display the Header Area *(WD 2.12)*
- Double-Space a Document *(WD 2.9)*
- E-mail a Document *(WD 2.54)*
- Enter and Format a Page Number *(WD 2.14)*
- Enter More Text *(WD 2.30)*
- Enter Name and Course Information *(WD 2.16)*
- Enter Works Cited Paragraphs *(WD 2.38)*
- Find a Synonym *(WD 2.48)*
- Find and Replace Text *(WD 2.43)*
- Find Text *(WD 2.45)*

- First-Line Indent Paragraphs *(WD 2.19)*
- Insert a Symbol Automatically *(WD 2.33)*
- Modify a Style *(WD 2.26)*
- Move Text *(WD 2.46)*
- Navigate to a Hyperlink *(WD 2.53)*
- Page Break Automatically *(WD 2.32)*
- Page Break Manually *(WD 2.35)*
- Print a Document *(WD 2.52)*
- Quit Word *(WD 2.54)*
- Reset Menus and Toolbars *(WD 2.7)*
- Save a Document *(WD 2.18)*
- Save a Document Again *(WD 2.52)*
- Select a Sentence *(WD 2.45)*
- Sort Paragraphs *(WD 2.40)*
- Start Word *(WD 2.6)*
- Use Shortcut Keys to Format Text *(WD 2.17)*
- Zoom Page Width *(WD 2.9)*

More About

Microsoft Certification

The Microsoft Office User Specialist (MOUS) Certification program provides an opportunity for you to obtain a valuable industry credential – proof that you have the Word 2000 skills required by employers. For more information, see Appendix D or visit the Shelly Cashman Series MOUS Web page at www.scsite.com/ off2000/cert.htm.

Apply Your Knowledge

1 Revising a Document

Instructions: Start Word. Open the document, Internet Paragraph, on the Data Disk. If you did not download the Data Disk, see the inside back cover for instructions for downloading the Data Disk or see your instructor.

The document is a paragraph of text. You are to move two sentences in the paragraph and change all occurrences of the word, Web, to the phrase, World Wide Web. The revised paragraph is shown in Figure 2-73.

> Although many people use the terms World Wide Web and Internet interchangeably, the World Wide Web is just one of the many services available on the Internet. The World Wide Web actually is a relatively new aspect of the Internet. While the Internet was developed in the late 1960s, the World Wide Web came into existence less than a decade ago – in the early 1990s. Since then, however, it has grown phenomenally to become the most widely used service on the Internet.

FIGURE 2-73

Perform the following tasks:

1. Press and hold the CTRL key. While holding the CTRL key, click in the third sentence, which begins, The Web actually is…, to select the sentence. Release the CTRL key.
2. Press and hold down the left mouse button. Drag the dotted insertion point to the left of the letter W in the second sentence beginning, While the Internet was…, and then release the mouse button to move the sentence. Click outside the selection to remove the highlight.
3. Click the Select Browse Object button on the vertical scroll bar and then click Find on the Select Browse Object menu.
4. When the Find and Replace dialog box displays, click the Replace tab. Type Web in the Find what text box, press the TAB key, and then type World Wide Web in the Replace with text box. Click the Replace All button.
5. Click the OK button in the Microsoft Word dialog box. Click the Close button in the Find and Replace dialog box.
6. Click File on the menu bar and then click Save As. Use the file name, Revised Internet Paragraph, and then save the document on your floppy disk.
7. Print the revised paragraph.

In the Lab

1 Preparing a Research Paper

Problem: You are a college student currently enrolled in an English composition class. Your assignment is to prepare a short research paper (400-425 words) about digital cameras. The requirements are that the paper be presented according to the MLA documentation style and have three references (Figures 2-74a through 2-74c shown below and on the next page). One of the three references must be from the Internet and formatted as a hyperlink on the Works Cited page.

Thornton 1

Anne Thornton

Ms. Baxter

English 105

March 12, 2001

Digital Cameras

Digital cameras allow computer users to take pictures and store the photographed images digitally instead of on traditional film. With some digital cameras, a user downloads the stored pictures from the digital camera to a computer using special software included with the camera. With others, the camera stores the pictures directly on a floppy disk or on a PC Card. A user then copies the pictures to a computer by inserting the floppy disk into a disk drive or the PC Card into a PC Card slot (Chambers and Norton 134). Once stored on a computer, the pictures can be edited with photo-editing software, printed, faxed, sent via electronic mail, included in another document, or posted to a Web site for everyone to see.

Three basic types of digital cameras are studio cameras, field cameras, and point-and-shoot cameras (*Shelly Cashman Series® Microsoft Word 2000 Project 2*). The most expensive and highest quality of the three, a studio camera, is a stationary camera used for professional studio work. Photojournalists frequently use field cameras because they are portable and have a variety of lenses and other attachments. As with the studio camera, a field camera can be quite expensive.

Reliable and lightweight, the point-and-shoot camera provides acceptable quality photographic images for the home or small business user. A point-and-shoot camera enables these users to add pictures to personalized greeting cards, a computerized photo album, a family

FIGURE 2-74a

(continued)

In the Lab

Preparing a Research Paper *(continued)*

Thornton 2

newsletter, certificates, awards, or a personal Web site. Because of its functionality, it is an ideal

camera for mobile users such as real estate agents, insurance agents, and general contractors.

The image quality produced by a digital camera is measured by the number of bits it

stores in a dot and the resolution, or number of dots per inch. The higher each number, the better

the quality, but the more expensive the camera. Most of today's point-and-shoot digital cameras

are at least 24-bit with a resolution ranging from 640 x 480 to 1024 x 960 (Walker 57-89). Home

and small business users can find an affordable camera with a resolution in this range that

delivers excellent detail for less than $400.

FIGURE 2-74b

Thornton 3

Works Cited

Chambers, John Q., and Theresa R. Norton. *Understanding Computers in the New Century.*

Chicago: Midwest Press, 2001.

Shelly Cashman Series® Word 2000 Project 2. Course Technology. 5 Mar. 2001.

http://www.scsite.com/wd2000/pr2/wc2.htm.

Walker, Marianne L. "Understanding the Resolutions of Digital Cameras and Imaging Devices."

Computing for the Home Feb. 2001: 57-89.

FIGURE 2-74c

Instructions:

1. If necessary, click the Show/Hide ¶ button on the Standard toolbar. Change all margins to one inch. Adjust line spacing to double. Create a header to number pages. If necessary, change the font size of all characters to 12 point. Type the name and course information at the left margin. Center and type the title. First-line indent all paragraphs in the paper.

2. Type the body of the paper as shown in Figure 2-74a on the previous page and Figure 2-74b. At the end of the body of the research paper, press the ENTER key and insert a manual page break.

3. Create the works cited page (Figure 2-74c).

4. Check the spelling of the paper at once.

5. Save the document on a floppy disk with Digital Camera Paper as the file name.

6. If you have access to the Web, test your hyperlink by clicking it.

7. Print the research paper. Above the title of your printed research paper, handwrite the number of words in the research paper.

2 **Preparing a Research Report with Footnotes**

Problem: You are a college student currently enrolled in an English composition class. Your assignment is to prepare a short research paper in any area of interest to you. The requirements are that the paper be presented according to the MLA documentation style and have three references. One of the three references must be from the Internet and formatted as a hyperlink on the works cited page. You decide to prepare a paper on virtual reality (Figures 2-75 below and on the next page).

Jameson 1

Casey Jameson

Mr. Brookfield

English 105

September 14, 2001

Virtual Reality

Virtual reality (VR) is the use of a computer to create an artificial environment that appears and feels like a real environment and allows users to explore a space and manipulate the environment. In its simplest form, a VR application displays what appears to be a three-dimensional view of a place or object, such as a landscape, building, molecule, or red blood cell, which users can explore. For example, architects can use VR software to show clients how a building will look after a construction or remodeling project.

In more advanced forms, VR software requires that users wear specialized headgear, body suits, and gloves to enhance the experience of the artificial environment (Vance and Reed 34-58). The headgear displays the artificial environment in front of a user's eyes.[1] The body suit and the gloves sense motion and direction, allowing a user to move through, pick up, or hold items displayed in the virtual environment. Experts predict that eventually the body suits will provide tactile feedback so users can experience the touch and feel of the virtual world.

Many games, such as flight simulators, use virtual reality. In these games, special visors allow users to see the computer-generated environment. As the user walks around the game's electronic landscape, sensors in the surrounding game machine record movements and change the view of the landscape accordingly.

_____

[1] According to Vance and Reed, patients in one dental office wear VR headsets to relax them during their visit with the dentist.

FIGURE 2-75a

(continued)

In the Lab

Preparing a Research Report with Footnotes *(continued)*

Jameson 2

Companies increasingly are using VR for more practical commercial applications, as well. Automobile dealers, for example, use virtual showrooms in which customers can view the exterior and interior of available vehicles. Airplane manufacturers use virtual prototypes to test new models and shorten product design time. Many firms use personal computer-based VR applications for employee training (*Shelly Cashman Series® Microsoft Word 2000 Project 2*). As computing power and the use of the Web increase, practical applications of VR continue to emerge in education, business, and entertainment.[2]

---

[2] Henry Davidson, a developer of VR applications, predicts that in the future, moviegoers will be able to pretend they are one of a movie's characters. In this environment, the VR technology will link the moviegoer's sensory system (sight, smell, hearing, taste, and touch) to the character's sensory system (Holloway 46-52).

FIGURE 2-75b

In the Lab

Part 1 Instructions: Perform the following tasks to create the research paper:

1. If necessary, click the Show/Hide ¶ button on the Standard toolbar. Change all margin settings to one inch. Adjust line spacing to double. Create a header to number pages. If necessary, change the font size of all characters to 12 point. Type the name and course information at the left margin. Center and type the title. First-line indent all paragraphs in the paper.

2. Type the body of the paper as shown in Figure 2-75a on page WD 2.59 and Figure 2-75b. At the end of the body of the research paper, press the ENTER key once and insert a manual page break.

3. Create the works cited page. Enter the works cited shown below as separate paragraphs and then sort the paragraphs.
   (a) *Shelly Cashman Series® Microsoft Word 2000 Project 2.* Course Technology. 3 Sep. 2001. http://www.scsite.com/wd2000/pr2/wc3.htm.
   (b) Holloway, April I. "The Future of Virtual Reality Applications." *Computers for Today, Tomorrow, and Beyond* Sep. 2001: 46-52.
   (c) Vance, Dale W., and Karen P. Reed. *The Complete Book of Virtual Reality.* Dallas: Worldwide Press, 2001.

4. Check the spelling of the paper.

5. Save the document on a floppy disk with Virtual Reality Paper as the file name.

6. If you have access to the Web, test your hyperlink by clicking it.

7. Print the research paper. Above the title of your printed research paper, handwrite the number of words, including the footnotes, in the research paper.

Part 2 Instructions: Perform the following tasks to modify the research paper:

1. Use Word to find a synonym of your choice for the word, eventually, in the second paragraph.

2. Change all occurrences of the word, artificial, to the word, simulated.

3. In the second footnote, change the word, link, to the word, connect.

4. Convert the footnotes to endnotes. You have learned that endnotes appear at the end of a document. *Hint:* Use Help to learn about converting footnotes to endnotes.

5. Modify the Endnote text style to 12-point font, double-spaced text with a first-line indent. Insert a page break so the endnotes are placed on a separate numbered page. Center the title, Endnotes, double-spaced above the notes.

6. Change the format of the note reference marks from Arabic numbers (1., 2., etc.) to capital letters (A., B., etc.). *Hint:* Use Help to learn about changing the number format of note reference marks.

7. Save the document on a floppy disk with Revised Virtual Reality Paper as the file name.

8. Print the revised research paper.

In the Lab

3 Composing a Research Paper from Notes

Problem: You have drafted the notes shown in Figure 2-76. Your assignment is to prepare a short research paper from these notes. Review the notes and then rearrange and reword them. Embellish the paper as you deem necessary. Add a footnote elaborating on a personal experience you have had. Present the paper according to the MLA documentation style.

Instructions: Perform the following tasks:

1. Change all margin settings to one inch. Adjust line spacing to double. Create a header to number pages. If necessary, change the font size of all characters to 12 point. Type the name and course information at the left margin. Center and type the title. First-line indent all paragraphs in the paper.

Productivity software makes people more efficient and effective in their daily activities. Three popular applications are (1) word processing, (2) spreadsheet, and (3) database.

Word Processing: Widely used application for creating, editing, and formatting text-based documents such as letters, memos, reports, fax cover sheet, mailing labels, and newsletters. Formatting features include changing font and font size, changing color of characters, organizing text into newspaper-style columns. Other features include adding clip art, changing margins, finding and replacing text, checking spelling and grammar, inserting headers and footers, providing a thesaurus, developing Web pages, and inserting tables. Source: "Evaluating Word Processing and Spreadsheet Software," an article in Computers Weekly, January 12, 2001 issue, pages 45-78, author Kimberly G. Rothman.

Spreadsheet: Used to organize data in rows and columns in a worksheet. Data is stored in cells, the intersection of rows and columns. Worksheets have more than 16 millions cells that can hold data. Cells can hold numbers, formulas, or functions. Formulas and functions perform calculations. When data in cells changes, the formulas and functions automatically recalculate formulas and display new values. Many spreadsheet packages allow you to create macros, which hold a series of keystrokes and instructions – a real timesaver. Most also include the ability to create charts, e.g. line charts, column charts, and pie charts, from the data. Source: same as for word processing software.

Database: Used to collect data and allow access, retrieval, and use of that data. Data stored in tables, which consists of rows (records) and columns (fields). Data can contain text, numbers, dates, or hyperlinks. When data is entered, it can be validated (compared to a set of stored rules or values to determine if the entered data is correct). Once the data is stored, you can sort it, query it, and generate reports from it. Sometimes called a database management system (DBMS). Source: Understanding Databases, a book published by Harbor Press in Detroit, Michigan, 2001, pages 35-56, authors Mark A. Greene and Andrea K. Peterson.

Microsoft Word 2000 is word processing software; Microsoft Excel 2000 is an example of spreadsheet software; and Microsoft Access 2000 is a database software package. Source: a Web site titled Shelly Cashman Series® Microsoft Word 2000 Project 2 sponsored by Course Technology; site visited on March 12, 2001; Web address is http://www.scsite.com/wd2000/pr2/wc4.htm.

FIGURE 2-76

2. Compose the body of the paper from the notes in Figure 2-76. Be sure to include a footnote as specified. At the end of the body of the research paper, press the ENTER key once and insert a manual page break. Create the works cited page from the listed sources. Be sure to sort the works.

3. Check the spelling and grammar of the paper. Save the document on a floppy disk with Software Research Paper as the file name. Print the research paper. Above the title of the printed research paper, handwrite the number of words, including the footnote, in the research paper.

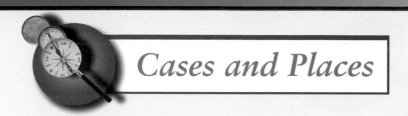

Cases and Places

The difficulty of these case studies varies:
▶ are the least difficult; ▶▶ are more difficult; and ▶▶▶ are the most difficult.

1 ▶ Project 1 of this book discussed the components of the Word document window. These components include the menu bar, toolbars, rulers, scroll bars, and status bar. In your own words, write a short research paper (400-450 words) that describes the purpose and functionality of one or more of these components. Use your textbook, Word Help, and any other resources available. Include at least two references and one explanatory note. Use the concepts and techniques presented in this project to format the paper.

2 ▶ Having completed two projects using Word 2000, you should be comfortable with some of its features. To reinforce your knowledge of Word's features, write a short research paper (400-450 words) that discusses a few of the features that you have learned. Features might include items such as checking spelling, inserting clip art, adding text using Click and Type, sorting paragraphs, and so on. Use your textbook, Word Help, and any other resources available. Include at least two references and one explanatory note. Use the concepts and techniques presented in this project to format the paper.

3 ▶▶ A pointing device is an input device that allows a user to control a pointer on a computer screen. Common pointing devices include the mouse, trackball, touchpad, pointing stick, joystick, touch screen, light pen, and graphics tablet. Using the school library, other textbooks, magazines, the Internet, or other resources, research two or more of these pointing devices. Then, prepare a brief research paper (400-450 words) that discusses the pointing devices. Include at least one explanatory note and two references, one of which must be a Web site on the Internet. Use the concepts and techniques presented in this project to format the paper.

4 ▶▶ A utility program, also called a utility, is a type of software that performs a specific task, usually related to managing a computer, its devices, or its programs. Popular utility programs are file viewers, file compression utilities, diagnostic utilities, disk scanners, disk defragmenters, uninstallers, backup utilities, antivirus programs, and screensavers. Using the school library, other textbooks, the Internet, magazines, or other resources, research two or more of these utility programs. Then, prepare a brief research paper (400-450 words) that discusses the utilities. Include at least one explanatory note and two references, one of which must be a Web site on the Internet. Use the concepts and techniques presented in this project to format the paper.

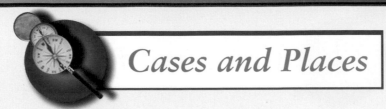

Cases and Places

5 ▶▶▶ Communications technologies have changed the way individuals interact, by allowing for instant and accurate information transfer, 24 hours a day. Today, uses of communications technology are all around and include e-mail, voice mail, fax, telecommuting, videoconferencing, groupware, global positioning systems (GPSs), bulletin board systems (BBSs), the Internet, the World Wide Web, e-commerce, and telephony. Using the school library, other textbooks, the Internet, magazines, or other resources, research two or more of these communications technologies. Then, prepare a brief research paper (400-450 words) that discusses the communications technologies. Include at least one explanatory note and two references, one of which must be a Web site on the Internet. Use the concepts and techniques presented in this project to format the paper.

6 ▶▶▶ In today's technology-rich world, a great demand for computer and information systems professionals exists and continues to grow. Career opportunities are available in many different areas including an information systems department, education and training, sales, service and repair, and consulting. Select an area of interest and research it. Obtain information about job titles, job functions, educational requirements, experience requirements, and salary ranges. Look through the classified section of a newspaper for job listings. Visit the career development and placement office at your school. Search the Web for employment opportunities at major companies. Then, prepare a brief research paper (400-450 words) on the career opportunities available. Indicate which ones you would pursue. Include at least two explanatory notes and three references, one of which must be a Web site on the Internet. Use the concepts and techniques presented in this project to format the paper.

7 ▶▶▶ The decision to purchase a personal computer is an important one – and finding and purchasing the right computer requires an investment of both time and money. In general, personal computers fall into three types: desktop computers, laptop computers, and handheld computers. Select one of these types of computers and shop for the best package deal. Many retailers offer software or additional hardware as part of a package deal. Visit or call a computer store. Search the Web for an online store. Look through newspapers or magazines for retailers, and obtain prices for their latest computer package deals. Then, prepare a brief research paper (400-450 words) on the various computer deals and recommend the one you feel is the best buy for the price. Include at least two explanatory notes and three references, one of which must be a Web site on the Internet. Use the concepts and techniques presented in this project to format the paper.

Microsoft **Word 2000**

Microsoft Word 2000

P R O J E C T

3

Using a Wizard to Create a Resume and Creating a Cover Letter with a Table

You will have mastered the material in this project when you can:

O B J E C T I V E S

- Create a resume using Word s Resume Wizard
- Identify the Word screen in print layout view
- Zoom text width
- Identify styles in a document
- Replace selected text with new text
- Insert a line break
- Use print preview to view, reduce the size of, and print a document
- Open a new document window
- Add color to characters
- Set and use tab stops
- Switch from one open Word document to another
- Collect and paste
- Insert a symbol
- Add a bottom border to a paragraph
- Identify the components of a business letter
- Create an AutoText entry
- Insert a nonbreaking space
- Insert an AutoText entry
- Create a bulleted list as you type
- Insert a Word table
- Enter data into a Word table
- Format a Word table
- Prepare and print an envelope address
- Close all open Word documents

Personalized Letters and Résumés

Get You the Job!

"**Y**oung physicist seeks teaching position at the university level. Ph.D. thesis submitted, awaiting acceptance. Works include papers on particle theory, quantum theory, and special theory of relativity. Family man, enjoys playing the violin and sailing. Contact A. Einstein."

Yes, *that* A. Einstein, who, in 1905, wrote by hand literally dozens of letters seeking employment as a teacher while he labored in relative obscurity at the Swiss patent office. The same year, he published three studies that set the world of science on its ear. Fame eventually helped, but persistence in his search paid off when he finally landed a teaching appointment at the University of Zurich after years as a patent clerk.

No one can tell whether Einstein might have met his goals more quickly if he would have had the benefit of modern word processing software, but certainly Microsoft Word would have made his life easier.

As you embark on your professional life, you have the advantage of using Word to prepare a resume and a personalized cover letter. In this project, you will learn these skills. Because employers review many resumes, the content of your resume is very important and its design and detail should represent you as the best candidate for the job. Providing a personalized cover letter with each resume enables you to elaborate on positive points in your resume and gives you an opportunity to show a potential employer your written communications skills.

Using the Résumé Wizard creates a resume that is tailored to your preferences. The Wizard provides the style, formats the resume with appropriate headings and spacing, and makes it easy for you to present your best qualities.

"Be studious in your profession, and you will be learned.
Be industrious and frugal, and you will be rich.
Be sober and temperate, and you will be healthy.
Be in general virtuous, and you will be happy.
At least you will, by such conduct, stand the best
chance for such consequences."

Benjamin Franklin

If good guidelines exist for doing something, then why not use them? This same practicality is built into the Résumé Wizard. Word provides the tools that eliminate the need to start from scratch every time, while you provide responses and supply the substance.

To understand the importance of using these guidelines, consider the meaning of the word represent: to bring clearly before the mind. When creating letters and résumés, which are two elements of business life that are fundamental to success, it is critical to bring a favorable image to mind. These documents must be crisp, to the point, and good-looking, because usually they are the first glimpse a prospective employer gets of a job-seeker.

Even if an individual's personal trip through the universe does not include physics or violins, a good résumé and cover letter may be the launch vehicles that start the journey.

Microsoft Word 2000

Using a Wizard to Create a Resume and Creating a Cover Letter with a Table

PROJECT 3

C A S E   P E R S P E C T I V E

Paulette Rose Brandon recently graduated from Illinois State College with a B.S. in Management, specializing in Marketing. She also has an A.S. in Business and an A.S. in Computer Technology. Ready to embark on a full-time career in computer sales management, Paulette knows she needs a resume and an accompanying cover letter to send to prospective employers. Because you work as an intern in the school s Office of Career Development, she has asked you to help her create a professional resume and cover letter.

While reading through the classified section of the *Chicago Times*, Paulette locates a computer sales management trainee position at Deluxe Computers that sounds perfect for her.

Paulette will use Word s Resume Wizard to create a resume. She will compose the cover letter to Mr. Carl Reed, personnel director at Deluxe Computers, being certain to include all essential business letter components. With her strong business sense and your resume writing expertise, you create an effective package that should ensure Paulette s success in obtaining the position.

Introduction

At some time in your professional life, you will prepare a resume along with a personalized cover letter to send to a prospective employer(s). In addition to some personal information, a **resume** usually contains the applicant's educational background and job experience. Because employers review many resumes for each vacant position, you should design your resume carefully so it presents you as the best candidate for the job. You also should attach a personalized cover letter to each resume you send. A **cover letter** enables you to elaborate on positive points in your resume; it also provides you with an opportunity to show a potential employer your written communication skills. Thus, it is important that your cover letter is written well and follows proper business letter rules.

Because composing documents from scratch is a difficult process for many people, Word provides templates and wizards to assist you in preparing documents. A **template** is similar to a form with prewritten text; that is, Word prepares the requested document with text and/or formatting common to all documents of this nature. By asking you several basic questions, a **wizard** prepares and formats a document for you based on your responses. Once Word creates a document from either a template or a wizard, you then fill in the blanks or replace prewritten words in the document.

Project Three   Resume and Cover Letter

Paulette Rose Brandon, a recent college graduate, is seeking a full-time position as a computer sales manager. Project 3 uses Word to produce her resume shown in Figure 3-1 and a personalized cover letter and envelope shown in Figure 3-2 on page WD 3.6.

More *About*

Resumes and Cover Letters

The World Wide Web contains a host of information, tips, and suggestions on writing resumes and cover letters. For a list of Web links to sites on writing resumes and cover letters, visit the Word 2000 More About Web page (www.scsite.com/wd2000/more.htm) and then click Links to Sites on Writing Resumes and Cover Letters.

223 Center Street
New Lenox, IL 60451

Phone (815) 555-2130
Fax (815) 555-2131
E-mail brandon@lenox.com

Paulette Rose Brandon

Objective	To obtain a sales management position for personal computers and related hardware and software products.
Education	1997 - 2001 Illinois State College Springfield, IL
	Marketing Management
	• B.S. in Management, May 2001
	• A.S. in Business, May 1999
	• A.S. in Computer Technology, December 1999
Computer experience	Software Applications: Microsoft Word, Microsoft Excel, Microsoft Access, Microsoft PowerPoint, Microsoft Outlook, Microsoft FrontPage, Microsoft Publisher, Microsoft Project, Microsoft Money, Corel WordPerfect, Broderbund Print Shop, Intuit Quicken, Intuit TurboTax, Visio Technical
	Hardware: IBM and compatible personal computers, Apple Macintosh personal computers, DEC Alpha minicomputer, IBM mainframe, laser printers, ink-jet printers, scanners, tape backup drives, Jaz® and Zip® drives, digital cameras, fax machines, modems, surge protectors, uninterruptible power supplies
	Programming Languages: BASIC, Visual Basic, COBOL, C, C++, RPG, SQL, JavaScript, HTML, XML
	Operating Systems: Windows, Mac OS, UNIX, Linux, VMS
Awards received	Dean's List, every semester
	Top Seller in Student Government Association Fund-raiser, 2001
	Carmon Management Scholarship, 1997-2001
	MOUS certification: Word and Excel
Interests and activities	The Marketing Club, 1999-2001
	Student Government Association, 1998-2001
	Plan to pursue Master's degree beginning fall 2002
Work experience	1999 - 2001 Illinois State College Springfield, IL
	Help Desk Consultant
	• Assist faculty and staff with software questions
	• Log hardware problems
	• Conduct software training sessions
Volunteer experience	Assist in various fund-raising events for school, church, and the community. Examples include phone-a-thons, magazine sales, car washes, and used equipment sales.

FIGURE 3-1

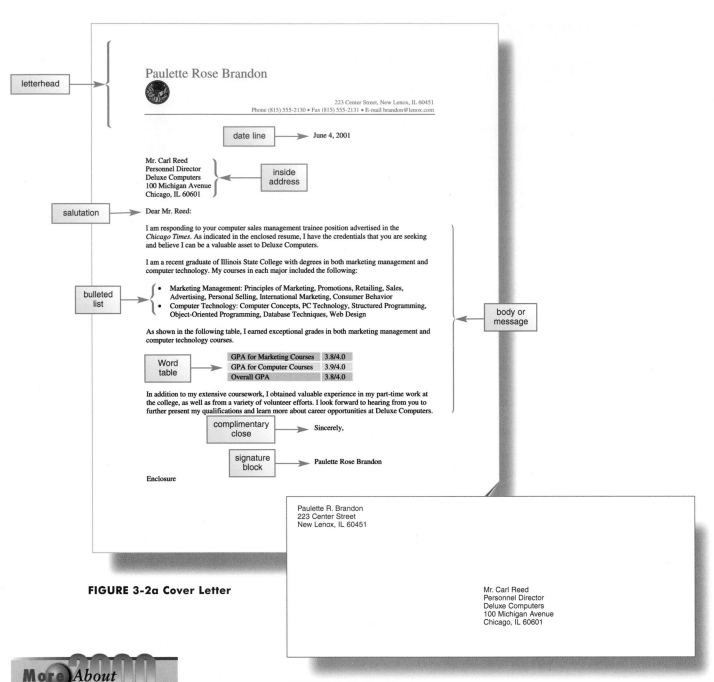

FIGURE 3-2a Cover Letter

FIGURE 3-2b Envelope

Using Word's Resume Wizard to Create a Resume

You can type a resume from scratch into a blank document window, or you can use the **Resume Wizard** and let Word format the resume with appropriate headings and spacing. Then, you can customize the resulting resume by filling in the blanks or selecting and replacing text.

When you use a wizard, Word displays a dialog box with the wizard's name in its title bar. A wizard's dialog box displays a list of **panel names** along its left side with the currently selected panel displaying on the right side of the dialog box (see Figure 3-4). Each panel presents a different set of options, in which you select preferences or enter text. You click the Next button to move from one panel to the next within the wizard's dialog box.

Perform the following steps to create a resume using the Resume Wizard. Because a wizard retains the settings selected by the last person that used the wizard, your selections initially may display differently. Be sure to verify that your settings match the screens shown in the following steps.

Steps **To Create a Resume Using Word's Resume Wizard**

1 **Click the Start button on the taskbar and then click New Office Document. If necessary, click the Other Documents tab when the New Office Document dialog box displays. Click the Resume Wizard icon.**

Office displays several wizard and template icons in the Other Documents sheet in the New Office Document dialog box (Figure 3-3). Icons without the word, wizard, are templates. If you click an icon, a sample of the resulting document displays in the Preview area.

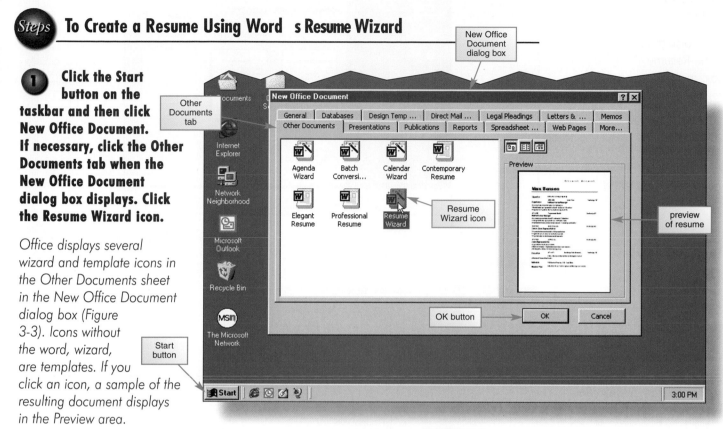

FIGURE 3-3

2 **Click the OK button. When the Resume Wizard dialog box displays, point to the Next button.**

After a few seconds, Word displays the Start panel of the Resume Wizard dialog box, informing you the Resume Wizard has started (Figure 3-4). Notice this dialog box has a Microsoft Word Help button you can click to obtain help while using this wizard. Depending on your system, the Word window may or may not be maximized behind the Resume Wizard dialog box.

FIGURE 3-4

3 **Click the Next button. When the Style panel displays, click Contemporary, if necessary, and then point to the Next button.**

Word displays the *Style panel* in the Resume Wizard dialog box, requesting the style of your resume (Figure 3-5). Word provides three styles of wizards and templates: Professional, Contemporary, and Elegant. A sample of each resume style displays in this panel.

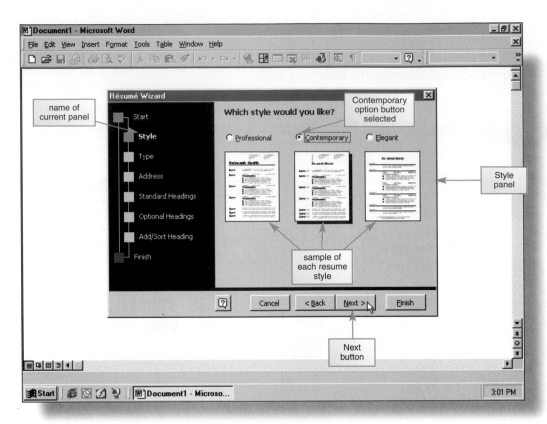

FIGURE 3-5

4 **Click the Next button. When the Type panel displays, click Entry-level resume, if necessary, and then point to the Next button.**

Word displays the *Type panel* in the Resume Wizard dialog box, asking for the type of resume that you want to create (Figure 3-6).

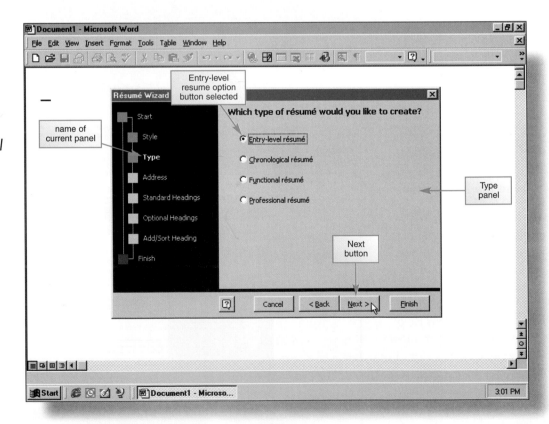

FIGURE 3-6

5 **Click the Next button.**

*Word displays the **Address panel** in the Resume Wizard dialog box, with the current name selected (Figure 3-7). The name displayed and selected in your Name text box will be different, depending on the name of the last person using the Resume Wizard.*

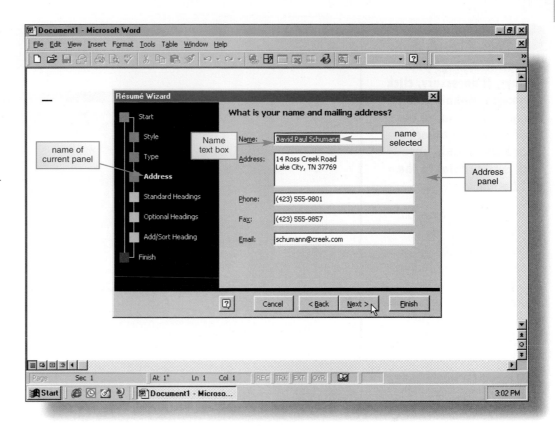

FIGURE 3-7

6 **With the name in the Name text box selected, type** Paulette Rose Brandon **and then press the TAB key. Type** 223 Center Street **and then press the ENTER key. Type** New Lenox, IL 60451 **and then press the TAB key. Type** (815) 555-2130 **and then press the TAB key. Type** (815) 555-2131 **and then press the TAB key. Type** brandon@lenox.com **and then point to the Next button.**

As you type the new text, it automatically replaces the selected text (Figure 3-8).

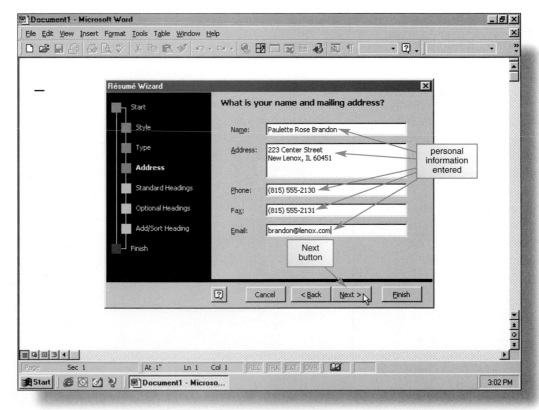

FIGURE 3-8

7 **Click the Next button. When the Standard Headings panel displays, if necessary, click Languages, Hobbies, and References to remove the check marks. All other check boxes should have check marks. Point to the Next button.**

Word displays the *Standard Headings panel* in the Resume Wizard dialog box, which requests the headings you want on your resume (Figure 3-9). You want all headings, except for these three: Languages, Hobbies, and References.

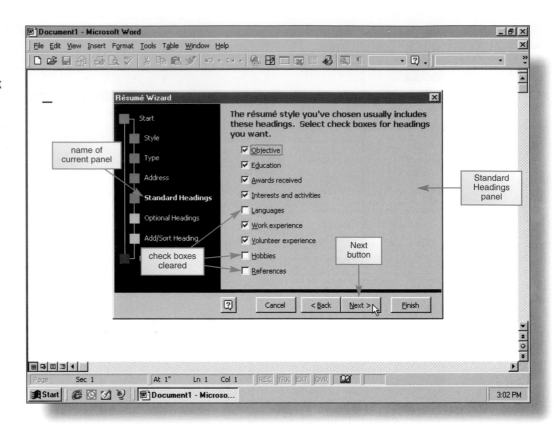

FIGURE 3-9

8 **Click the Next button. Point to the Next button in the Optional Headings panel.**

Word displays the *Optional Headings panel* in the Resume Wizard dialog box, which allows you to choose additional headings for your resume (Figure 3-10). All of these check boxes should be empty because none of these headings is required on your resume.

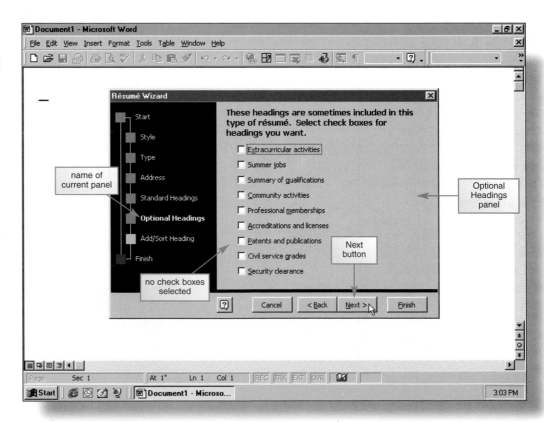

FIGURE 3-10

9 **Click the Next button. When the Add/Sort Heading panel displays, type** Computer experience **in the additional headings text box. Point to the Add button.**

*Word displays the **Add/Sort Heading panel** in the Resume Wizard dialog box, which allows you to enter any additional headings you want on your resume (Figure 3-11).*

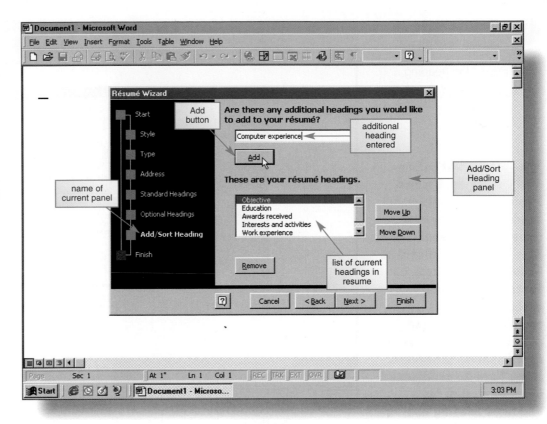

FIGURE 3-11

10 **Click the Add button. Scroll to the bottom of the list of resume headings and then click Computer experience. Point to the Move Up button.**

The Computer experience heading is selected (Figure 3-12). You can rearrange the order of the headings on your resume by selecting a heading and then clicking the appropriate button (Move Up button or Move Down button).

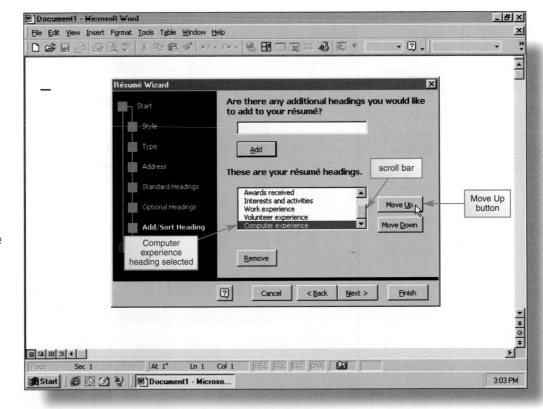

FIGURE 3-12

11 **Click the Move Up button four times.**

Word moves the heading, Computer experience, above the Awards received heading (Figure 3-13).

12 **If the last person using the Resume Wizard included additional headings, you may have some unwanted headings. Your heading list should be as follows: Objective, Education, Computer experience, Awards received, Interests and activities, Work experience, and Volunteer experience. If you have an additional heading(s), click the unwanted heading and then click the Remove button.**

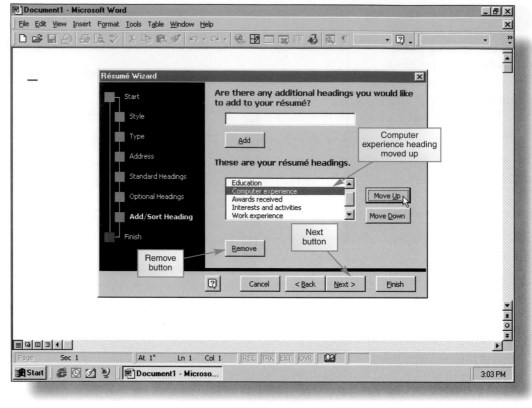

FIGURE 3-13

13 **Click the Next button. When the Finish panel displays, point to the Finish button.**

Word displays the Finish panel in the Resume Wizard dialog box, which indicates the wizard is ready to create your document (Figure 3-14).

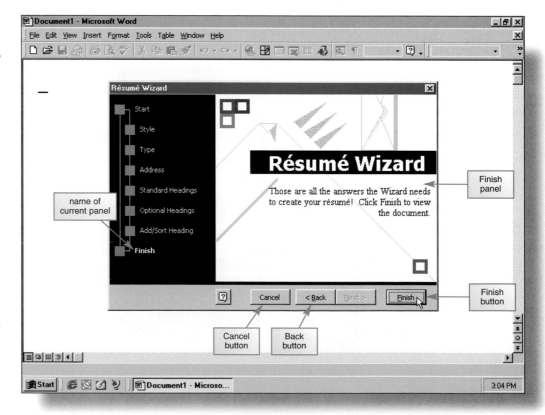

FIGURE 3-14

14 Click the Finish button. If the Word window is not maximized, click its Maximize button. If the Office Assistant displays, click its Cancel button. To close the Office Assistant, if necessary, right-click it and then click Hide on the shortcut menu.

Word creates an entry-level contemporary style resume layout (Figure 3-15). You are to personalize the resume as indicated.

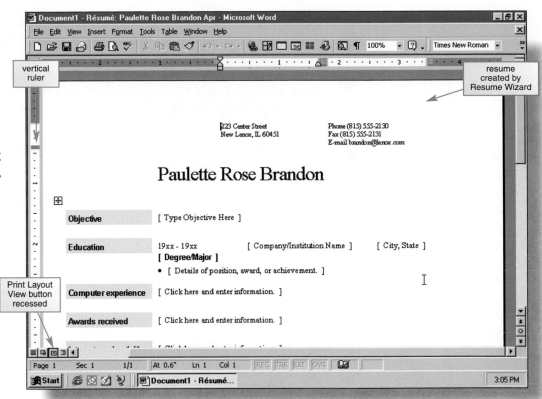

FIGURE 3-15

When you create a resume using the Resume Wizard (see Figure 3-14), you can click the Back button in any panel of the Resume Wizard dialog box to change any of the previous options you selected. To exit from the Resume Wizard and return to the document window without creating the resume, click the Cancel button in any panel of the Resume Wizard dialog box.

In addition to the Resume Wizard, Word provides many other wizards to assist you in creating documents: agenda for a meeting, calendar, envelope, fax cover sheet, legal pleading, letter, mailing label, memorandum, and Web page.

Word displays the resume in the document window in print layout view. You can tell you are in print layout view by looking at the Word window (Figure 3-15). Notice that in print layout view, the **Print Layout View button** on the horizontal scroll bar is recessed. Also, notice that a **vertical ruler** displays at the left edge of the document window, in addition to the horizontal ruler at the top of the window.

Your screen was in normal view when you created documents in Project 1 and for most of Project 2. In Project 2, when you created the header, you were in print layout view. In both normal view and print layout view, you can type and edit text. The difference is that **print layout view** shows you exactly how the printed page will print. That is, in print layout view, Word places the entire piece of paper in the document window, showing precisely the positioning of the text, margins, headers, footers, and footnotes on the printed page.

Resetting Menus and Toolbars

To set the menus and toolbars so they appear exactly as shown in this book, you should reset your menus and toolbars as outlined in Appendix C or follow the steps on the next page.

Other **Ways**

1. Right-click Start button, click Open, double-click New Office Document, click Other Documents tab, double-click Resume Wizard icon

2. Click New Office Document button on Microsoft Office Shortcut Bar, click Other Documents tab, double-click Resume Wizard icon

3. In Microsoft Word, on File menu click New, click Other Documents tab, double-click Resume Wizard icon

TO RESET MENUS AND TOOLBARS

1 Click View on the menu bar and then point to Toolbars. Click Customize on the Toolbars submenu.

2 When the Customize dialog box displays, click the Options tab, make sure the top three check boxes have check marks and then click the Reset my usage data button. When the Microsoft Word dialog box displays, click the Yes button.

3 Click the Toolbars tab. Click Standard in the Toolbars list and then click the Reset button. When the Reset Toolbar dialog box displays, click the OK button.

4 Click Formatting in the Toolbars list and then click the Reset button. When the Reset Toolbar dialog box displays, click the OK button. Click the Close button.

Word resets the menus and toolbars.

To see the entire resume created by the Resume Wizard, you should print the resume.

TO PRINT THE RESUME CREATED BY THE RESUME WIZARD

1 Double-click the move handle on the Standard toolbar to display the entire toolbar. Ready the printer and then click the Print button on the Standard toolbar.

2 When the printer stops, retrieve the hard copy resume from the printer.

The printed resume is shown in Figure 3-16.

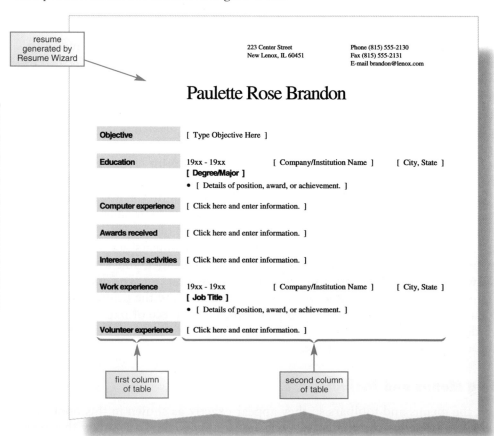

<table>
<tr><td></td><td colspan="2">first column of table</td><td>second column of table</td></tr>
</table>

FIGURE 3-16

Personalizing the Resume

The next step is to personalize the resume. Where Word has indicated, you type the objective, education, computer experience, awards received, interests and activities, work experience, and volunteer experience next to the respective headings. In the education and work experience sections, you select and replace text to customize these sections. The following pages show how to personalize the resume generated by the Resume Wizard.

Displaying Formatting Marks

As you have learned, it is helpful to display **formatting marks** that indicate where in the document you pressed the ENTER key, SPACEBAR, and other keys. If formatting marks do not display already on your screen, follow this step to display them.

TO DISPLAY FORMATTING MARKS

 If the Show/Hide ¶ button on the Standard toolbar is not already recessed, click it.

Word displays formatting marks in the document window, and the Show/Hide ¶ button on the Standard toolbar is recessed (see Figure 3-17 on the next page).

Tables

When the Resume Wizard prepares a resume, it arranges the body of the resume as a table. A Word **table** is a collection of rows and columns. As shown in Figure 3-16, the section headings (Objective, Education, Computer experience, Awards received, Interests and activities, Work experience, and Volunteer experience) are placed in the first column of the table; the details for each of these sections are placed in the second column of the table. Thus, this table contains two columns (see Figure 3-17 on the next page). It also contains seven rows – one row for each section of the resume.

The intersection of a row and a column is called a **cell**, and cells are filled with text. Each cell has an **end-of-cell mark**, which is a formatting mark, that you use to select and format cells. You have learned that formatting marks do not print on a hard copy.

To see clearly the rows, columns, and cells in a Word table, some users prefer to show gridlines. As illustrated in Figure 3-17, **gridlines** help identify the rows and columns in a table. If you want to display gridlines in a table, position the insertion point somewhere in the table, click Table on the menu bar, and then click **Show Gridlines**. If you want to hide the gridlines, click somewhere in the table, click Table on the menu bar, and then click **Hide Gridlines**.

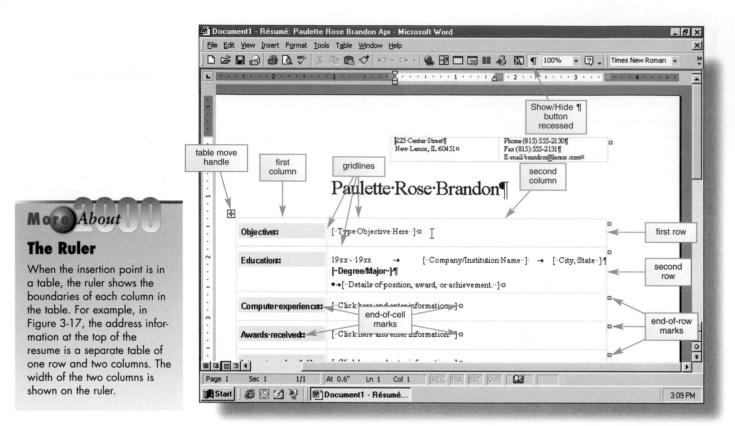

FIGURE 3-17

The upper-left corner of the table displays the **table move handle**, which you drag to move the table to a new location. You also can resize a table, add or delete rows or columns in a table, and format a table. These and other features of tables are discussed in more depth when you create the cover letter later in this project.

Zooming Text Width

In Projects 1 and 2, your screen was in normal view and you used the zoom page width command to display text on the screen as large as possible without extending the right margin beyond the right edge of the document window. When you are in print layout view, the zoom page width command extends the edges of the paper to the margins —making the text smaller on the screen. To make the text as large as possible on the screen in print layout view, you should **zoom text width** as shown in the following steps.

To Zoom Text Width

 Click the Zoom box arrow on the Standard toolbar and then point to Text Width in the Zoom list (Figure 3-18).

2 **Click Text Width.**

Word extends the text to the right edge of the document window (see Figure 3-19 on the next page).

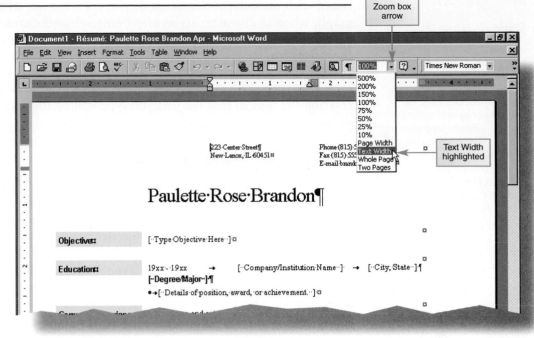

FIGURE 3-18

Other **Ways**

1. On View menu click Zoom, select Text Width, click OK button

Word computes a zoom percentage based on a variety of settings. The percentage that displays in your Zoom box may be different, depending on your system configuration. Notice in Figure 3-18 that the Zoom list contains more options when the Word window is in print layout view than in normal view.

The next step is to bold the name, Paulette Rose Brandon, in the resume as described in the following steps.

TO BOLD TEXT

1 Drag through the name, Paulette Rose Brandon, to select it.

2 Double-click the move handle on the Formatting toolbar to display the entire toolbar. Click the Bold button on the Formatting toolbar.

Word bolds the name, Paulette Rose Brandon (see Figure 3-19 on the next page).

Styles

When you use a wizard to create a document, Word formats the document using styles. You learned in Project 2 that a **style** is a customized format that you can apply to text. Recall that the formats defined by a style include character formatting, such as the font and font size, and paragraph formatting, such as line spacing and text alignment.

The Style box on the Formatting toolbar displays the name of the style associated with the location of the insertion point. You can identify many of the characteristics assigned to a style by looking at the Formatting toolbar. For example, in Figure 3-19 on the next page, the insertion point is in a paragraph formatted with the Objective style, which uses the 10-point Times New Roman font for the characters.

More About

Styles

To apply a different style to a paragraph, click in the paragraph, click the Style box arrow on the Formatting toolbar, and then click the desired paragraph style. To apply a different style to characters, select the characters, click the Style box arrow on the Formatting toolbar, and then click the desired character style.

If you click the Style box arrow on the Formatting toolbar, the list of styles associated with the current document displays. Paragraph styles affect an entire paragraph, whereas character styles affect only selected characters. In the Style list, **paragraph style** names are followed by a proofreader's paragraph mark (¶), and **character style** names are followed by an underlined letter a (<u>a</u>).

In Project 2, you changed the formats assigned to a style by changing the Footnote Text style. You also may select the appropriate style from the Style list before entering the text so that the text you type will be formatted according to the selected style.

Selecting and Replacing Text

The next step in personalizing the resume is to select text that the Resume Wizard inserted into the resume and replace it with personal information. The first heading on the resume is the objective. You enter the objective where the Resume Wizard inserted the words, Type Objective Here, which is called **placeholder text**.

To replace text in Word, select the text to be removed and then type the desired text. To select the placeholder text, Type Objective Here, you click it. Then, you type the objective. As soon as you begin typing, the selected placeholder text is deleted; thus, you do not have to delete the selection before you begin typing. Perform the following steps to enter the objective into the resume.

 To Select and Replace Placeholder Text

1 **Click the placeholder text, Type Objective Here.**

Word highlights the placeholder text in the resume (Figure 3-19). Notice the style is Objective in the Style box on the Formatting toolbar.

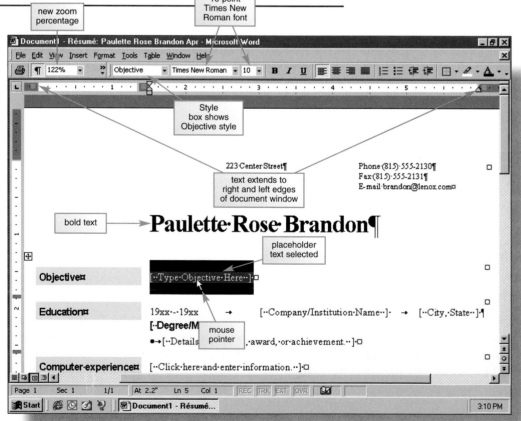

FIGURE 3-19

2 **Type** To obtain a sales management position for personal computers and related hardware and software products.

Word replaces the high-lighted placeholder text, Type Objective Here, with the objective you type (Figure 3-20). Your document may wordwrap on a different word depending on the type of printer you are using.

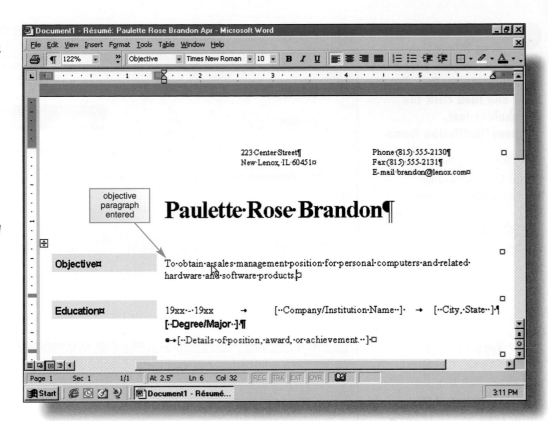

FIGURE 3-20

The next step in personalizing the resume is to replace the wizard's words and phrases in the education section of the resume with your own words and phrases as shown in the following steps.

 To Select and Replace Resume Wizard Supplied Text

1 **If necessary, scroll down to display the entire education section of the resume. Drag through the xx in the first 19xx of the education section.**

Word selects the xx in the first year (Figure 3-21).

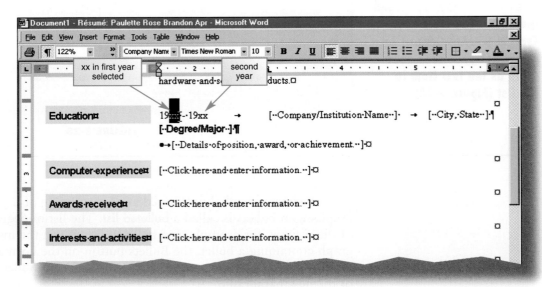

FIGURE 3-21

2 **Type** 97 **and then drag through the 19xx in the second year of the education section. Type** 2001 **and then click the placeholder text, Company/Institution Name.**

Word highlights the placeholder text, Company/Institution Name (Figure 3-22). The years now display as 1997 - 2001 in the education section.

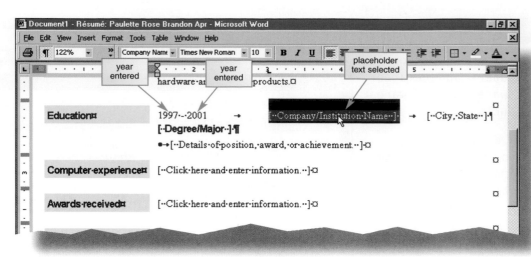

FIGURE 3-22

3 **Type** Illinois State College **and then click the placeholder text, City, State. Type** Springfield, IL **and then click the placeholder text, Degree/Major. Type** Marketing Management **and then click the placeholder text, Details of position, award, or achievement. Type** B.S. in Management, May 2001 **and then press the ENTER key. Type** A.S. in Business, May 1999 **and then press the ENTER key. Type** A.S. in Computer Technology, December 1999 **as the last item in the list (Figure 3-23).**

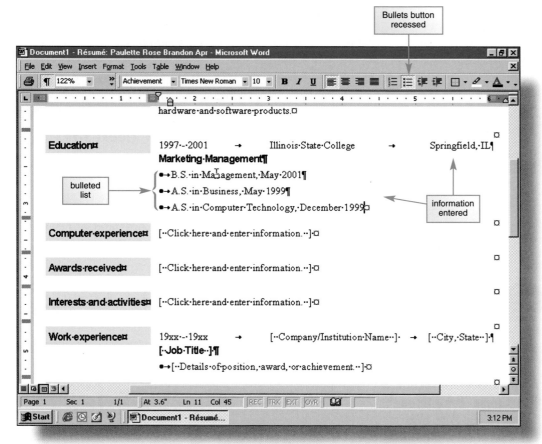

FIGURE 3-23

A **bullet** is a symbol positioned at the beginning of a paragraph. A list of paragraphs with bullets is called a **bulleted list**. The list of degrees in the education section of the resume, for example, is a bulleted list. When the insertion point is in a paragraph containing a bullet, the Bullets button on the Formatting toolbar is recessed. In a bulleted list, each time you press the ENTER key, a bullet displays at the beginning of the new paragraph.

The next step is to enter the computer experience section of the resume as described in the following steps.

TO ENTER PLACEHOLDER TEXT

1 If necessary, scroll down to display the computer experience section of the resume. Click the placeholder text, Click here and enter information, to select it.

2 Type the first paragraph of computer experience (software applications) as shown in Figure 3-24.

3 Press the ENTER key. Type the second paragraph of computer experience (hardware) as shown in Figure 3-24.

4 Press the ENTER key. Type the third paragraph of computer experience (programming languages) as shown in Figure 3-24.

5 Press the ENTER key. Type the fourth paragraph of computer experience (operating systems) as shown in Figure 3-24. Do not press the ENTER key at the end of this line.

The computer experience section of the resume is entered (Figure 3-24).

More About

The Registered Trademark Symbol

To automatically enter the registered trademark symbol, type (r). Or, press ALT+CTRL+R. Or, click Insert on the menu bar, click Symbol, click the Special Characters tab, click Registered in the Character list, click the Insert button, and then click the Close button.

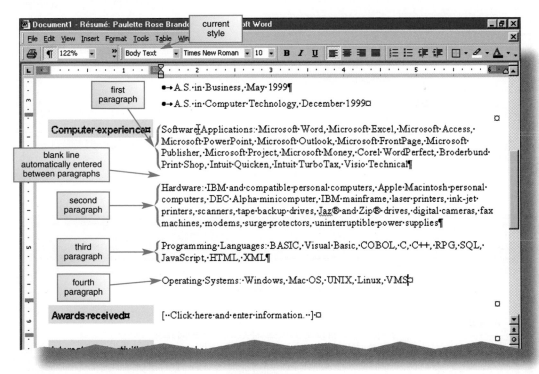

FIGURE 3-24

Entering a Line Break

The next step in personalizing the resume is to enter the awards received section. The style used for the characters in the awards received section of the resume is the Objective style. A paragraph formatting characteristic of the Objective style is that when you press the ENTER key, the insertion point advances downward at least 11 points, which leaves nearly an entire blank line between each paragraph. For example, each time you pressed the ENTER key in the computer experience section, Word placed a blank line between each paragraph (Figure 3-24).

You want the lines within the awards received section to be close to each other (see Figure 3-1 on page WD 3.5). Thus, you will not press the ENTER key between each award received. Instead, you will create a **line break**, which advances the insertion point to the beginning of the next physical line– ignoring any paragraph formatting instructions. Perform the following steps to enter the awards received section using a line break, instead of a paragraph break, between each line.

Steps **To Enter a Line Break**

1 If necessary, scroll down to display the awards received section of the resume. In the awards received section, click the placeholder text, Click here and enter information. **Type** Dean's List, every semester **and then press the SHIFT+ENTER keys.**

Word inserts a line break character, which is a formatting mark, after the named award and moves the insertion point to the beginning of the next physical line (Figure 3-25).

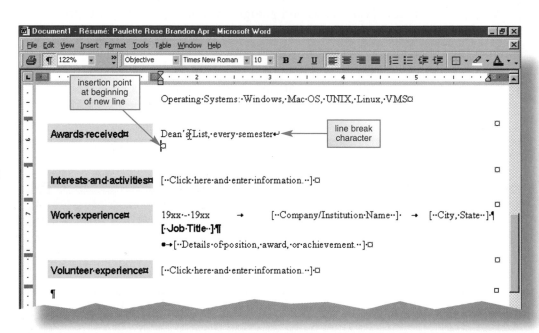

FIGURE 3-25

2 **Type** Top Seller in Student Government Association Fundraiser, 2001 **and then press the SHIFT+ENTER keys. Type** Carmon Management Scholarship, 1997-2001 **and then press the SHIFT+ENTER keys. Type** MOUS certification: Word and Excel **as the last award. Do not press the SHIFT+ENTER keys at the end of this line.**

The awards received section is entered (Figure 3-26).

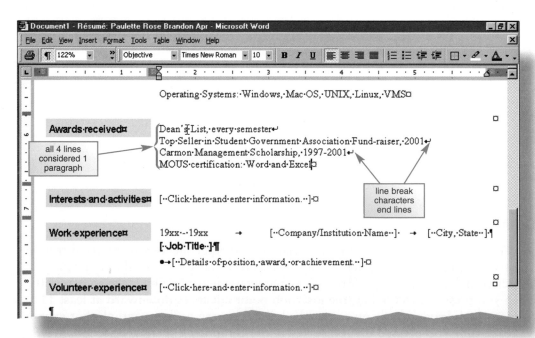

FIGURE 3-26

Enter the remaining text for the resume as described in the following steps.

TO ENTER THE REMAINING SECTIONS OF THE RESUME

1 If necessary, scroll down to display the interests and activities section of the resume. Click the placeholder text, Click here and enter information. Type `The Marketing Club, 1999-2001` and then press the SHIFT+ENTER keys.

2 Type `Student Government Association, 1998-2001` and then press the SHIFT+ENTER keys.

3 Type `Plan to pursue Master's degree beginning fall 2002` as the last activity. Do not press the SHIFT+ENTER keys at the end of this line.

4 If necessary, scroll down to display the work experience section of the resume. Drag through the xx in the first 19xx, type 99 and then drag through the 19xx in the second year. Type 2001 as the year.

5 Click the placeholder text, Company/Institution Name. Type `Illinois State College` as the new text. Click the placeholder text, City, State. Type `Springfield, IL` as the city and state.

6 Click the placeholder text, **Job Title**. Type `Help Desk Consultant` as the title.

7 Click the placeholder text, Details of position, award, or achievement. Type `Assist faculty and staff with software questions` and then press the ENTER key. Type `Log hardware problems` and then press the ENTER key. Type `Conduct software training sessions` as the last item in the list.

8 If necessary, scroll down to display the volunteer experience section of the resume. Click the placeholder text, Click here and enter information. Type `Assist in various fund-raising events for school, church, and the community. Examples include phone-a-thons, magazine sales, car washes, and used equipment sales.` Do not press the ENTER key at the end of this line.

The interests and activities, work experience, and volunteer experience sections of the resume are complete (Figure 3-27).

More About

References

Do not state "References Available Upon Request" on your resume; nor should references be listed on the resume. Employers assume you will give references, if asked, and this information simply clutters a resume. Often you are asked to list references on your application. Be sure to give your references a copy of your resume.

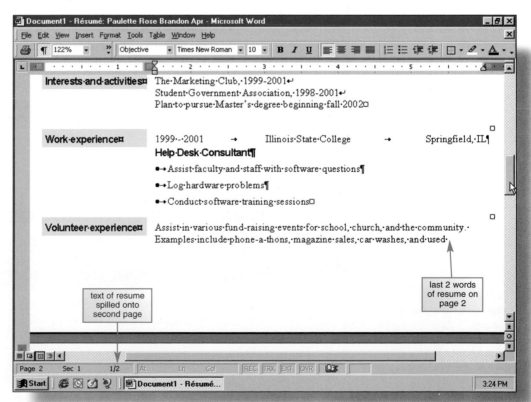

FIGURE 3-27

Print Preview

To magnify a page in print preview, be sure the Magnifier button is recessed on the Print Preview toolbar and then click in the document to zoom in or out. Magnifying a page has no effect on the printed document. To edit a document in print preview, be sure the Magnifier button is not recessed and then edit the text.

Notice in Figure 3-27 on the previous page that the last two words of the resume spilled onto a second page. The next section illustrates how to shrink the resume so it fits on a single page.

Viewing and Printing the Resume in Print Preview

To see exactly how a document will look when you print it, you should display it in **print preview**. Print preview displays the entire document in reduced size on the Word screen. In print preview, you can edit and format text, adjust margins, view multiple pages, reduce the document to fit on a single page, and print the document.

If a document *spills* onto a second page by just a line or two, you can try to shrink the document so it fits onto a single page using the **Shrink to Fit button** in print preview. In the previous steps, the last two words of the resume spilled onto a second page. Perform the following steps to view the resume, display both pages of the resume, shrink the resume, and finally print the resume in print preview.

To Print Preview a Document

1 **Double-click the move handle on the Standard toolbar to display the entire toolbar. Point to the Print Preview button on the Standard toolbar (Figure 3-28).**

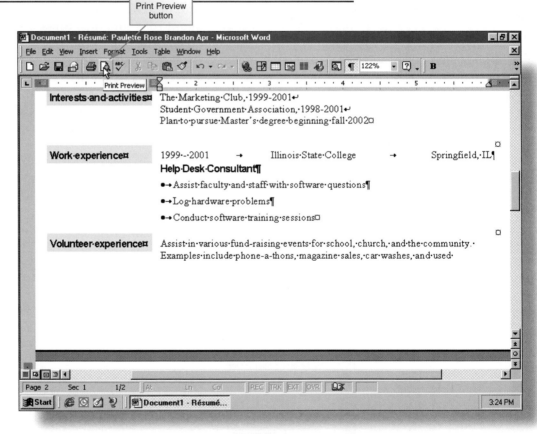

FIGURE 3-28

2 **Click the Print Preview button.**

Word displays the document in print preview. The **Print Preview toolbar** *displays below the menu bar; the Standard and Formatting toolbars disappear from the screen. Depending on your settings, your screen may display one or two pages in the Preview window.*

3 **Click the Multiple Pages button on the Print Preview toolbar. Point to the icon in the first row and second column of the grid.**

Word displays a **grid** *so you can select the number of pages to display (Figure 3-29). With the current selection, Word will display one row of two pages (1 x 2) – or two pages side by side.*

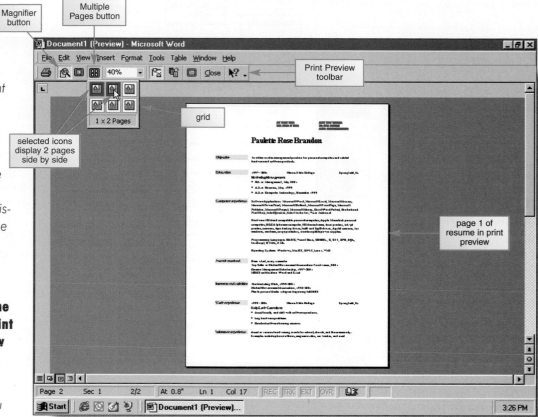

FIGURE 3-29

4 **Click the icon in the first row and second column of the grid. Point to the Shrink to Fit button on the Print Preview toolbar.**

Word displays the two pages of the resume side by side (Figure 3-30).

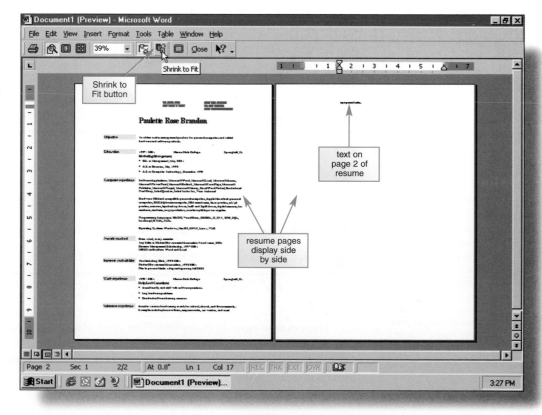

FIGURE 3-30

5 **Click the Shrink to Fit button.**

Word shrinks the resume to a single page by reducing font sizes (Figure 3-31).

6 **Click the Print button on the Print Preview toolbar. When the printer stops, retrieve the printout.**

Word prints the resume on the printer (see Figure 3-1 on page WD 3.5).

7 **Click the Close Preview button on the Print Preview toolbar.**

Word returns to the document window, displaying the resume.

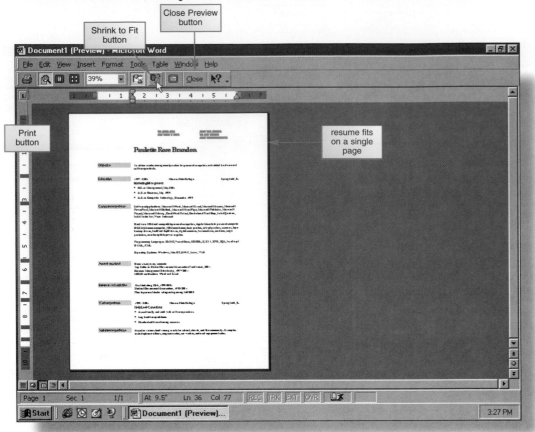

FIGURE 3-31

Other Ways

1. On File menu click Print Preview
2. Press CTRL+F2

Saving the Resume

Because the resume now is complete, you should save it. For a detailed example of the procedure summarized below, refer to pages WD 1.26 through WD 1.28 in Project 1.

TO SAVE A DOCUMENT

1 Insert your floppy disk into drive A.

2 Click the Save button on the Standard toolbar.

3 Type Brandon Resume in the File name text box. Do not press the ENTER key.

4 Click the Save in box arrow and then click 3½ Floppy (A:).

5 Click the Save button in the Save As dialog box.

Word saves the document on a floppy disk in drive A with the file name, Brandon Resume.

The resume now is complete. The next step in Project 3 is to create a cover letter to send with the resume to a potential employer. Do not close the Brandon Resume. You will use it again later in this project to copy the address, telephone, fax, and e-mail information.

More About

Printing

If you want to save ink, print faster, or decrease printer overrun errors, lower the printer resolution. Click File on the menu bar, click Print, click the Properties button in the Print dialog box, click the Graphics tab, click the Resolution box arrow, click a lower resolution than displayed currently, click the Apply button, click the OK button, and then click the Close button.

Creating a Letterhead

You have created a resume to send to prospective employers. Along with the resume, you will attach a personalized cover letter. You would like the cover letter to have a professional looking letterhead (see Figure 3-2a on page WD 3.6). The following pages describe how to use Word to create a letterhead.

In many businesses, letterhead is preprinted on stationery that is used by everyone throughout the corporation. For personal letters, the expense of preprinted letterhead can be costly. Thus, you can create your own letterhead and save it in a file. When you want to create a letter with the letterhead, you simply open the letterhead file and then save the file with a new name, preserving the original letterhead file.

The steps on the following pages illustrate how to create a personal letterhead file.

More About

Letterhead Design

Letterhead designs vary. Some are centered at the top of the page, while others have text or graphics aligned with the left and right margins. Another style places the company's name and logo at the top of the page with the address and other information at the bottom. Well-designed letterheads add professionalism to correspondence.

Opening a New Document Window

The resume currently displays in the document window. You want to leave the resume open because you intend to use it again during this Word session. Thus, you want to work with two documents at the same time: the resume and the letterhead. Each of these documents will display in a separate document window. Perform the following steps to open a new document window for the letterhead file.

Steps: To Open a New Document Window

1 Point to the New Blank Document button on the Standard toolbar (Figure 3-32).

2 Click the New Blank Document button.

Word opens a new document window (see Figure 3-33 on the next page).

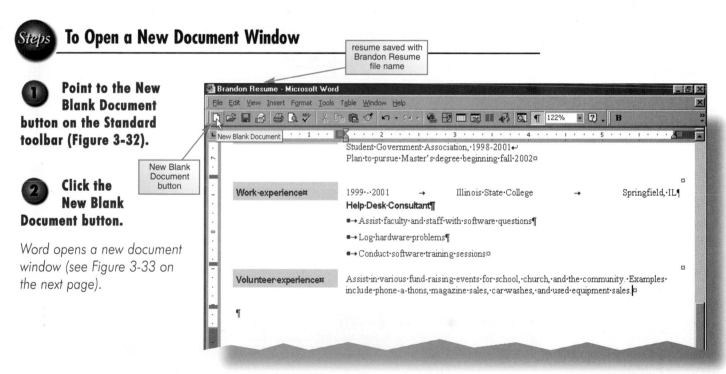

resume saved with Brandon Resume file name

New Blank Document button

FIGURE 3-32

The Brandon Resume document still is open. The program buttons on the taskbar display the names of the open Word document windows. In Figure 3-33 on the next page, the Brandon Resume is open and Document2 is open. The Document2 button on the taskbar is recessed, indicating that it is the active document displayed in the document window.

Other Ways

1. On File menu click New, click General tab, double-click Blank Document icon

The name in the letterhead is to be a font size of 20. Perform the following steps to change the font size.

TO CHANGE THE FONT SIZE

1 Double-click the move handle on the Formatting toolbar to display the entire toolbar. Click the Font Size box arrow on the Formatting toolbar.

2 Scroll to and then click 20 in the Font Size list.

Word changes the displayed font size to 20 (Figure 3-33).

Adding Color to Characters

The characters in the letterhead are to be green. Perform the following steps to change the color of the characters before you enter them.

Steps **To Color Characters**

1 **Point to the Font Color button arrow on the Formatting toolbar (Figure 3-33).**

The color that displays below the letter A on the Font Color button is the most recently used color for characters; thus, the color on your button may differ from this figure.

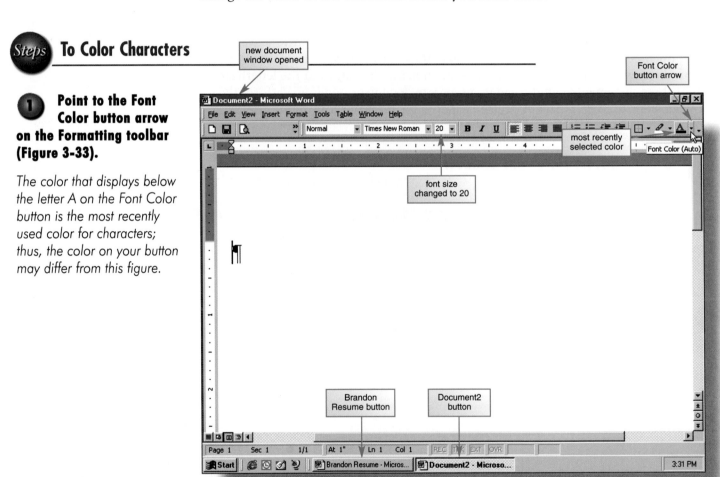

FIGURE 3-33

2 **Click the Font Color button arrow. Point to Green on the color palette.**

Word displays a list of available colors on the color palette (Figure 3-34). Automatic is the default color, which usually is black.

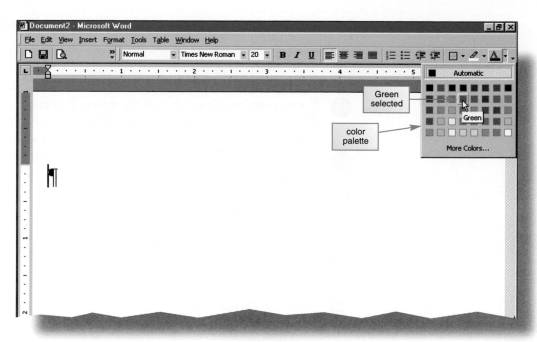

FIGURE 3-34

3 **Click Green. Type** Paulette Rose Brandon **and then press the ENTER key.**

Word displays the first line of the letterhead in green (Figure 3-35).

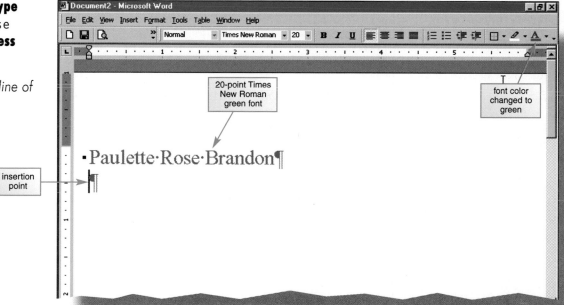

FIGURE 3-35

Notice the paragraph mark on line 2 is green. Recall that each time you press the ENTER key, formatting is carried forward to the next paragraph. If, for some reason, you wanted to change the text back to black at this point, you would click the Font Color button arrow on the Formatting toolbar and then click Automatic.

Other Ways

1. Right-click paragraph mark or selected text, click Font on shortcut menu, click Font tab, click Font Color box arrow, click desired color, click OK button

2. On Format menu click Font, click Font tab, click Font Color box arrow, click desired color, click OK button

The next step is to insert a graphic of a rose and resize it as described in the following steps.

TO ENTER AND RESIZE A GRAPHIC

1 If necessary, scroll up so that the name, Paulette Rose Brandon, is positioned at the top of the document window. With the insertion point below the name, click Insert on the menu bar, point to Picture, and then click Clip Art.

2 When the Insert ClipArt window opens, click the Search for clips text box. Type rose and then press the ENTER key.

3 Click the clip of the rose that matches the one shown in Figure 3-36. Click the Insert clip button on the Pop-up menu. Click the Close button on the Insert ClipArt window's title bar.

4 Click the graphic to select it. Drag the upper-right corner sizing handle diagonally toward the center of the graphic until the selection rectangle is positioned approximately as shown in Figure 3-36.

5 Click the paragraph mark to the right of the graphic to position the insertion point to the right of the graphic.

Word inserts the clip art and resizes it to approximately one-fourth of its original size (Figure 3-36).

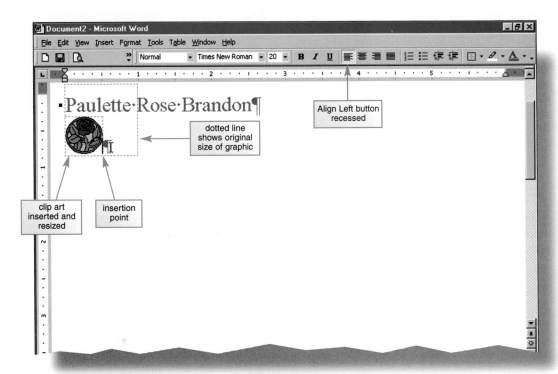

FIGURE 3-36

Setting Tab Stops Using the Tabs Dialog Box

The graphic of the rose is left-aligned (Figure 3-36). The address is to be positioned at the right margin of the same line. If you click the Align Right button, the graphic will be right-aligned. In Word, a paragraph cannot be both left-aligned and right-aligned. To place text at the right margin of a left-aligned paragraph, you set a tab stop at the right margin.

Word, by default, places **tab stops** at every .5" mark on the ruler (see Figure 3-38). These default tabs are indicated on the horizontal ruler by small **tick marks**. You also can set your own custom tab stops. When you set a **custom tab stop**, Word clears all default tab stops to the left of the custom tab stop. You also can specify how the text will align at a tab stop: left, centered, right, or decimal. Word stores tab settings in the paragraph mark at the end of each paragraph. Thus, each time you press the ENTER key, any custom tab stops are carried forward to the next paragraph.

In this letterhead, you want the tab stop to be right-aligned with the right margin; that is, at the 6" mark on the ruler. One method of setting custom tab stops is to click on the ruler at the desired location of the tab stop. You cannot, however, click at the right margin location. Thus, use the Tabs dialog box to set this custom tab stop as shown in the following steps.

 To Set Custom Tab Stops Using the Tabs Dialog Box

1 With the insertion point positioned between the paragraph mark and the graphic, click Format on the menu bar and then point to Tabs (Figure 3-37).

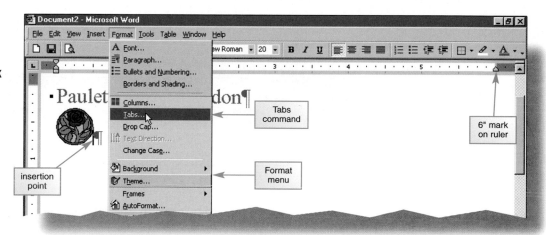

FIGURE 3-37

2 Click Tabs. When the Tabs dialog box displays, type 6 in the Tab stop position text box and then click Right in the Alignment area. Point to the Set button.

Word displays the Tabs dialog box (Figure 3-38).

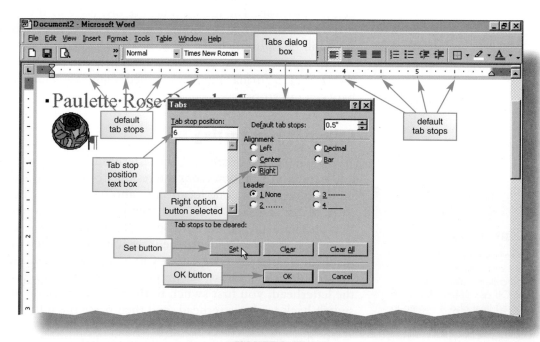

FIGURE 3-38

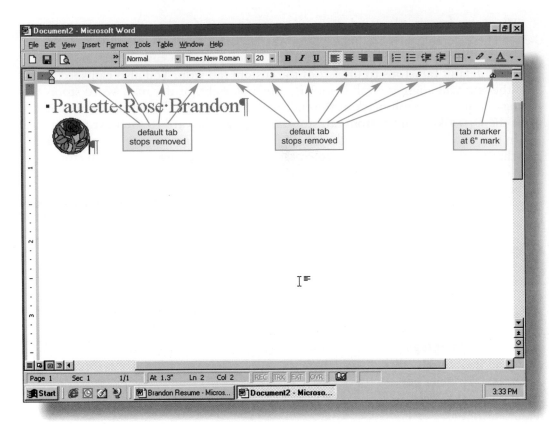

3 **Click the Set button and then click the OK button.**

*Word places a **tab marker** at the 6" mark on the ruler and removes all default tab stops to the left of the tab marker (Figure 3-39).*

FIGURE 3-39

Other Ways

1. Click button on left of ruler until desired tab stop alignment displays and then click ruler

Tab Stop Alignment

If you have a series of numbers that you want aligned on the decimal point, such as dollar amounts, use a decimal-aligned tab stop for the data.

More About

Clipboards

The Windows Clipboard holds only one item at a time. When you collect multiple items on the Office Clipboard, the last copied item also is copied to the Windows Clipboard. When you clear the Office Clipboard, the Windows Clipboard also is cleared.

When you set a custom tab stop, the tab marker on the ruler reflects the tab stop alignment. A capital letter L indicates a left-aligned tab stop; a mirror image of a capital letter L indicates a right-aligned tab stop; an upside down T indicates a centered tab stop; and an upside down T with a dot next to it indicates a decimal-aligned tab stop. The tab markers are discussed as they are presented in these projects. The tab marker on the ruler in Figure 3-39 indicates text entered at that tab stop will be right-aligned.

To move from one tab stop to another, you press the TAB key. When you press the TAB key, a formatting mark, called a **tab character**, displays in the empty space between tab stops.

Collecting and Pasting

The next step in creating the letterhead is to copy the address, telephone, fax, and e-mail information from the resume to the letterhead. When you want to copy multiple items from one location to another, you use the Office Clipboard to copy these items, or **collect** them, and then paste them in a new location. You have learned that **pasting** is the process of copying an item from the Office Clipboard into the document at the location of the insertion point. When you paste text into a document, the contents of the Office Clipboard are not erased.

To copy the address, telephone, fax, and e-mail information from the resume to the letterhead, you first switch to the resume, copy the items to the Office Clipboard, switch back to the letterhead, and then paste the information into the letterhead. The following pages illustrate this process.

Follow these steps to switch from the letterhead to the resume.

Steps **To Switch from One Open Document to Another**

1 **Point to the Brandon Resume - Microsoft Word button on the taskbar (Figure 3-40).**

2 **Click the Brandon Resume - Microsoft Word button.**

Word switches from the cover letter to the resume (see Figure 3-41 below).

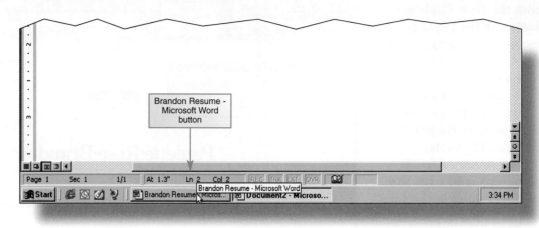

FIGURE 3-40

Other **Ways**

1. On Window menu click document name

You copy multiple items to the Office Clipboard so you can paste them later. Each copied item displays as an icon on the Clipboard toolbar, as shown in these steps.

Steps **To Collect Items**

1 **Press CTRL + HOME to display the top of the resume. Click View on the menu bar, point to Toolbars, and then point to Clipboard (Figure 3-41).**

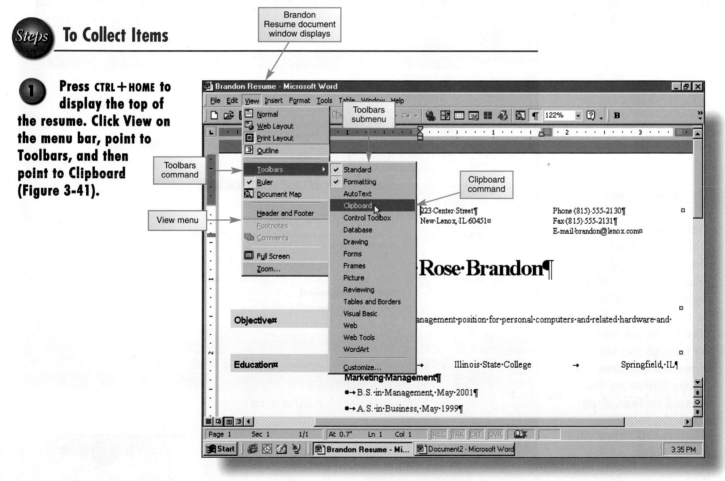

FIGURE 3-41

2 **Click Clipboard. If it is not dimmed, click the Clear Clipboard button on the Clipboard toolbar. If necessary, drag the Clipboard toolbar's title bar so the toolbar does not cover the address information in the resume. Drag through the street address, 223 Center Street (do not select the paragraph mark after the address). Point to the Copy button on the Clipboard toolbar.**

The Clipboard toolbar displays in the document window (Figure 3-42). The street address is selected.

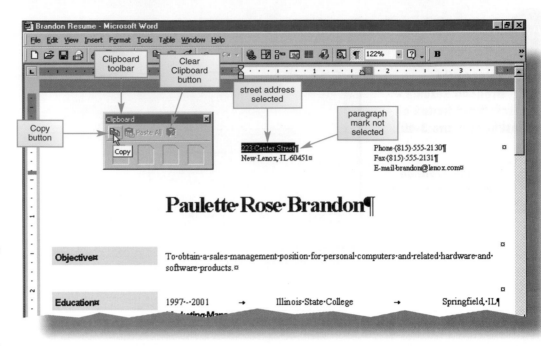

FIGURE 3-42

3 **Click the Copy button on the Clipboard toolbar.**

Word places a copy of the street address on the Office Clipboard and displays an icon that represents the copied item on the Clipboard toolbar.

4 **Drag through the city, state, and postal code information and then click the Copy button on the Clipboard toolbar. Drag through the telephone information and then click the Copy button on the Clipboard toolbar. Drag through the fax information and then click the Copy button on the Clipboard toolbar. Drag through the e-mail information and then click the Copy button on the Clipboard toolbar (Figure 3-43).**

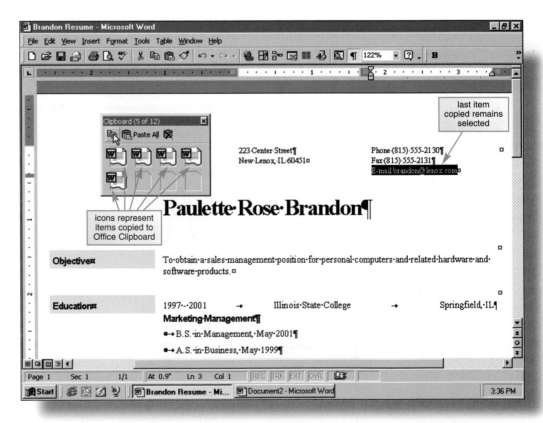

FIGURE 3-43

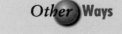

Other Ways

1. Click the Copy button on the Standard toolbar two consecutive times

The Office Clipboard can store up to 12 items at one time. When you copy a thirteenth item, Word deletes the first item to make room for the new item. When you point to the icons on the Clipboard toolbar, the first 50 characters of text in the item display as a ScreenTip.

Perform the following steps to paste the items from the Office Clipboard into the letterhead.

Steps **To Paste from the Office Clipboard**

1 **Click the Document2 - Microsoft Word button on the taskbar to display the letterhead document window.**

2 **With the insertion point between the paragraph mark and the rose graphic, press the TAB key.**

Word displays the letterhead with the Clipboard toolbar in the middle of the Word window (Figure 3-44). The insertion point is positioned at the 6" mark on the ruler, which is the location of the right-aligned tab stop. The right-pointing arrow is a tab character that displays each time you press the TAB key.

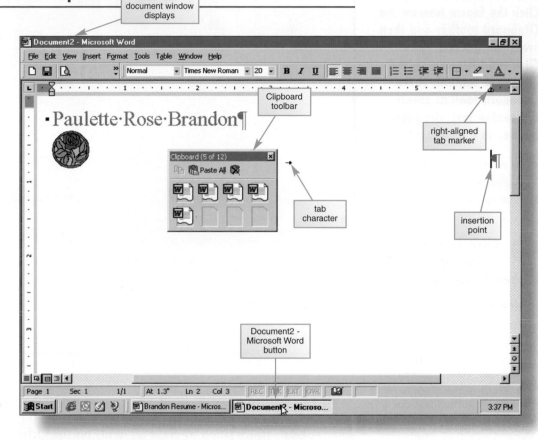

FIGURE 3-44

3 **Click the first icon on the Clipboard toolbar.**

Word pastes the contents of the clicked item at the location of the insertion point (Figure 3-45). Notice the text is aligned with the right margin because of the right-aligned tab stop.

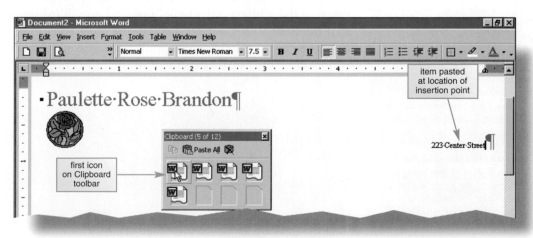

FIGURE 3-45

4 Press the COMMA key and then the SPACEBAR. Click the second icon on the Clipboard toolbar and the press the ENTER key. Press the TAB key. Click the third icon on the Clipboard toolbar and then press the SPACEBAR twice. Click the fourth icon on the Clipboard toolbar and then press the SPACEBAR twice. Click the fifth icon on the Clipboard toolbar. If the Clipboard toolbar covers the pasted text, drag the toolbar to a new location.

Word pastes all items from the Office Clipboard into the letterhead (Figure 3-46).

5 Click the Close button on the Clipboard toolbar.

Word removes the Clipboard toolbar from the window.

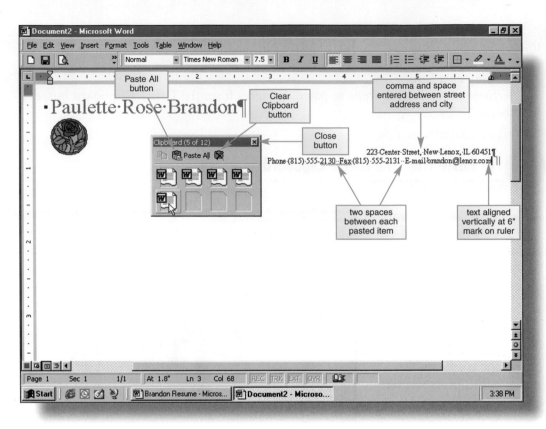

FIGURE 3-46

More *About*

Office Clipboard

Depending on your Office Clipboard usage, clicking either the Copy button or the Cut button on the Standard toolbar twice in succession may display the Clipboard toolbar. You can click the Copy button on the Standard toolbar or the Copy button on the Clipboard toolbar to collect items on the Office Clipboard.

If you wanted to paste all items in a row without any characters or formatting in between them, you would click the Paste All button on the Clipboard toolbar. If, for some reason, you wanted to erase all items on the Office Clipboard, click the Clear Clipboard button on the Clipboard toolbar (Figure 3-46).

The next step is to change the font size to 9 and the color of the characters to green in the address, telephone, fax, and e-mail information in the letterhead. Recall that the Font Color button displays the most recently used color, which is green, in this case. When the color you want to use displays on the Font Color button, you simply click the button as shown in the following steps.

To Color More Characters the Same Color

1 **Drag through the address, telephone, fax, and e-mail information in the letterhead, including both paragraph marks at the end of the lines. Click the Font Size box arrow on the Formatting toolbar and then click 9 in the Font Size list. Point to the Font Color button on the Formatting toolbar (Figure 3-47).**

2 **Click the Font Color button. Click inside the selected text to remove the highlight.**

Word changes the color of the selected characters to green (see Figure 3-48).

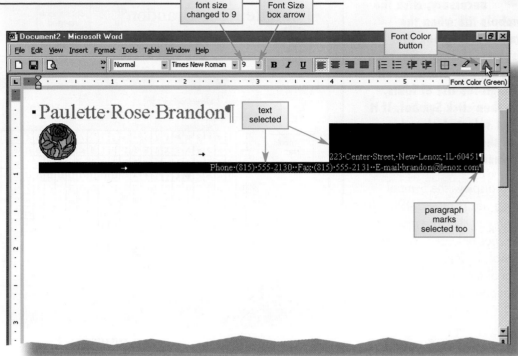

FIGURE 3-47

Inserting Symbols into a Document

To visually separate the telephone and fax information in the letterhead, you want a small round dot to display between them. Likewise, you want a small round dot to display between the fax and e-mail information. To insert symbols, such as dots, letters in the Greek alphabet, and mathematical characters, you can use the Symbol dialog box, as shown in the following steps.

To Insert a Symbol into Text

1 **Click where you want to insert the symbol, in this case, the space between the telephone and fax information. Click Insert on the menu bar and then point to Symbol (Figure 3-48).**

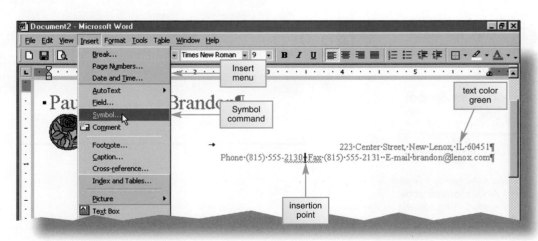

FIGURE 3-48

> **Other Ways**
>
> 1. Right-click paragraph mark or selected text, click Font on shortcut menu, click Font tab, click Font Color box arrow, click desired color, click OK button
> 2. On Format menu click Font, click Font tab, click Font Color box arrow, click desired color, click OK button

2 **Click Symbol. If necessary, click the Symbols tab when the Symbol dialog box first displays. If necessary, click the Font box arrow, scroll through the list of fonts, and then click Symbol. If it is not selected already, click the dot symbol. Click the Insert button.**

Word displays the Symbol dialog box (Figure 3-49). When you click a symbol, it becomes enlarged. The dot symbol displays in the document at the location of the insertion point.

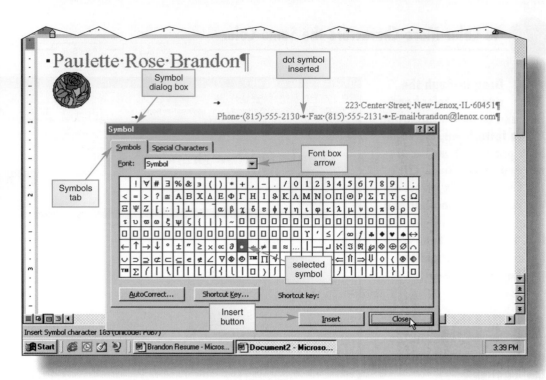

FIGURE 3-49

3 **Click where you want to insert the next symbol, in this case, the space between the fax and e-mail information in the document window. With the dot symbol still selected in the dialog box, click the Insert button. Point to the Close button in the Symbol dialog box.**

Word inserts the selected symbol at the location of the insertion point (Figure 3-50).

4 **Click the Close button in the Symbol dialog box.**

Word closes the Symbol dialog box.

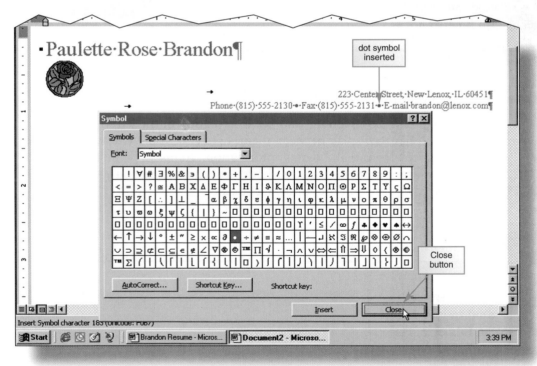

FIGURE 3-50

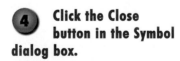

1. Type ALT+0 (zero) followed by ANSI character code for symbol using numeric keypad

You also can insert ANSI (American National Standards Institute) characters into a document by entering the ANSI code directly into the document. The **ANSI characters** are a predefined set of characters, including both characters on the keyboard and special characters, such as the dot symbol. To enter the ANSI code, make sure the NUM LOCK key is on. Press and hold the ALT key and then type the numeral zero followed by the ANSI code for the characters. You *must* use the numeric keypad when entering the ANSI code. For a complete list of ANSI codes, see your Microsoft Windows documentation.

Adding a Bottom Border to a Paragraph

To add professionalism to the letterhead, you would like to draw a horizontal line from the left margin to the right margin immediately below the telephone, fax, and e-mail information. In Word, you can draw a solid line, called a **border**, at any edge of a paragraph. That is, borders may be added above or below a paragraph, to the left or right of a paragraph, or any combination of these sides.

When adding a border to a paragraph, it is important that you have an extra paragraph mark below the paragraph you intend to border. Otherwise, each time you press the ENTER key, the border will be carried forward to each subsequent paragraph. If you forget to do this after you have added a border, simply click the Undo button on the Standard toolbar and begin again.

Perform the following steps to add a bottom border to the paragraph containing telephone, fax, and e-mail information.

More About

Special Characters

In addition to symbols, you can insert special characters including a variety of dashes, hyphens, spaces, apostrophes, and quotation marks through the Symbol dialog box. Click Insert on the menu bar, click Symbol, click the Special Characters tab, click the desired character in the Character list, click the Insert button, and then click the Close button.

Steps **To Add a Bottom Border to a Paragraph**

1 **Press the END key to move the insertion point to the end of the line and then press the ENTER key to create a paragraph mark below the line you want to border. Press CTRL+Z to undo the AutoFormat of the e-mail address. Press the UP ARROW key to reposition the insertion point in the paragraph that will contain the border. Point to the Border button arrow on the Formatting toolbar.**

The name of this button changes depending on the last border type added. In this figure, it is the Outside Border button (Figure 3-51).

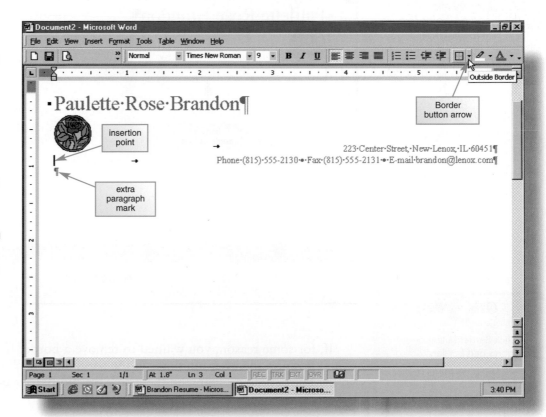

FIGURE 3-51

2 **Click the Border button arrow and then point to the Bottom Border button.**

*Word displays the border palette (Figure 3-52). Using the **border palette**, you can add a border to any edge of a paragraph.*

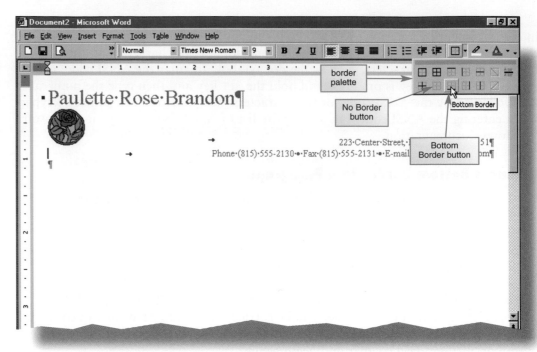

FIGURE 3-52

3 **Click the Bottom Border button.**

Word places a bottom border below the paragraph containing the insertion point (Figure 3-53). The Border button on the Formatting toolbar now displays the icon for a bottom border.

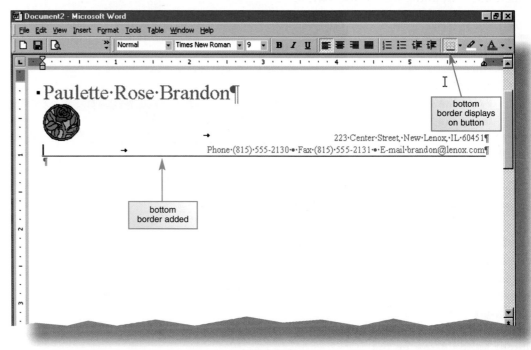

FIGURE 3-53

If, for some reason, you wanted to remove a border from a paragraph, you would position the insertion point in the paragraph, click the Border button arrow on the Formatting toolbar, and then click the No Border button (Figure 3-52) on the border palette.

Perform the following step to change the color of the text below the border back to Automatic (black).

TO CHANGE COLOR OF TEXT

1. Press the DOWN ARROW key.

2. Click the Font Color button arrow and then click Automatic.

Word changes the color of the paragraph mark below the border to black (see Figure 3-54 on page WD 3.43).

Now that you have created your letterhead, you should save it in a file.

TO SAVE THE LETTERHEAD

1. Insert your floppy disk into drive A.

2. Double-click the move handle on the Standard toolbar to display the entire toolbar. Click the Save button on the Standard toolbar.

3. Type the file name Brandon Letterhead in the File name text box.

4. If necessary, click the Save in box arrow and then click 3½ Floppy (A:).

5. Click the Save button in the Save As dialog box.

Word saves the document on a floppy disk in drive A with the file name, Brandon Letterhead.

Each time you wish to create a letter, you would open your letterhead file (Brandon Letterhead) and then immediately save it with a new file name. By doing this, your letterhead file will remain unchanged for future use.

Creating a Cover Letter

You have created a letterhead for your cover letter. The next step is to compose the cover letter. The following pages outline how to use Word to compose a cover letter with a bulleted list and a table.

Components of a Business Letter

During your professional career, you will create many business letters. A **cover letter** is one type of business letter. All business letters contain the same basic components. When preparing business letters, you should include all essential elements. **Essential business letter elements** include the date line, inside address, message, and signature block (see Figure 3-2a on the page WD 3.6). The **date line**, which consists of the month, day, and year, is positioned two to six lines below the letterhead. The **inside address**, placed three to eight lines below the date line, usually contains the addressee's courtesy title plus full name, business affiliation, and full geographical address. The **salutation**, if present, begins two lines below the last line of the inside address. The body of the letter, the **message**, begins two lines below the salutation. Within the message, paragraphs are single-spaced with double-spacing between paragraphs. Two lines below the last line of the message, the **complimentary close** displays. Capitalize only the first word in a complimentary close. Type the **signature block** at least four lines below the complimentary close, allowing room for the author to sign his or her name.

Borders

If you do not want the border of the current paragraph to extend to the margins, drag the right or left indent markers inward on the ruler to narrow the border.

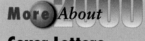

Letterhead Contents

All letterheads should contain the following items: complete legal name of company, group, or individual; full street address including any building, room, suite number, or post office box; city, state, and postal code. Other items sometimes found in a letterhead include a logo, department name, telephone number, fax number, e-mail address, and Web address.

Cover Letters

You should always send a personalized cover letter with a resume. A cover letter should highlight aspects of your background relevant to the position. Because it often is difficult to recall past achievements and activities, you should keep a personal file containing documents that outline your accomplishments.

Table 3-1	Common Business Letter Styles
LETTER STYLES	**FEATURES**
Block	All components of the letter begin flush with the left margin.
Modified Block	The date, complimentary close, and signature block are centered, positioned approximately ½″ to the right of center, or at the right margin. All other components of the letter begin flush with the left margin.
Modified Semi-Block	The date, complimentary close, and signature block are centered, positioned approximately ½″ to the right of center, or at the right margin. The first line of each paragraph in the body of the letter is indented ½″ to 1″ fom the left margin. All other components of the letter begin flush with the left margin.

You can follow many different styles when you create business letters. The cover letter in this project follows the **modified block style**. Table 3-1 outlines the differences between three common styles of business letters.

Saving the Cover Letter with a New File Name

The document in the document window currently has the name Brandon Letterhead, the name of the personal letterhead. Because you want the letterhead to remain unchanged, save the document with a new file name as described in these steps.

More About

Templates

As an alternative to saving the letterhead as a Word document, you could save it as a template by clicking the Save as type box arrow in the Save As dialog box and then clicking Document Template. To use the template, click File on the menu bar, click New, click the General tab, and then click the template icon or name.

TO SAVE THE DOCUMENT WITH A NEW FILE NAME

1 If necessary, insert your floppy disk into drive A.

2 Click File on the menu bar and then click Save As.

3 Type the file name Brandon Cover Letter in the File name text box.

4 If necessary, click the Save in box arrow and then click 3½ Floppy (A:).

5 Click the Save button in the Save As dialog box.

Word saves the document on a floppy disk in drive A with the file name, Brandon Cover Letter (see Figure 3-54).

The font size of characters in the resume is 10. You want the size of the characters in the cover letter to be slightly larger, yet close to the size of those in the resume. Perform the following steps to increase the font size of characters in the cover letter to 11.

TO INCREASE THE FONT SIZE

1 If necessary, click the paragraph mark below the border to position the insertion point below the border.

2 Double-click the move handle on the Formatting toolbar to display the entire toolbar. Click the Font Size box arrow on the Formatting toolbar and then click 11 in the Font Size list.

The font size of characters in the cover letter is 11 (see Figure 3-54).

More About

Bar Tabs

To insert a vertical line at a tab stop, set a bar tab. To do this, click the button at the left edge of the horizontal ruler until its icon changes to a Bar Tab icon (a vertical bar) and then click the location on the ruler. Or, click Bar in the Alignment area of the Tabs dialog box.

Setting Tab Stops Using the Ruler

The first required element of the cover letter is the date line, which is positioned three lines below the letterhead. The month, day, and year in the date line begins 3.5 inches from the left margin, which is one-half inch to the right of center. Thus, you should set a custom tab stop at the 3.5″ mark on the ruler.

Earlier you used the Tabs dialog box to set a tab stop because you could not use the ruler to set a tab stop at the right margin. In the following steps, you set a left-aligned tab stop using the ruler.

Steps: To Set Custom Tab Stops Using the Ruler

1 **Press the ENTER key twice. If necessary, click the button at the left edge of the horizontal ruler until it displays the left tab icon. Point to the 3.5" mark on the ruler.**

Each time you click the button at the left of the horizontal ruler, its icon changes (Figure 3-54). The left tab icon looks like a capital letter L.

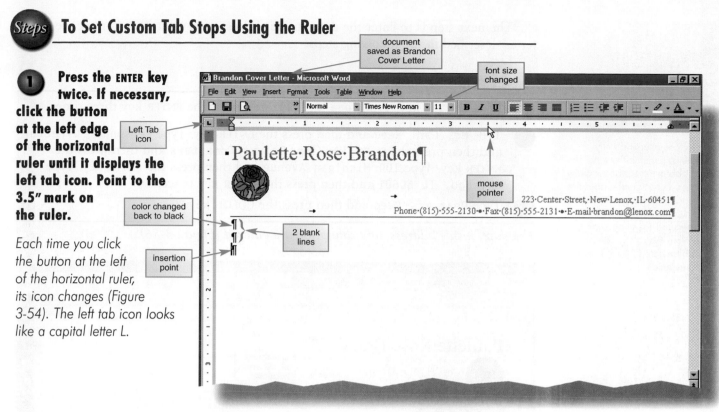

FIGURE 3-54

2 **Click the 3.5" mark on the ruler.**

Word places a left tab marker at the 3.5" mark on the ruler (Figure 3-55). The text you enter at this tab stop will be left-aligned.

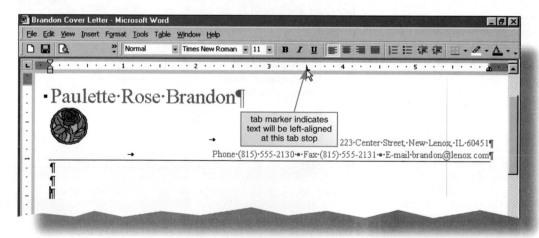

FIGURE 3-55

If, for some reason, you wanted to move a custom tab stop, you would drag the tab marker to the desired location on the ruler. If you wanted to change the alignment of a custom tab stop, you could remove the existing tab stop and then insert a new one as described in the steps above. To remove a custom tab stop, point to the tab marker on the ruler and then drag the tab marker down and out of the ruler. You also could use the Tabs dialog box to change an existing tab stop's alignment or position. You have learned that you click Format on the menu bar and then click Tabs to display the Tabs dialog box.

Other Ways

1. On Format menu click Tabs, enter tab stop position, click appropriate alignment, click OK button

The next step is to enter the date, inside address, and salutation in the cover letter as described in the following steps.

TO ENTER THE DATE, INSIDE ADDRESS, AND SALUTATION

1 Press the TAB key. Type June 4, 2001 and press the ENTER key three times.

2 Type Mr. Carl Reed and then press the ENTER key. Type Personnel Director and then press the ENTER key. Type Deluxe Computers and then press the ENTER key. Type 100 Michigan Avenue and then press the ENTER key. Type Chicago, IL 60601 and then press the ENTER key twice.

3 Type Dear Mr. Reed and then press the COLON key (:).

The date, inside address, and salutation are entered (Figure 3-56).

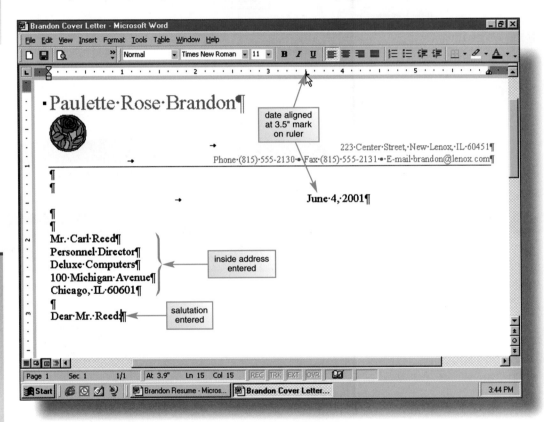

FIGURE 3-56

Creating an AutoText Entry

If you use the same text frequently, you can store the text in an **AutoText entry** and then use the stored entry throughout this document, as well as future documents. That is, you type the entry only once, and for all future occurrences of the text, you access the stored entry as you need it. In this way, you avoid entering the text inconsistently or incorrectly in different locations throughout the same document. Follow these steps to create an AutoText entry for the prospective employer's company name.

Steps To Create an AutoText Entry

1 **Drag through the text to be stored, in this case, Deluxe Computers. Be sure not to select the paragraph mark at the end of the text. Click Insert on the menu bar and then point to AutoText. Point to New on the AutoText submenu.**

Word highlights the company name, Deluxe Computers, in the inside address (Figure 3-57). Notice the paragraph mark is not part of the selection.

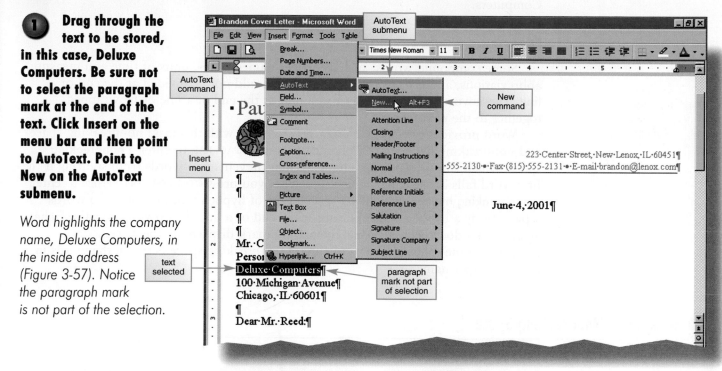

FIGURE 3-57

2 **Click New on the AutoText submenu. When the Create AutoText dialog box displays, type dc and then point to the OK button.**

Word displays the Create AutoText dialog box (Figure 3-58). In this dialog box, Word proposes a name for the AutoText entry, which usually is the first word(s) of the selection. You change it to a shorter name, dc.

3 **Click the OK button. If Word displays a dialog box, click the Yes button.**

Word stores the AutoText entry and closes the AutoText dialog box.

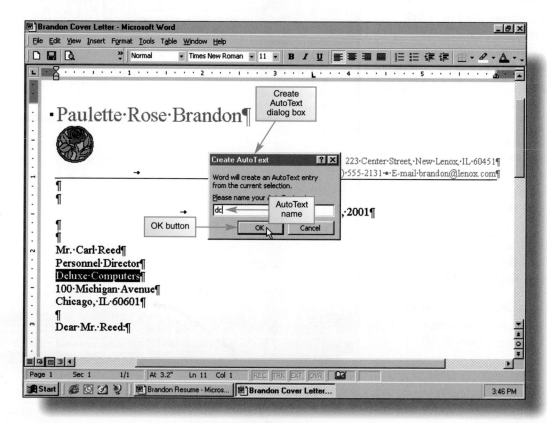

FIGURE 3-58

The name, dc, has been stored as an AutoText entry. Later in the project, you will use the AutoText entry, dc, instead of typing the company name, Deluxe Computers.

Entering a Nonbreaking Space

Some compound words, such as proper names, dates, units of time and measure, abbreviations, and geographic destinations, should not be divided at the end of a line. These words either should fit as a unit at the end of a line or be wrapped together to the next line.

Word provides two special characters to assist with this task: nonbreaking space and nonbreaking hyphen. You press CTRL+SHIFT+SPACEBAR to enter a **nonbreaking space**, which is a special space character that prevents two words from splitting if the first word falls at the end of a line. Likewise, you press CTRL+SHIFT+HYPHEN to enter a **nonbreaking hyphen**, which is a special type of hyphen that prevents two words separated by a hyphen from splitting at the end of a line. When you enter these characters into a document, a special formatting mark displays on the screen.

Perform the following steps to enter a nonbreaking space between the words in the newspaper name.

To Insert a Nonbreaking Space

1 **Scroll the salutation to the top of the document window. Click after the colon in the salutation and then press the ENTER key twice. If the Office Assistant displays, click its Cancel button. Type** I am responding to your computer sales management trainee position advertised in the **and then press the SPACEBAR. Press CTRL+I to turn on italics. Type** Chicago **and then press CTRL+SHIFT+SPACEBAR.**

Word enters a nonbreaking space after the word, Chicago (Figure 3-59).

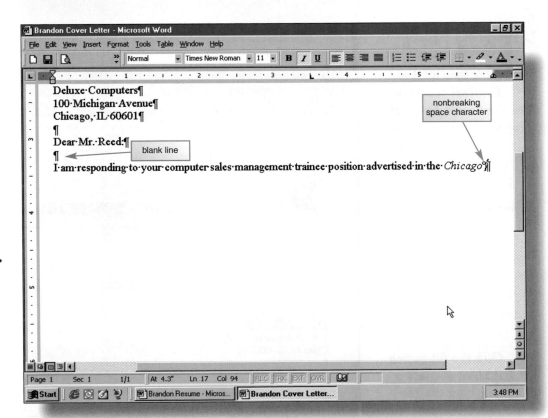

FIGURE 3-59

Type Times **and then press** CTRL+I **to turn off italics. Press the** PERIOD **key.**

Word wraps the two words in the newspaper title, Chicago Times, to the next line (Figure 3-60).

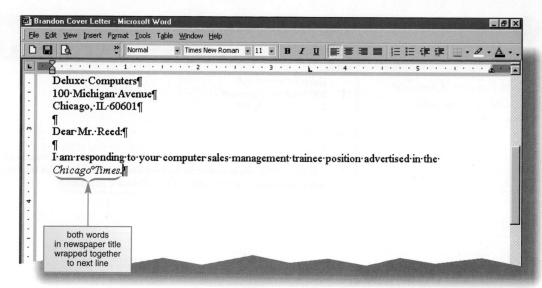

FIGURE 3-60

Inserting an AutoText Entry

At the end of the next sentence in the body of the cover letter, you want to put the company name, Deluxe Computers. Recall that earlier in this project, you stored an AutoText entry name of dc for Deluxe Computers. Thus, you will type the AutoText entry's name and then instruct Word to replace the AutoText entry's name with the stored entry of Deluxe Computers. Perform the following steps to insert an AutoText entry.

Other Ways

1. On Insert menu click Symbol, click Special Characters tab, click Nonbreaking Space in Character list, click Insert button, click Close button

Steps **To Insert an AutoText Entry**

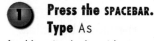 **Press the** SPACEBAR. **Type** As indicated in the enclosed resume, I have the credentials that you are seeking and believe I can be a valuable asset to dc **as shown in Figure 3-61.**

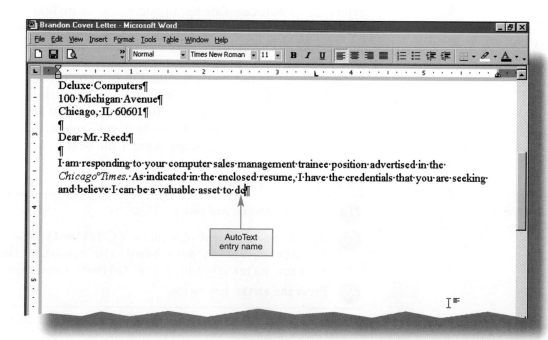

FIGURE 3-61

Press F3. Press the
PERIOD key.

Word replaces the characters,
dc, with the stored AutoText
entry, Deluxe Computers
(Figure 3-62).

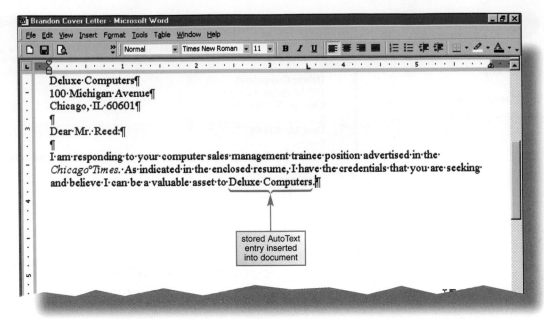

FIGURE 3-62

Pressing F3 instructs Word to replace the AutoText entry name with the stored AutoText entry. In Project 2, you learned how to use the AutoCorrect feature, which enables you to insert and also create AutoCorrect entries (just as you did for this AutoText entry). The difference between an AutoCorrect entry and an AutoText entry is that the AutoCorrect feature makes corrections for you automatically as soon as you press the SPACEBAR or a punctuation mark key, whereas you must press F3 or click the AutoText command to instruct Word to make an AutoText correction.

If you watch the screen as you type, you may discover that AutoComplete tips display on the screen. As you type, Word searches the list of AutoText entry names and if one matches your typing, Word displays its complete name above your typing as an **AutoComplete tip**. In addition to AutoText entries, Word proposes AutoComplete tips for the current date, a day of the week, a month, and so on. If your screen does not display AutoComplete tips, click Tools on the menu bar, click AutoCorrect, click the AutoText tab, click Show AutoComplete tip for AutoText and dates to select it, and then click the OK button. To view the complete list of entries, click Tools on the menu bar, click AutoCorrect, click the AutoText tab, and then scroll through the list of entries. To ignore an AutoComplete tip proposed by Word, simply continue typing to remove the AutoComplete tip from the screen.

Perform the following steps to enter the next paragraph into the cover letter.

TO ENTER A PARAGRAPH

1 Press the ENTER key twice.

2 Type I am a recent graduate of Illinois State College with degrees in both marketing management and computer technology. My courses in each major included the following and then press the COLON key.

3 Press the ENTER key twice.

The paragraph is entered (Figure 3-63 on page WD 3.50).

AutoFormat As You Type

As you type text into a document, Word automatically formats it for you. Table 3-2 outlines commonly used AutoFormat As You Type options and their results.

Table 3-2 Commonly Used AutoFormat As You Type Options		
TYPED TEXT	*AUTOFORMAT FEATURE*	*EXAMPLE*
Quotation marks or apostrophes	Changes straight quotation marks or apostrophes to curly ones	"the" becomes "the"
Text, a space, one hyphen, one or no spaces, text, space	Changes the hyphen to an en dash	ages 20 - 45 becomes ages 20 — 45
Text, two hyphens, text, space	Changes the two hyphens to em dash	Two types--yellow and red becomes Two types—yellow and red
Web address followed by space or ENTER key	Formats address as a hyperlink	www.scsite.com becomes www.scsite.com
Three hyphens, underscores, equal signs, asterisks, tildes, or number signs and then ENTER key	Places a border above a paragraph	--- Hyphens converted to line becomes _____ Hyphens converted to line
Number followed by a period, hyphen, right parenthesis, or greater than sign and then a space or tab followed by text	Creates a numbered list when you press the ENTER key	1. Word 2. Excel becomes 1. Word 2. Excel
Asterisk, hyphen, greater than sign and then a space or tab followed by text	Creates a bulleted list when you press the ENTER key	* Standard toolbar * Formatting toolbar becomes • Standard toolbar • Formatting toolbar
Fraction and then a space or hyphen	Converts the entry to a fraction-like notation	1/2 becomes ½
Ordinal and then a space or hyphen	Makes the original a superscript	3rd becomes 3rd

You can type a list and then place the bullets on the paragraphs at a later time, or you can use Word's AutoFormat As You Type feature to bullet the paragraphs as you type them. Because your fingers are on the keyboard already, perform the steps on the next page to add bullets automatically to a list as you type.

More About

AutoFormat

For an AutoFormat option to work as expected, it must be turned on. To check if an AutoFormat option is enabled, click Tools on the menu bar, click AutoCorrect, click the AutoFormat As You Type tab, select the appropriate check boxes, and then click the OK button. For example, Format beginning of list item like the one before it and Automatic bulleted lists should both contain check marks for automatic bullets.

Steps: **To Bullet a List as You Type**

1 **Press the ASTERISK key (*) and then press the SPACEBAR.**
Type Marketing Management: Principles of Marketing, Promotions, Retailing, Sales, Advertising, Personal Selling, International Marketing, Consumer Behavior **as the first list item (Figure 3-63).**

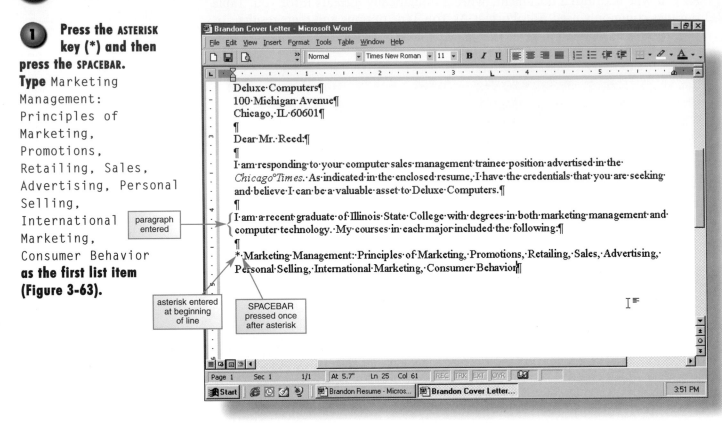

FIGURE 3-63

2 **Press the ENTER key.**

Word converts the asterisk to a bullet character, places another bullet on the second list item, and indents the two bulleted paragraphs.

3 **Type** Computer Technology: Computer Concepts, PC Technology, Structured Programming, Object-Oriented Programming, Database Techniques, Web Design **and then press the ENTER key.**

Word places a bullet on the next line (Figure 3-64).

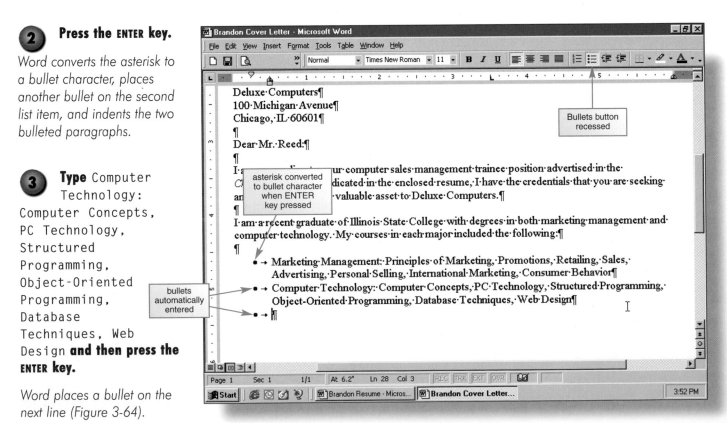

FIGURE 3-64

Press the ENTER key.

Word removes the lone bullet because you pressed the ENTER key twice (Figure 3-65). The Bullets button no longer is recessed.

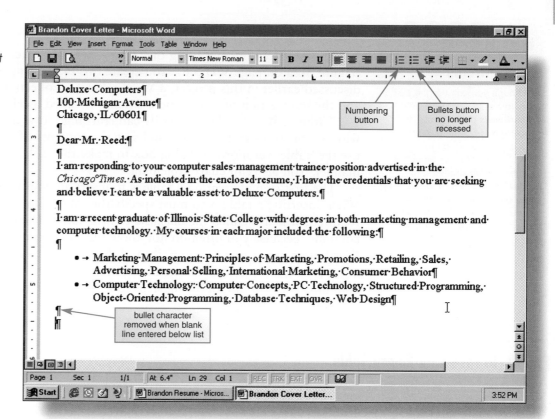

FIGURE 3-65

When the insertion point is in a bulleted list, the Bullets button on the Formatting toolbar is recessed. To instruct Word to stop bulleting paragraphs, you press the ENTER key twice or click the Bullets button.

If you know before you type a list that it is to be numbered, you can add numbers as you type, just as you can add bullets as you type. To number a list, type the number one followed by a period and then a space (1.) at the beginning of the first item and then type your text. When you press the ENTER key, Word places the number two (2.) at the beginning of the next line automatically. As with bullets, press the ENTER key twice at the end of the list or click the Numbering button on the Formatting toolbar to stop numbering (Figure 3-66).

Perform the following steps to enter the next paragraph into the cover letter.

TO ENTER A PARAGRAPH

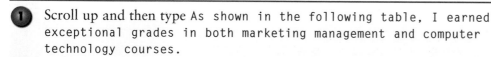

1 Scroll up and then type As shown in the following table, I earned exceptional grades in both marketing management and computer technology courses.

2 Press the ENTER key twice.

The paragraph is entered (see Figure 3-66 on the next page).

Other Ways

1. Select list, click Bullets button on Formatting toolbar
2. Select list, right-click selection, click Bullets and Numbering on shortcut menu, click Bulleted tab, click desired bullet type, click OK button
3. Select list, on Format menu click Bullets and Numbering, click Bulleted tab, click desired bullet type, click OK button

More About

Outline Numbered Lists

To create an outline numbered list, click Format on the menu bar, click Bullets and Numbering, click the Outline Numbered tab, and then click a style that does not contain the word 'Heading.' To promote or demote a list item to the next or previous levels, click the Increase Indent and Decrease Indent buttons on the Formatting toolbar.

More About

Word Tables

Although you can use the TAB key to create a table, many Word users prefer to use its table feature. With a Word table, you can arrange numbers in columns. For emphasis, tables can be shaded and have borders. Word tables can be sorted, and you can have Word add the contents of an entire row or column.

Creating a Table with the Insert Table Button

The next step in composing the cover letter is to place a table listing your GPAs (Figure 3-2a on page WD 3.6). You create this table using Word's table feature. As discussed earlier in this project, a Word table is a collection of rows and columns, and the intersection of a row and a column is called a cell.

Within a Word table, you easily can rearrange rows and columns, change column widths, sort rows and columns, and sum the contents of rows and columns. You can use the Table AutoFormat dialog box to make the table display in a professional manner. You also can chart table data.

The first step in creating a table is to insert an empty table into the document. When inserting a table, you must specify the total number of rows and columns required, which is called the **dimension** of the table. The table in this project has two columns. Because you often do not know the total number of rows in a table, many Word users create one row initially and then add rows as they need them. The first number in a dimension is the number of rows, and the second is the number of columns. Perform the following steps to insert a 1 x 2 table; that is, a table with one row and two columns.

Steps To Insert an Empty Table

1 Double-click the move handle on the Standard toolbar. Click the Insert Table button on the Standard toolbar. Point to the cell in the first row and second column of the grid to highlight the first two cells in the first row of the grid.

*Word displays a **grid** to define the dimension of the desired table (Figure 3-66). Word will insert the table immediately above the insertion point.*

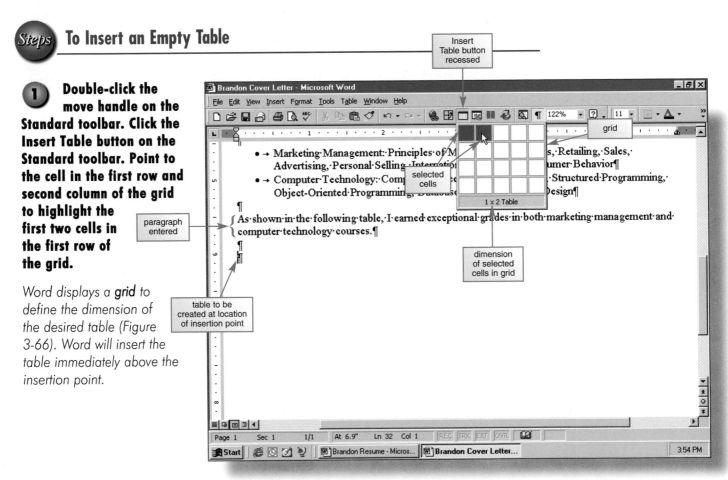

FIGURE 3-66

2 Click the cell in the first row and second column of the grid.

Word inserts an empty 1 × 2 table into the document (Figure 3-67). The insertion point is in the first cell (row 1 and column 1) of the table.

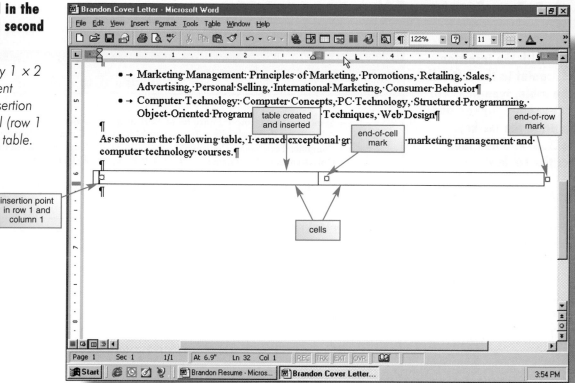

FIGURE 3-67

As you learned earlier in this project, each row of a table has an end-of-row mark, which you use to add columns to the right of a table. Each cell has an end-of-cell mark, which you use to select a cell. The end-of-cell mark currently is left-aligned; thus it is positioned at the left edge of each cell. You can use any of the paragraph formatting buttons on the Formatting toolbar to change the alignment of the text within the cells. For example, if you click the Align Right button on the Formatting toolbar, the end-of-cell mark and any entered text will display at the right edge of the cell.

For simple tables, such as the one just created, Word users click the Insert Table button to create a table. For more complex tables, such as one with a varying number of columns per row, Word has a Draw Table feature that allows you to use a pencil pointer to draw a table on the screen. Project 4 discusses the Draw Table feature.

Entering Data into a Word Table

The next step is to enter data into the empty table. Cells are filled with data. The data you enter within a cell wordwraps just as text does between the margins of a document. To place data into a cell, you click the cell and then type. To advance rightward from one cell to the next, press the TAB key. When you are at the rightmost cell in a row, also press the TAB key to move to the first cell in the next row; do not press the ENTER key. The ENTER key is used to begin a new paragraph within a cell.

To add new rows to a table, press the TAB key with the insertion point positioned in the bottom right corner cell of the table. Perform the steps on the next page to enter data into the table.

Other Ways

1. On Table menu point to Insert, click Table, enter number of columns, enter number of rows, click OK button

More About 2000

Draw Table

To use Draw Table, click the Tables and Borders button on the Standard toolbar to change the mouse pointer to a pencil. Use the pencil to draw from one corner to the opposite diagonal corner to define the perimeter of the table. Then, draw the column and row lines inside the perimeter. To remove a line, use the Eraser button on the Tables and Borders toolbar.

Steps **To Enter Data into a Table**

1 **With the insertion point in the left cell** of the table, type `GPA for Marketing Courses` **and then press the TAB key. Type** `3.8/4.0` **and then press the TAB key.**

Word enters the table data into the first row of the table and adds a second row to the table (Figure 3-68). The insertion point is positioned in the first cell of the second row.

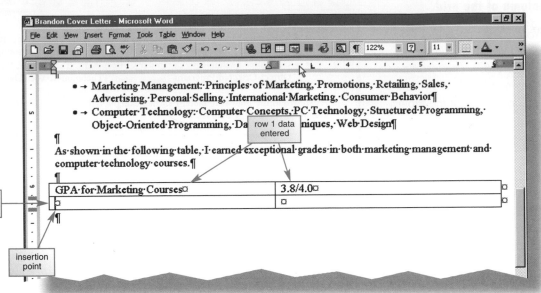

FIGURE 3-68

2 **Type** `GPA for Computer Courses` **and then press the TAB key. Type** `3.9/4.0` **and then press the TAB key. Type** `Overall GPA` **and then press the TAB key. Type** `3.8/4.0` **as shown in Figure 3-69.**

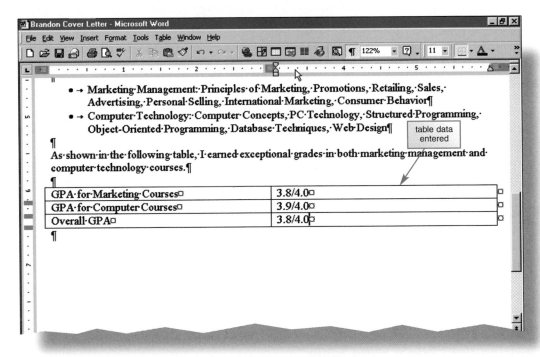

FIGURE 3-69

More About

Tabs

Because the TAB key advances the insertion point from one cell to the next in a table, press the CTRL+TAB keys to insert a tab character into a cell.

You modify the contents of cells just as you modify text in a document. To delete the contents of a cell, select the cell contents by pointing to the left edge of a cell, clicking when the mouse pointer changes direction, and then pressing the DELETE key. To modify text in a cell, click in the cell and then correct the entry. You can double-click the OVR indicator on the status bar to toggle between insert and overtype modes. You also may drag and drop or cut and paste the contents of cells.

Formatting a Table

Although you can format each row, column, and cell of a table individually, Word provides a Table AutoFormat feature that contains predefined formats for tables. Perform the following steps to format the entire table using Table AutoFormat.

More About

Table Commands

If a Table command is dimmed on the Table menu, it is likely that the insertion point is not in the table.

 To AutoFormat a Table

1 With the insertion point in the table, click Table on the menu bar and then point to Table AutoFormat (Figure 3-70).

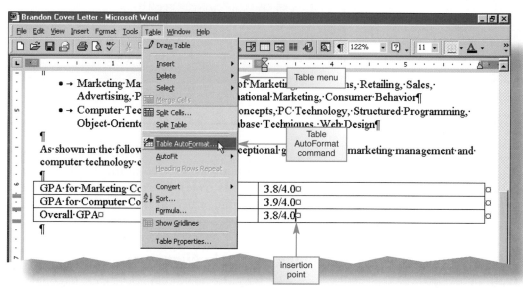

FIGURE 3-70

2 Click Table AutoFormat. When the Table AutoFormat dialog box displays, scroll through the Formats list and then click Contemporary. If necessary, click Heading rows in the Apply special formats to area to remove the check mark. Be sure the remaining check boxes match Figure 3-71.

Word displays the Table AutoFormat dialog box (Figure 3-71). This table does not have a heading row.

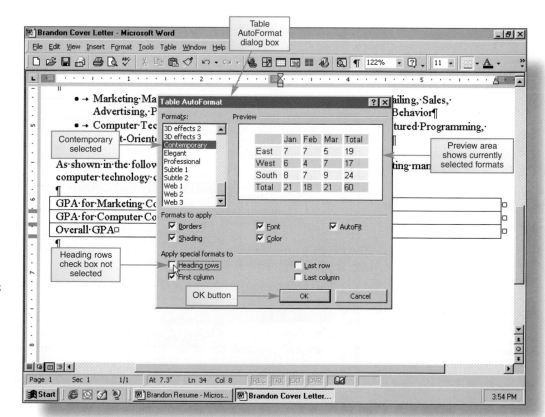

FIGURE 3-71

3 **Click the OK button.**

Word formats the table according to the Contemporary format (Figure 3-72).

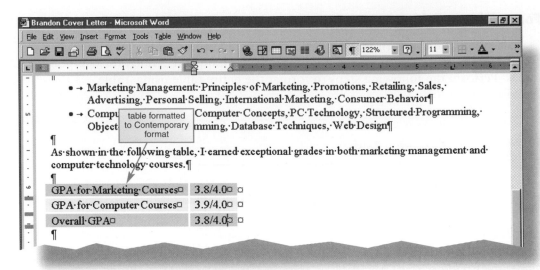

FIGURE 3-72

Other Ways

1. Click Table AutoFormat button on Tables and Borders toolbar

Because AutoFit was selected in the Table AutoFormat dialog box (see Figure 3-71 on the previous page), Word automatically adjusted the widths of the columns based on the amount of text in the table. In this case, Word reduced the size of the column widths.

Changing the Table Alignment

When you first create a table, it is left-aligned; that is, flush with the left margin. This table should be centered. To center a table, you first must select the entire table and then center it using the Center button on the Formatting toolbar, as shown in the following steps.

 Steps **To Select a Table**

1 **With the insertion point in the table, click Table on the menu bar, point to Select, and then point to Table (Figure 3-73).**

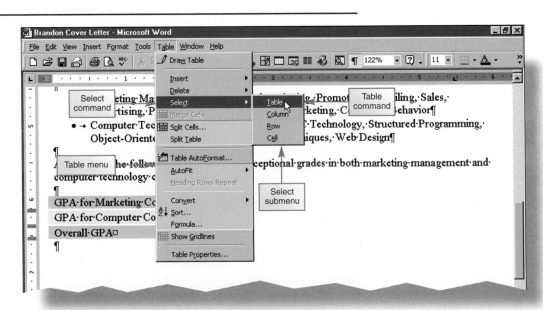

FIGURE 3-73

② Click Table.

Word highlights the contents of the entire table.

③ Double-click the move handle on the Formatting toolbar. Click the Center button on the Formatting toolbar.

Word centers the table between the left and right margins (Figure 3-74).

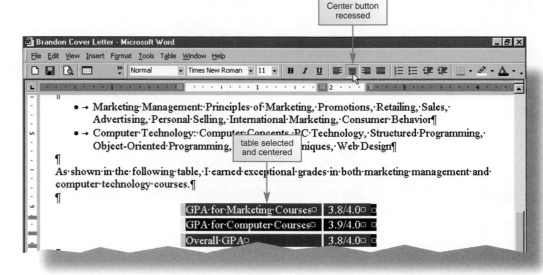

FIGURE 3-74

Perform the following steps to enter the remainder of the cover letter.

TO ENTER THE REMAINDER OF THE COVER LETTER

① Click the paragraph mark below the table. Press the ENTER key. Type the paragraph shown in Figure 3-75, making certain you use the AutoText entry, dc, to insert the company name.

② Press the ENTER key twice. Press the TAB key. Type Sincerely and then press the COMMA key.

③ Press the ENTER key four times. Press the TAB key. Type Paulette Rose Brandon and then press the ENTER key twice.

④ Type Enclosure as the final text.

The cover letter text is complete (Figure 3-75).

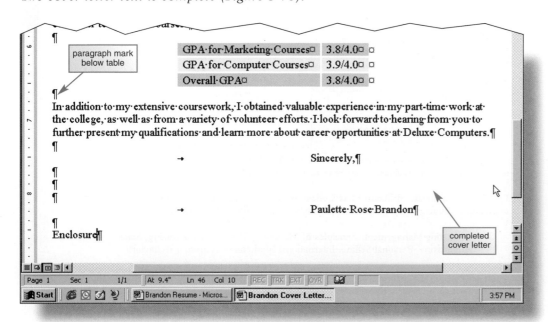

FIGURE 3-75

Saving Again and Printing the Cover Letter

The cover letter for the resume now is complete. You should save the cover letter again and then print it as described in the following steps.

TO SAVE A DOCUMENT AGAIN

1 Double-click the move handle on the Standard toolbar. Click the Save button on the Standard toolbar.

Word saves the cover letter with the same file name, Brandon Cover Letter.

TO PRINT A DOCUMENT

1 Click the Print button on the Standard toolbar.

The completed cover letter prints as shown in Figure 3-2a on page WD 3.6.

Preparing and Printing an Envelope Address

The final step in this project is to prepare and print an envelope address, as shown in the following steps.

More About

Printing

Use a laser printer to print the resume and cover letter on standard letter-size white or ivory paper. Be sure to print a copy for yourself. And read it - especially before the interview. Most likely, the interviewer will have copies in hand, ready to ask you questions about the contents of both the resume and cover letter.

Steps **To Prepare and Print an Envelope Address**

1 Scroll through the cover letter to display the inside address in the document window. Drag through the inside address to select it. Click Tools on the menu bar and then point to Envelopes and Labels (Figure 3-76).

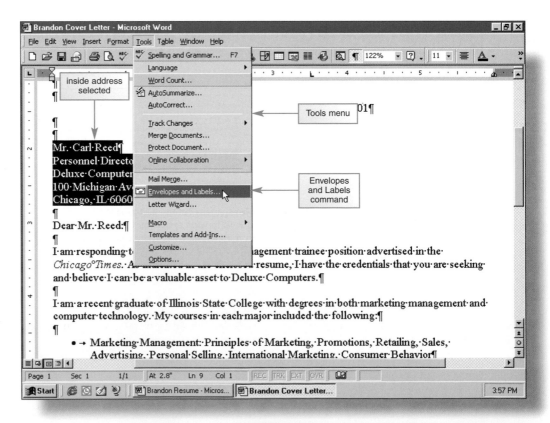

FIGURE 3-76

2 **Click Envelopes and Labels. When the Envelopes and Labels dialog box displays, if necessary, click the Envelopes tab. Click the Return address text box. Type** Paulette R. Brandon **and then press the ENTER key. Type** 223 Center Street **and then press the ENTER key. Type** New Lenox, IL 60451 **and then point to the Print button in the Envelopes and Labels dialog box.**

Word displays the Envelopes and Labels dialog box (Figure 3-77). The selected inside address displays in the Delivery address text box.

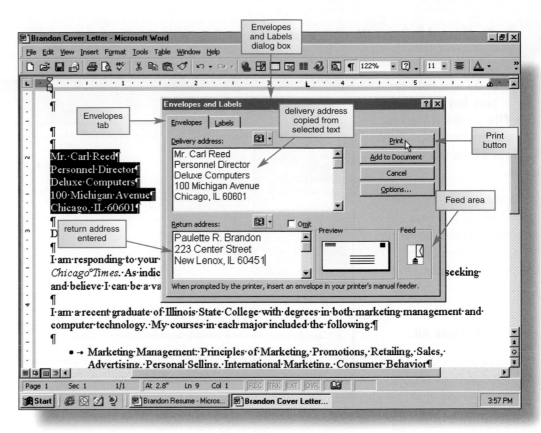

FIGURE 3-77

3 **Insert an envelope into your printer as shown in the Feed area of the Envelopes and Labels dialog box and then click the Print button in the dialog box. If a Microsoft Word dialog box displays, click the No button.**

Word prints the envelope (Figure 3-78).

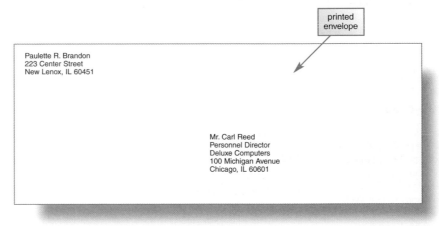

FIGURE 3-78

Instead of printing an envelope, you can print a mailing label. To do this, click the Labels tab in the Envelopes and Labels dialog box.

Currently, you have two documents open: the resume and cover letter. When you are finished with both documents, you may wish to close them. Instead of closing each one individually, you can close all open files at once as shown in the steps on the next page.

More About

Office Supplies

For more information on where to obtain supplies for printing documents, visit the Word 2000 More About Web page (www.scsite.com/wd2000/more.htm) and then click Online Office Supplies.

Steps **To Close All Open Word Documents**

 1 **Press and hold the SHIFT key and then click File on the menu bar. Release the SHIFT key. Point to Close All on the File menu.**

Word displays a Close All command, instead of a Close command, on the File menu because you pressed the SHIFT key when clicking the menu name (Figure 3-79).

 2 **Click Close All.**

Word closes all open documents and displays a blank document window. If at this point you wanted to begin a new document, you would click the New Blank Document button on the Standard toolbar.

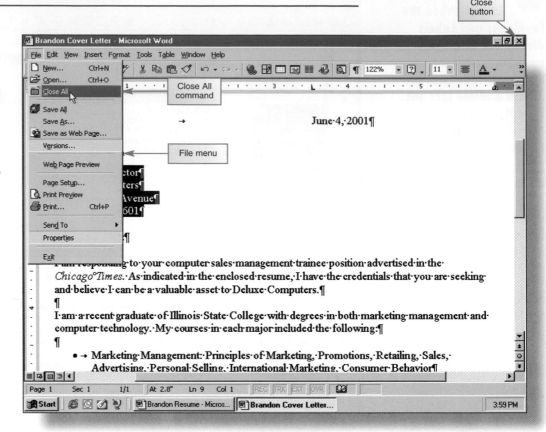

FIGURE 3-79

 **More** *About*

Quick Reference

For a table that lists how to complete the tasks covered in this book using the mouse, menu, shortcut menu, and keyboard, visit the Shelly Cashman Series Office Web page (www.scsite.com/off2000/qr.htm) and then click Microsoft Word 2000.

The final step in this project is to quit Word as described in the step below.

TO QUIT WORD

1 Click the Close button in the Word window.

The Word window closes.

C A S E   P E R S P E C T I V E   S U M M A R Y

With your resume writing expertise and Paulette's business sense, you have created an effective resume and cover letter. Paulette immediately staples the two documents together, places them in the envelope, adds necessary postage, and delivers the envelope to the post office. As she places her cover letter and resume in the mail, Paulette dreams about a career at Deluxe Computers. She plans to wait one week to hear from Mr. Reed, the personnel director at Deluxe Computers. If he has not contacted her in that time, Paulette plans to follow up with a telephone call to him.

Project Summary

Project 3 introduced you to creating a resume using a wizard and creating a cover letter with a letterhead, a bulleted list, and a table. You used the Resume Wizard to create a resume, and then used several formatting techniques to personalize the resume. You viewed, reduced the size of, and printed the resume in print preview. You created a letterhead and then created the cover letter. While creating the letterhead, you learned how to add color to characters, set custom tab stops, collect and paste between documents, add a symbol to a document, and add a border to a paragraph. You created an AutoText entry, which you used when you personalized the cover letter. Finally, you prepared and printed an envelope.

What You Should Know

Having completed this project, you now should be able to perform the following tasks:

▶ Add a Bottom Border to a Paragraph (*WD 3.39*)
▶ AutoFormat a Table (*WD 3.55*)
▶ Bold Text (*WD 3.17*)
▶ Bullet a List as You Type (*WD 3.50*)
▶ Change Color of Text (*WD 3.41*)
▶ Change the Font Size (*WD 3.28*)
▶ Close All Open Word Documents (*WD 3.60*)
▶ Collect Items (*WD 3.33*)
▶ Color Characters (*WD 3.28*)
▶ Color More Characters the Same Color (*WD 3.37*)
▶ Create a Resume Using Word's Resume Wizard (*WD 3.7*)
▶ Create an AutoText Entry (*WD 3.45*)
▶ Display Formatting Marks (*WD 3.15*)
▶ Enter a Line Break (*WD 3.22*)
▶ Enter a Paragraph (*WD 3.48, WD 3.51*)
▶ Enter and Resize a Graphic (*WD 3.30*)
▶ Enter Data into a Table (*WD 3.54*)
▶ Enter Placeholder Text (*WD 3.21*)
▶ Enter the Date, Inside Address, and Salutation (*WD 3.44*)
▶ Enter the Remainder of the Cover Letter (*WD 3.57*)
▶ Enter the Remaining Sections of the Resume (*WD 3.23*)
▶ Increase the Font Size (*WD 3.42*)
▶ Insert a Nonbreaking Space (*WD 3.46*)
▶ Insert a Symbol into Text (*WD 3.37*)
▶ Insert an AutoText Entry (*WD 3.47*)
▶ Insert an Empty Table (*WD 3.52*)
▶ Open a New Document Window (*WD 3.27*)
▶ Paste from the Office Clipboard (*WD 3.35*)
▶ Prepare and Print an Envelope Address (*WD 3.58*)
▶ Print a Document (*WD 3.58*)
▶ Print Preview a Document (*WD 3.24*)

▶ Print the Resume Created by the Resume Wizard (*WD 3.14*)
▶ Quit Word (*WD 3.60*)
▶ Reset Menus and Toolbars (*WD 3.14*)
▶ Save a Document (*WD 3.26*)
▶ Save a Document Again (*WD 3.58*)
▶ Save the Document with a New File Name (*WD 3.42*)
▶ Save the Letterhead (*WD 3.41*)
▶ Select a Table (*WD 3.56*)
▶ Select and Replace Placeholder Text (*WD 3.18*)
▶ Select and Replace Resume Wizard Supplied Text (*WD 3.19*)
▶ Set Custom Tab Stops Using the Ruler (*WD 3.43*)
▶ Set Custom Tab Stops Using the Tabs Dialog Box (*WD 3.31*)
▶ Switch From One Open Document to Another (*WD 3.33*)
▶ Zoom Text Width (*WD 3.17*)

More About

Microsoft Certification

The Microsoft Office User Specialist (MOUS) Certification program provides an opportunity for you to obtain a valuable industry credential - proof that you have the Word 2000 skills required by employers. For more information, see Appendix D or visit the Shelly Cashman Series MOUS Web page at www.scsite.com/off2000/cert.htm.

Apply Your Knowledge

➕ **Project Reinforcement at www.scsite.com/off2000/reinforce.htm**

1 Working with a Table

Instructions: Start Word. Open the document, Expenses Table, on the Data Disk. If you did not download the Data Disk, see the inside back cover for instructions for downloading the Data Disk or see your instructor.

The document is a Word table that you are to edit and format. The revised table is shown in Figure 3-80.

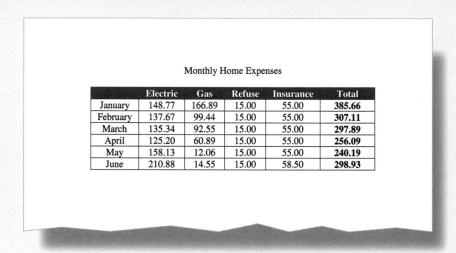

Monthly Home Expenses

	Electric	Gas	Refuse	Insurance	Total
January	148.77	166.89	15.00	55.00	**385.66**
February	137.67	99.44	15.00	55.00	**307.11**
March	135.34	92.55	15.00	55.00	**297.89**
April	125.20	60.89	15.00	55.00	**256.09**
May	158.13	12.06	15.00	55.00	**240.19**
June	210.88	14.55	15.00	58.50	**298.93**

FIGURE 3-80

Perform the following tasks:

1. With the insertion point in the table, click Table on the menu bar and then click Table AutoFormat. In the Table AutoFormat dialog box, scroll to and then click Grid 8 in the Formats list. All check boxes should have check marks except for these two: Last row and Last column. Click the OK button.

2. Select the Phone column by pointing to the top of the column until the mouse pointer changes to a downward pointing arrow and then clicking. Right-click in the selected column and then click Delete Columns on the shortcut menu to delete the Phone column.

3. Add a new row to the table for June as follows: Electric– 210.88; Gas– 14.55; Refuse– 15.00; Insurance – 58.50.

4. With the insertion point in the table, click Table on the menu bar, point to Select, and then click Table. Double-click the move handle on the Formatting toolbar. Click the Center button on the Formatting toolbar to center the table.

5. Click in the rightmost column, Insurance. Click Table on the menu bar, point to Insert, and then click Columns to the Right. Type Total as the new column's heading.

6. Position the insertion point in the January Total cell (second row, sixth column). Click Table on the menu bar and then click Formula. When the Formula dialog box displays, be sure the formula is =SUM(LEFT) and then click the OK button to place the Total expenses for January in the cell. Repeat for each month s total expense. For these expenses, you will need to edit the formula so it reads =SUM(LEFT) instead of =SUM(ABOVE).

7. Select the cells containing the total expense values and then click the Bold button on the Formatting toolbar.

8. Click File on the menu bar and then click Save As. Use the file name, Revised Expenses, to save the document on your floppy disk.

9. Print the revised table.

In the Lab

1 Using Word's Resume Wizard to Create a Resume

Problem: You are a student at University of Tennessee expecting to receive your Bachelor of Science degree in Restaurant/Hotel Management this May. As the semester end is approaching quickly, you are beginning a search for full-time employment upon graduation. You prepare the resume shown in Figure 3-81 using Word's Resume Wizard.

Instructions:

1. Use the Resume Wizard to create a resume. Select the Contemporary style for the resume. Use the name and address information in Figure 3-81 when the Resume Wizard requests it.
2. Personalize the resume as shown in Figure 3-81. When entering multiple lines in the Awards received, Memberships, Languages, and Hobbies sections, be sure to enter a line break at the end of each line, instead of a paragraph break.
3. Check the spelling of the resume.
4. Save the resume on a floppy disk with Schumann Resume as the file name.
5. View the resume from within print preview. If the resume exceeds one page, use print preview to shrink it to a page. Print the resume.

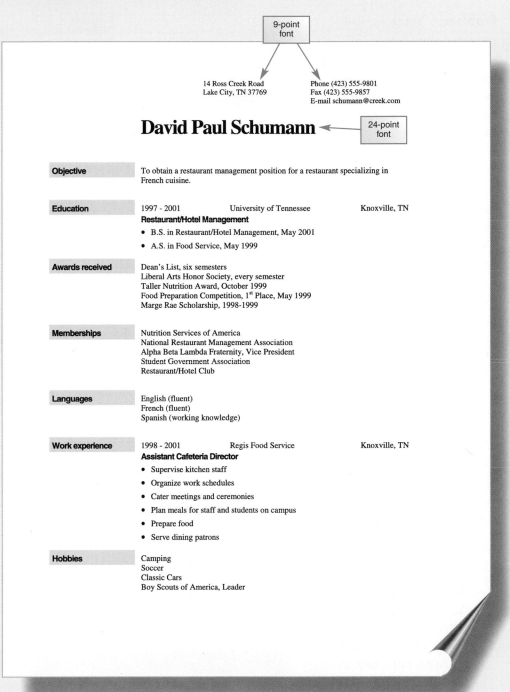

FIGURE 3-81

In the Lab

2 Creating a Cover Letter with a Table

Problem: You have just prepared the resume shown in Figure 3-81 on the previous page and now are ready to create a cover letter to send to a prospective employer. In yesterday's edition of the *West Coast Tribune*, you noticed an advertisement for a restaurant manager at Worldwide Hotels and Suites. You prepare the cover letter shown in Figure 3-82 to send with your resume.

Instructions:

1. Create the letterhead shown at the top of Figure 3-82. Save the letterhead with the file name, Schumann Letterhead.

2. Create the letter shown in Figure 3-82 using the modified block style. Set a tab stop at the 3.5" mark on the ruler for the date line, complimentary close, and signature block. After entering the inside address, create an AutoText entry for Worldwide Hotels and Suites, and use the AutoText

---

20-point indigo font

letterhead

David Paul Schumann

9-point indigo font

14 Ross Creek Road, Lake City, TN 37769
Phone (423) 555-9801 • Fax (423) 555-9857 • E-mail schumann@creek.com

clip keywords: hands on serving tray

April 18, 2001

Ms. Amy Leonard
Food Service Director
Worldwide Hotels and Suites
202 Park Boulevard
Richmond, CA 98993

11-point font

Dear Ms. Leonard:

I am responding to your advertisement in the *West Coast Tribune* for the restaurant manager position that will be opening in June. I have enclosed my resume for your consideration.

I will be graduating from the University of Tennessee in May. My courses in restaurant management and nutrition included the following:

- Restaurant Management: Introduction to Food Service, Restaurant Management, Food Service Marketing, Computers in Food Service, Food Production, Food Safety
- Nutrition: Food Planning and Preparation, Nutrition Essentials, Diet Planning, Nutrition Problems, Nutrition for Health

Through my part-time work for the university for Regis Food Service, I have first-hand experience with many aspects of food service. My annual reviews were outstanding. The following table lists my overall rating for each review.

Academic Year	Rating
2000-2001	5.0/5.0
1999-2000	4.8/5.0
1998-1999	4.5/5.0

Given my coursework and experience, I feel I would be a valuable asset to your organization. I look forward to hearing from you to schedule an interview and to discuss my career opportunities with Worldwide Hotels and Suites.

Sincerely,

David Paul Schumann

Enclosure

FIGURE 3-82

---

entry whenever you have to enter the company name, Worldwide Hotels and Suites. Center the table and format it using the Elegant format in the Table AutoFormat dialog box.

3. Save the letter on a floppy disk with Schumann Cover Letter as the file name.

4. Check the spelling of the cover letter. Save the cover letter again with the same file name.

In the Lab

5. View the cover letter from within print preview. If the cover letter exceeds one page, use print preview to shrink it to a single page. Print the cover letter.

6. Prepare and print an envelope address and mailing label using the inside address and return address in the cover letter.

3 Using Wizards to Compose a Personal Cover Letter and Resume

Problem: You are currently in the market for a new job and are ready to prepare a resume and cover letter.

Instructions: Obtain a copy of last Sunday's newspaper. Look through the classified section and cut out a want ad in an area of interest. Assume you are in the market for the position being advertised. Use the Resume Wizard to create a resume. Use the Letter Wizard to create the cover letter. Display the Letter Wizard by clicking Tools on the menu bar and then clicking Letter Wizard. *Hint:* Use Help for assistance in using the Letter Wizard. Use the want ad for the inside address and your personal information for the return address. Try to be as accurate as possible when personalizing the resume and cover letter. Submit the want ad with your cover letter and resume.

Cases and Places

The difficulty of these case studies varies:
▶ are the least difficult; ▶▶ are more difficult; and ▶▶▶ are the most difficult.

1 ▶ Your boss has asked you to create a calendar for October so he can post it on the office bulletin board. Use the Calendar Wizard in the Other Documents sheet of the New Office Document dialog box. Use the following settings in the wizard: boxes & borders style, landscape print direction, leave room for a picture, October 2001 for both the start and end date. With the calendar on the screen, click the current graphic and delete it. Insert a clip art image of a haunted house or a similar seasonal graphic and then resize the image so it fits in the entire space for the graphic.

2 ▶ You have been asked to prepare the agenda for the next monthly department meeting. Use the Agenda Wizard in the Other Documents sheet of the New Office Document dialog box. Use the following settings in the wizard: style – modern; meeting date – 4/18/2001; meeting time – 2:00 p.m.; title – Monthly Meeting; meeting location – Conference Room B; headings – Please read and Please bring; names on agenda – Meeting called by, Note taker, and Attendees; Topics, People, and Minutes – Approve March Minutes, C. Dolby, 5; Department News, E. Jones, 10; Budget Status, J. Peterson, 15; Annual Kick-Off Dinner, T. Greeson, 15; New Business, Floor, 15; add a form for recording the minutes. On the agenda created by the wizard, add the following names in the appropriate spaces: C. Dolby called the meeting; R. Wilson will be the note taker; all people listed in this assignment will be attending – including you. Also, attendees should bring the 2001 Budget Report and read the March Minutes.

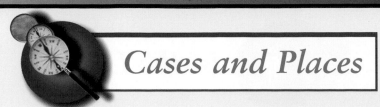

Cases and Places

3 ▶ You notice that Word has a Letter Wizard, which you can begin by clicking Tools on the menu bar and then clicking Letter Wizard. To assist you with letter preparation, you decide to prepare the letter shown in Figure 3-82 on page WD 3.64 using the Letter Wizard. How does the document prepared using the Letter Wizard differ from the one created from scratch? Do you prefer using a wizard or composing a letter from scratch?

4 ▶▶ A potential employer has asked you to fax your cover letter and resume so she may review it immediately. Use the Fax Wizard and the following settings: create the fax cover sheet with a note and print the fax so you can send it on a separate fax machine. It must be faxed to K. J. Buchham at Jade Enterprises (One Main Street, Cambridge, MA 02142; telephone 617-555-0098; fax 617-555-0099). Each is one page in length. Fax a copy to T. R. Green at the same number. In the fax, write a message informing K. J. Buchham that your cover letter and resume are attached and if she has any questions, she can contact you. Use your own name, address, and telephone information in the fax.

5 ▶▶ As chairperson of the Annual Company Picnic, you look for volunteers to assist with various activities. You have compiled a list of jobs for the picnic: prepare fliers, distribute fliers, plan meal and order food, plan and organize games, plan children's activities, reserve park pavilion, setup on day of picnic, and cleanup on day of picnic. You prepare a memorandum asking fellow employees for their assistance. A copy of the memo should be sent to Howard Bender. Use the Memo Wizard, together with the concepts and techniques presented in this project, to create and format the interoffice memorandum.

6 ▶▶▶ You have been asked to locate a speaker for this year's commencement address at your school. Locate the address of someone you feel would be a highly respected and enthusiastic speaker for the commencement address. Using Word's Letter Wizard, write the individual a letter inviting him or her to speak at the commencement. In the letter, present a background of your school, the student body, the staff, and any other aspects of your school that would make this speaker want to attend your commencement. Be sure to list the date, time, and location of the commencement in the letter. Apply the concepts and techniques presented in this project to personalize the letter.

7 ▶▶▶ Many individuals place their resumes on the World Wide Web for potential employers to see. Find a resume on the Web that you believe could be improved if it were designed differently. Print the resume. Using the text on the resume, Word's Resume Wizard, and the techniques presented in this project, create a new resume that would be more likely to catch a potential employer's attention. Turn in both the resume from the Web and your newly designed version of the resume.

Microsoft **Word 2000**

Microsoft Word 2000

Creating Web Pages Using Word

CASE PERSPECTIVE

In Project 3, Paulette Rose Brandon created her resume (Figure 3-1 on page WD 3.5). Paulette graduated with you from Illinois State College. She was proficient in business, and you excelled at Internet skills. Recently, Paulette has been surfing the Internet on her own and has discovered that many people have their own personal Web pages with links to other Web sites and Web pages such as resumes and schedules. These personal Web pages are very impressive. To make herself more attractive to a potential employer, Paulette has asked you to help her create a personal Web page that contains a hyperlink to her resume. To do this, she must save her resume as a Web page. Paulette also wants her Web page to contain two more hyperlinks: one to her favorite Web site (www.scsite.com) and another to her e-mail address. This way, potential employers easily can send her a message.

To complete this Web Feature, you will need the resume created in Project 3 so you can save it as a Web page and then use the resulting Web page as a hyperlink destination. (If you did not create the resume, see your instructor for a copy.)

Introduction

Word provides two techniques for creating Web pages. If you have an existing Word document, you can save it as a Web page. If you do not have an existing Word document, you can create a new Web page by using a Web page template or the Web Page Wizard, which provides customized templates you can modify easily. In addition to these Web tools, Word has many other **Web page authoring** features. For example, you can include frames, hyperlinks, sounds, videos, pictures, scrolling text, bullets, horizontal lines, check boxes, option buttons, list boxes, text boxes, and scripts on Web pages.

In this Web Feature, you save the resume created in Project 3 as a Web page. You then use Word's Web Page Wizard to create another Web page that contains two frames (Figure 1a on the next page). A **frame** is a rectangular section of a Web page that can display another separate Web page. Thus, a Web page that contains multiple frames can display multiple Web pages simultaneously. Word stores all frames associated with a Web page in a single file called the **frames page**. The frames page is not visible on the screen; it simply is a container for all frames associated with a Web page. When you open the frames page in Word or a Web browser, all frames associated with the Web page display on the screen.

In this Web Feature, the file name of the frames page is Brandon Personal Web Page. When you initially open this frames page, the left frame contains the title Paulette Rose Brandon and two hyperlinks – My Resume and My Favorite Site; the right frame displays Paulette's resume (Figure 1a). You have learned that a hyperlink is a shortcut that allows a user to jump easily and quickly to another location in the same document or to other documents or Web pages. The My Resume hyperlink is a connection to the resume, and the My Favorite Site hyperlink is a connection to www.scsite.com.

When you click the My Favorite Site hyperlink, the www.scsite.com Web site displays in the right frame (Figure 1b). When you click the My Resume hyperlink, the resume displays in the right frame. The resume itself contains a hyperlink to an e-mail address. When you click the e-mail address, Word opens your e-mail program automatically with the recipient's address (brandon@lenox.com) already filled in (Figure 1c). You simply type a message and then click the Send button, which places the message in the Outbox or sends it if you are connected to an e-mail server.

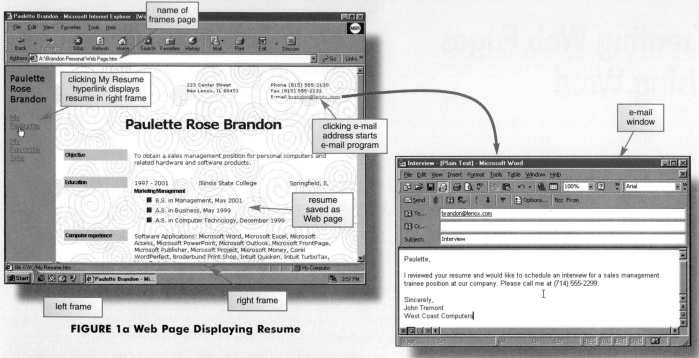

FIGURE 1a Web Page Displaying Resume

FIGURE 1c E-mail Program

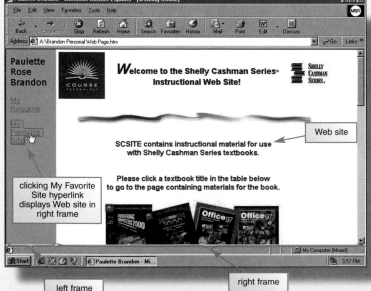

FIGURE 1b Web Page Displaying Web Site

Once you have created Web pages, you can publish them. **Publishing** is the process of making Web pages available to others, for example on the World Wide Web or on a company's intranet. In Word, you can publish Web pages by saving them to a Web folder or to an FTP location. The procedures for publishing Web pages in Microsoft Office are discussed in Appendix B.

Because this Web Feature is for instructional purposes, you create and save your frames page and associated Web pages on a floppy disk rather than to the Web. Saving these pages to the floppy disk may be a slow process – please be patient.

Saving a Word Document as a Web Page

Once you have created a Word document, you can save it as a Web page so that it can be published and then viewed by a Web browser, such as Internet Explorer. Perform the following steps to save the resume created in Project 3 as a Web page.

Steps To Save a Word Document as a Web Page

1 Start Word and then open the Brandon Resume created in Project 3. Reset your toolbars as described in Appendix C. Click File on the menu bar and then point to Save as Web Page (Figure 2).

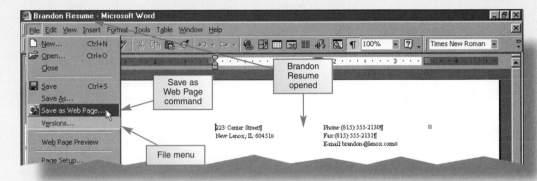

FIGURE 2

2 Click Save as Web Page. When the Save As dialog box displays, type Brandon Resume Web Page in the File name text box and then, if necessary, change the Save in location to 3½ Floppy (A:) as shown in Figure 3.

3 Click the Save button in the Save As dialog box.

Word displays the Brandon Resume Web Page in the Word window (see Figure 4 on the next page).

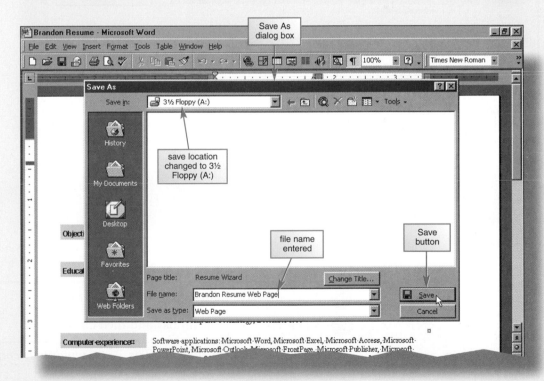

FIGURE 3

Word switches to Web layout view and also changes some of the toolbar buttons and menu commands to provide Web page authoring features. For example, the Standard toolbar now displays a New Web Page button (Figure 4 on the next page). The Web Layout View button on the horizontal scroll bar is recessed.

The resume displays on the Word screen similar to how it will display in a Web browser. Some of Word's formatting features are not supported by Web pages; thus, your Web page may display slightly different from the original Word document.

Formatting the E-mail Address as a Hyperlink

You want the e-mail address in your resume to be formatted as a hyperlink so that when someone clicks the e-mail address on your Web page, his or her e-mail program opens automatically with your e-mail address already filled in.

You have learned that when you press the SPACEBAR or ENTER key after a Web or e-mail address, Word automatically formats it as a hyperlink. Perform the following steps to format the e-mail address as a hyperlink.

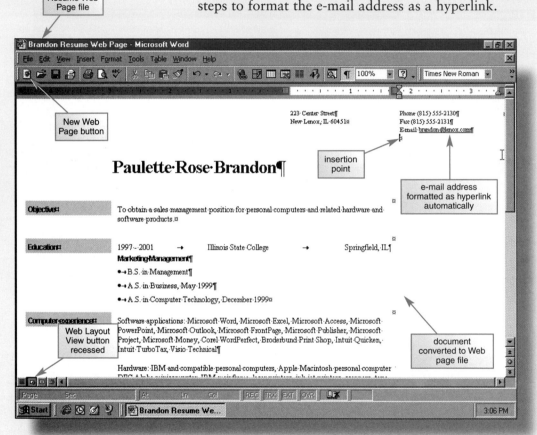

FIGURE 4

TO FORMAT A HYPERLINK AUTOMATICALLY

1 Position the insertion point immediately after the e-mail address; that is, after the m in com.

2 Press the ENTER key.

Word automatically formats the e-mail address as a hyperlink; that is, it is colored blue and underlined (Figure 4).

You are now finished modifying the Brandon Resume Web Page file. Thus, perform the following steps to save the file again and then close it.

TO SAVE AND CLOSE A WEB PAGE

1 Click the Save button on the Standard toolbar.

2 Click File on the menu bar and then click Close.

Word saves the file and closes it. The Word window is empty.

More About

Web Page Design

For more information on guidelines for designing Web pages, visit the Word 2000 More About Web page (www.scsite.com/wd2000/more.htm) and then click Web Page Design.

Using Word's Web Page Wizard to Create a Web Page

In the previous section, you saved an existing Word document as a Web page. Next, you want to create a brand new Web page. You can create a Web page from scratch using a Web page template or you can use the **Web Page Wizard**. Because this is your first experience creating a new Web page with frames, you should use the Web Page Wizard as shown in the following steps.

Steps **To Create a Web Page Using the Web Page Wizard**

1 **Click File on the menu bar and then click New. If necessary, click the Web Pages tab when the New dialog box first displays. Point to the Web Page Wizard icon.**

Word displays several Web page template icons and the Web Page Wizard in the Web Pages sheet (Figure 5).

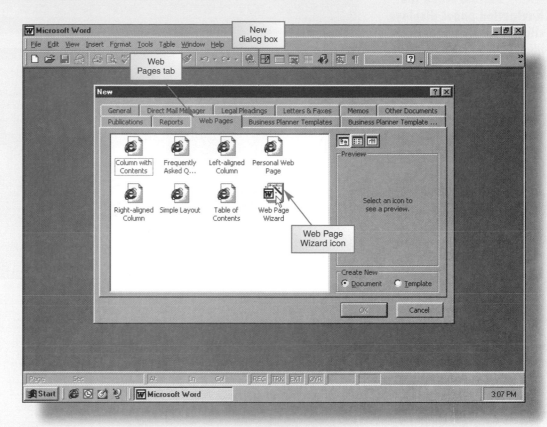

FIGURE 5

2 **Double-click the Web Page Wizard icon. When the Start panel displays in the Web Page Wizard dialog box, click the Next button. When the Title and Location panel displays, type** Paulette Brandon **in the Web site title text box. Press the TAB key and then type** a: **in the Web site location text box.**

Word displays the Title and Location panel in the Web Page Wizard dialog box (Figure 6). In this dialog box, the title you enter displays in the Web browser's title bar.

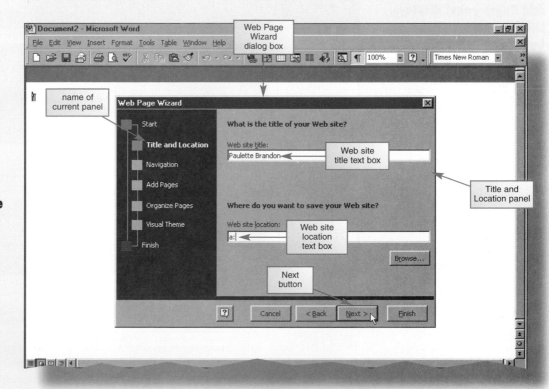

FIGURE 6

3 **Click the Next button. When the Navigation panel displays, click Vertical frame, if necessary, and then point to the Next button.**

Word displays the *Navigation panel* in the Web Page Wizard dialog box (Figure 7). In this dialog box, you select the placement of hyperlinks on your Web page(s).

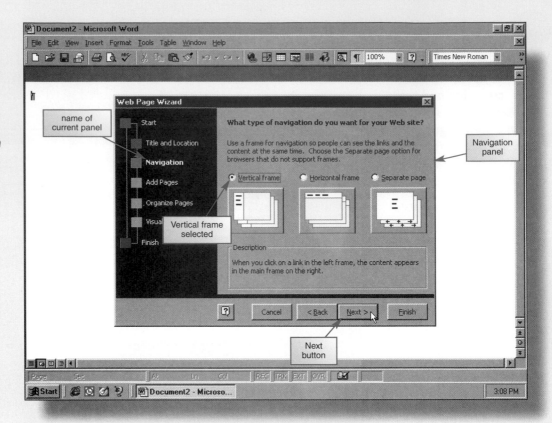

FIGURE 7

4 **Click the Next button. When the Add Pages panel displays, click the Remove Page button three times and then point to the Add Existing File button.**

Word displays the *Add Pages panel* that initially lists three Web page names: Personal Web Page, Blank Page 1, and Blank Page 2. You do not want any of these Web page names on your Web page; thus, you remove them (Figure 8). You will click the Add Existing File button to add Brandon Resume Web Page to the list.

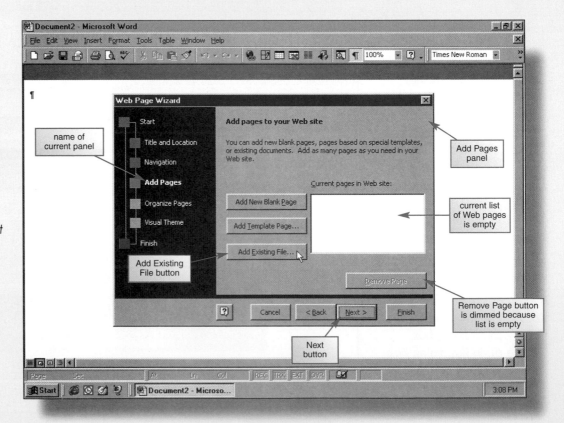

FIGURE 8

5 Click the Add Existing File button to display the Open dialog box. If necessary, change the Look in location to 3½ Floppy (A:). Click Brandon Resume Web Page and then point to the Open button in the Open dialog box (Figure 9).

6 Click the Open button in the Open dialog box.

The wizard adds Brandon Resume Web Page to the list in the Add Pages panel.

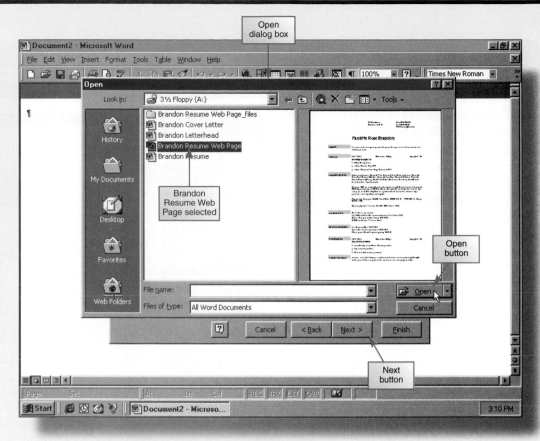

FIGURE 9

7 Click the Next button in the Add Pages panel. When the Organize Pages panel displays, click the Rename button. When the Rename Hyperlink dialog box displays, type My Resume in the text box. Point to the OK button.

In the Organize Pages panel in the Web Page Wizard, you specify the sequence and names of the hyperlinks to be in the left frame of the Web page (Figure 10).

8 Click the OK button.

Word renames the hyperlink to My Resume.

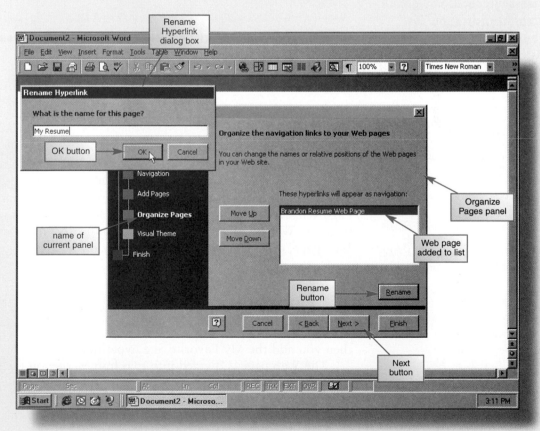

FIGURE 10

9 Click the Next button. If the displayed theme in the Visual Theme panel is not Spiral, click the Browse Themes button. When the Theme dialog box displays, scroll to and then click Spiral in the Choose a Theme list. Click the OK button.

*Word displays the **Visual Theme** panel in the Web Page Wizard dialog box (Figure 11). A **theme** is a collection of defined design elements and color schemes.*

10 Click the Next button. When the Finish panel displays, click the Finish button. If the Office Assistant displays a message about navigation features, click the Yes button. If a Frames toolbar displays in your document window, click its Close button to remove it from the screen.

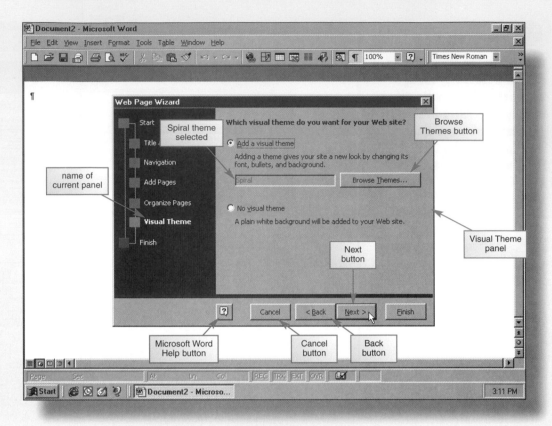

FIGURE 11

After about a minute, Word displays a layout of the Web pages (see Figure 12). The My Resume hyperlink displays in a frame on the left and the resume displays in a frame on the right.

Other Ways

1. On Start menu click New Office Document, click Web Pages tab, double-click Web Page Wizard icon
2. Click New Office Document button on Microsoft Office Shortcut Bar, click Web Pages tab, double-click Web Page Wizard icon

When creating a Web page using the Web Page Wizard, you can click the Back button (Figure 11) in any panel of the Web Page Wizard dialog box to change any previously entered information. For help with entering information into the Web Page Wizard, click the Microsoft Word Help button in the appropriate panel. To exit from the Web Page Wizard and return to the document window without creating the Web page, click the Cancel button in any of the Web Page Wizard dialog boxes.

Modifying a Web Page

The next step is to modify the Web pages. First, you make the left frame smaller and then you add the My Favorite Site hyperlink.

The Web page is divided into two frames, one on the left and one on the right. A **frame border** separates the frames. When you point to the frame border, the mouse pointer shape changes to a double-headed arrow.

You want to make the left frame narrower. To do this, you drag the frame border as illustrated in the following steps.

Steps To Resize a Web Page Frame

1 **Point to the frame border.**

The mouse pointer shape changes to a double-headed arrow and Word displays the ScreenTip, Resize (Figure 12).

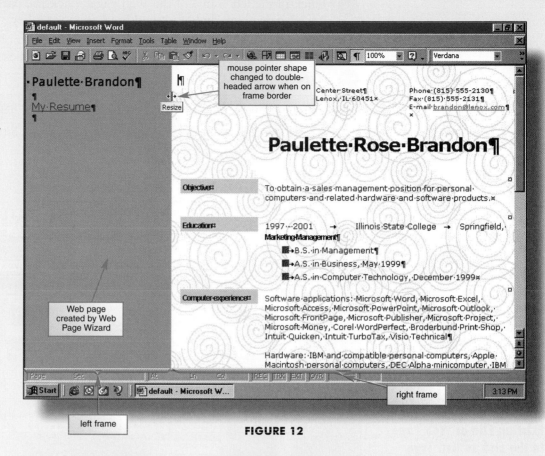

FIGURE 12

2 **Drag the frame border to the left until it is positioned under the r in Brandon (Figure 13).**

Word narrows the left frame and widens the right frame (see Figure 14 on the next page).

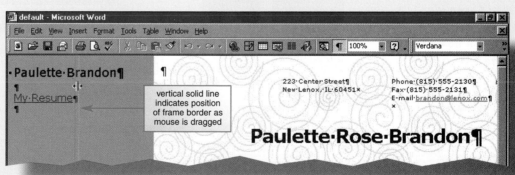

FIGURE 13

In the left frame, you want to add a My Favorite Site hyperlink. You used the Web Page Wizard to link the My Resume hyperlink to the Web page file called Brandon Resume Web Page, which means when you click the My Resume link in the left frame, the Brandon Resume Web Page file displays in the right frame. Similarly, when you click the My Favorite Site hyperlink, you want a Web site to display in the right frame.

The first step is to enter the hyperlink text into the left frame as described in the steps on the next page.

More About 2000

Highlighting

To add color to an online document or e-mail communication, highlight the text. Highlighting alerts the reader to the text's importance, much like a highlight marker does in a textbook. To highlight text, select it, click the Highlight button arrow on the Formatting toolbar, and then click the desired highlight color.

TO ENTER AND FORMAT TEXT

1 Click in the left frame of the Web page. Click the paragraph mark below the My Resume hyperlink and then press the ENTER key.

2 Double-click the move handle on the Formatting toolbar to display the entire toolbar. Click the Font Size box arrow and then click 12.

3 Type My Favorite Site as the text.

Word enters the text, My Favorite Site, in the left frame using a font size of 12.

Perform the following steps to link the My Favorite Site text to a Web site.

Steps **To Add a Hyperlink**

1 **Drag through the My Favorite Site text. Double-click the move handle on the Standard toolbar to display the entire toolbar. Click the Insert Hyperlink button on the Standard toolbar. When the Insert Hyperlink dialog box displays, if necessary, click Existing File or Web Page in the Link to list. Type** http://www.scsite.com **in the Type the file or Web page name text box (Figure 14).**

2 **Click the OK button.**

Word formats the My Favorite Site text as a hyperlink that when clicked displays the associated Web site in the right frame (see Figure 1b on page WDW 1.2).

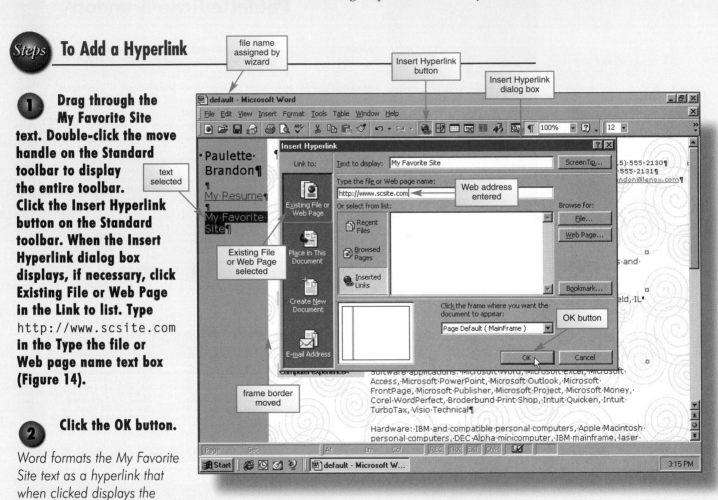

FIGURE 14

Other Ways

1. Right-click selected text, point to Hyperlink on shortcut menu, click Edit hyperlink on Hyperlink submenu

If you wanted to edit an existing hyperlink, you would drag through the hyperlink text and then click the Insert Hyperlink button on the Standard toolbar. Word will display the Edit Hyperlink dialog box instead of the Insert Hyperlink dialog box. Other than the title bar, these two dialog boxes are the same.

The Resume Wizard assigned the file name, default, to this frames page (Figure 14). Save the frames page with a new name as described in the following steps.

TO SAVE THE FRAMES PAGE WITH A NEW FILE NAME

1. Insert your floppy disk into drive A.

2. Click File on the menu bar and then click Save As.

3. Type the file name Brandon Personal Web Page in the File name text box. Do not press the ENTER key.

4. If necessary, click the Save in box arrow and then click 3½ Floppy (A:).

5. Click the Save button in the Save As dialog box.

Word saves the frames page and associated frames on a floppy disk in drive A with the file name Brandon Personal Web Page.

Viewing the Web Page in Your Default Browser

To see how the Web page looks in your default browser without actually connecting to the Internet, you use the **Web Page Preview command.** That is, if you click File on the menu bar and then click Web Page Preview, Word opens your Web browser in a separate window and displays the open Web page file in the browser window.

From the browser window, you can test your hyperlinks to be sure they work—before you publish them to the Web. For example, in the left frame, click the My Favorite Site link to display the Web site www.scsite.com in the right frame. (If you are not connected to the Internet, your browser will connect you and then display the Web site.) Click the My Resume link to display the Brandon Resume Web Page in the right frame. Click the e-mail address to open your e-mail program with the address, brandon@lenox.com, entered in the recipient's address box. When finished, close the browser window.

The next step is to quit Word.

TO QUIT WORD

1. Click the Close button at the right edge of Word's title bar.

The Word window closes.

Editing a Web Page from Your Browser

One of the powerful features of Office 2000 is the ability to edit a Web page directly from Internet Explorer. The steps on the next page illustrate how to open your Web page in Internet Explorer and then edit it from Internet Explorer.

Web Pages

Use horizontal lines to separate sections of a Web page. To add a horizontal line at the location of the insertion point, click Format on the menu bar, click Borders and Shading, click the Horizontal Line button, click the desired line type in the Horizontal Line dialog box, and then click the Insert Clip button on the Pop-up menu.

HTML

If you wish to view the HTML source code associated with the Web page you have created, click View on the menu bar and then click HTML Source, which starts the HTML Source Editor. To close the HTML Source Editor, click File on the menu bar and then click Exit.

Microsoft Certification

The Microsoft Office User Specialist (MOUS) Certification program provides an opportunity for you to obtain a valuable industry credential - proof that you have the Word 2000 skills required by employers. For more information, see Appendix D or visit the Shelly Cashman Series MOUS Web page at www.scsite.com/off2000/cert.htm.

Steps

To Edit a Web Page from Your Browser

1
Click the Start button on the taskbar, point to Programs, and then click Internet Explorer. When the Internet Explorer window displays, type a:Brandon Personal Web Page.htm **in the Address Bar and then press the ENTER key. Point to the Edit with Microsoft Word for Windows button on the toolbar.**

Internet Explorer opens the Brandon Personal Web Page and displays it in the browser window (Figure 15). Internet Explorer determines the Office program you used to create the Web page and associates that program with the Edit button.

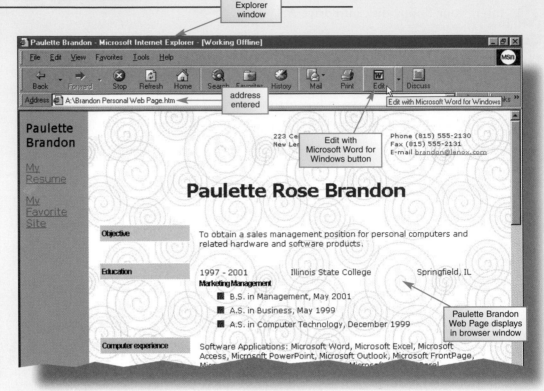

FIGURE 15

2
Click the Edit with Microsoft Word for Windows button.

Internet Explorer starts Microsoft Word and displays the Brandon Personal Web Page in the Word window.

3
In the left frame, click immediately to the left of the B in Brandon. Type Rose **and then press the SPACEBAR.**

Paulette's middle name displays in the left frame of the Web page (Figure 16).

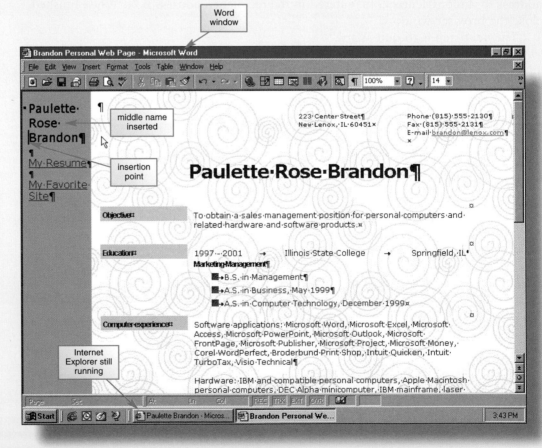

FIGURE 16

4 Click the Save button on the Standard toolbar. Click the Close button at the right edge of Word's title bar.

Word saves the revised Web page and, after about a minute, the Word window closes.

5 When the Internet Explorer window redisplays, click the Refresh button on the toolbar.

Internet Explorer displays the revised Web page (Figure 17).

6 Click the Close button at the right edge of the Internet Explorer window.

The Internet Explorer window closes.

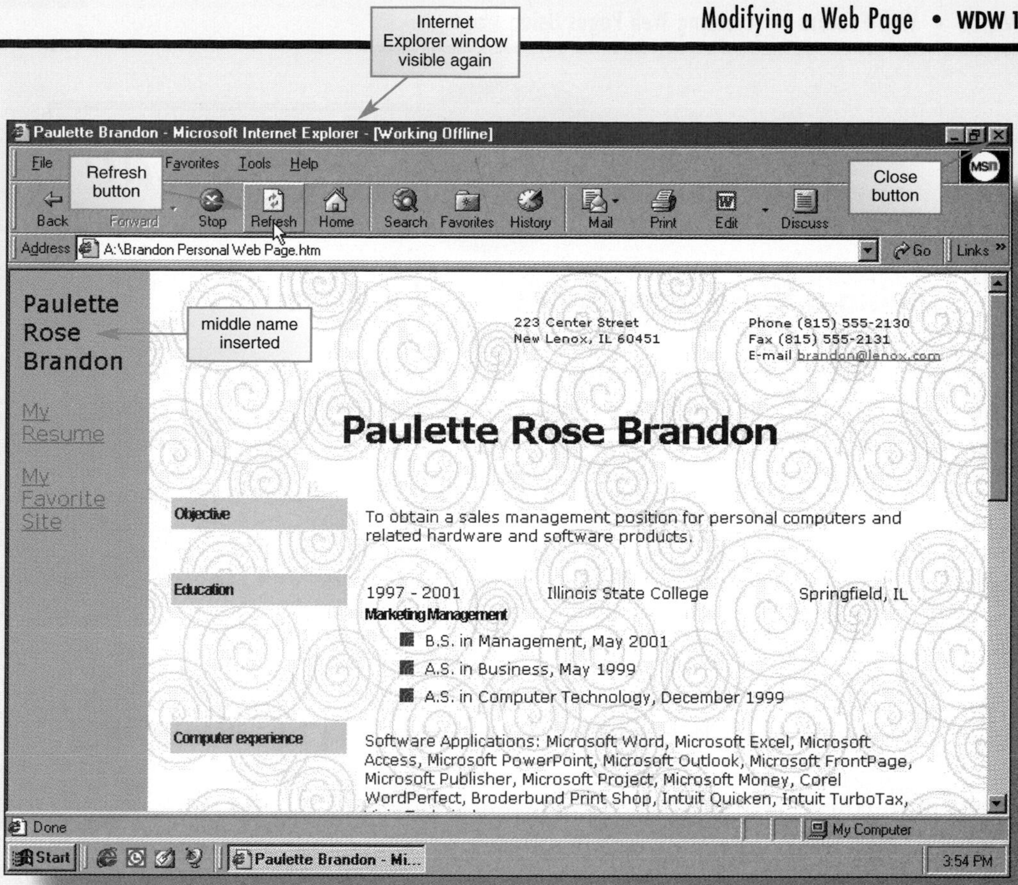
Internet Explorer window visible again
Paulette Brandon - Microsoft Internet Explorer - [Working Offline]
Refresh button
Close button
A:\Brandon Personal Web Page.htm
Paulette Rose Brandon
middle name inserted
My Resume
My Favorite Site
223 Center Street
New Lenox, IL 60451
Phone (815) 555-2130
Fax (815) 555-2131
E-mail brandon@lenox.com
Paulette Rose Brandon
Objective
To obtain a sales management position for personal computers and related hardware and software products.
Education
1997 - 2001 Illinois State College Springfield, IL
Marketing Management
B.S. in Management, May 2001
A.S. in Business, May 1999
A.S. in Computer Technology, December 1999
Computer experience
Software Applications: Microsoft Word, Microsoft Excel, Microsoft Access, Microsoft PowerPoint, Microsoft Outlook, Microsoft FrontPage, Microsoft Publisher, Microsoft Project, Microsoft Money, Corel WordPerfect, Broderbund Print Shop, Intuit Quicken, Intuit TurboTax,
Done
My Computer
Paulette Brandon - Mi...
3:54 PM

FIGURE 17

If the right edge of the resume wraps when you display it in the browser, you can follow the steps above to edit it in Word and drag the right border of the resume table to the right.

The final step is to make your Web pages and associated files available to others on your network, on an intranet, or on the World Wide Web. See Appendix B and then talk to your instructor about how you should do this for your system.

More About

Quick Reference

For a table that lists how to complete the tasks covered in this book using the mouse, menu, shortcut menu, and keyboard, visit the Shelly Cashman Series Office Web page (www.scsite.com/off2000/qr.htm) and then click Microsoft Word 2000.

CASE PERSPECTIVE SUMMARY

Paulette is thrilled with her personal Web pages. They look so professional! Paulette now is ready to publish the Web pages and associated files to the World Wide Web. After talking with her ISP's technical support staff, she learns she can use Word to save a copy of her Web page files directly on her ISP's Web server. You are familiar with this feature of Word and assist Paulette with this task. Next, she connects to the Web and displays her personal Web pages from her browser. Paulette is quite impressed with herself!

Web Feature Summary

This Web Feature introduced you to creating a Web page by saving an existing Word document as a Web Page file. You also created a new Web page with frames using the Web Page Wizard and then modified this Web page. You created a hyperlink to an e-mail address, one to a Web page file, and another to a Web site.

In the Lab

1 Saving a Word Document as a Web Page

Problem: You created the research paper shown in Figure 2-74 on pages WD 2.57 and WD 2.58 in Project 2. You decide to save this research paper as a Web page.

Instructions:

1. Open the Digital Camera Paper shown in Figure 2-74. (If you did not create the research paper, see your instructor for a copy.) Then, save the paper as a Web page using the file name Digital Camera Web Page.
2. Print the Web page. Click File on the menu bar and then click Web Page Preview to view the Web page in your browser. Close the browser window. Quit Word.

2 Creating a Web Page with a Hyperlink to a Web Site

Problem: You created the resume shown in Figure 3-81 on page WD 3.63 in Project 3. You decide to create a personal Web page with a link to this resume. Thus, you also must save the resume as a Web page.

Instructions:

1. Open the Schumann Resume shown in Figure 3-81. (If you did not create the resume, see your instructor for a copy.) Then, save the resume as a Web page using the file name Schumann Resume Web Page. Convert the e-mail address to a Web page by clicking immediately to the right of the address and pressing the ENTER key. Save the Web page again.
2. Create a personal Web page with frames using the Web Page Wizard. Use the following settings as the wizard requests them: apply vertical frame navigation; create a hyperlink to the Schumann Resume Web Page; change the name of the hyperlink to My Resume; select a visual theme you like best.
3. Insert a hyperlink called My Favorite Site and link it to your favorite Web address.
4. Save the Web page. Test your Web page links. Print the Web page. Click File on the menu bar and then click Web Page Preview to view the Web page in your browser. Close the browser window. Quit Word.

3 Creating a Personal Web Page

Problem: You have decided to create your own personal Web page using the Personal Home Page template in the Web Page Wizard.

Instructions:

1. Create your own personal Web page using the Web Page Wizard. Use Horizontal frame as your navigation method. When the Add Pages panel displays, keep the Personal Web Page, and delete Blank Page 1 and Blank Page 2. Select a theme you like best.
2. Personalize the Personal Web Page as indicated on the template. For each bullet in the Favorite Links section, enter a URL of a site on the Web that interests you.
3. Save the Web page. Test your Web page links.
4. Ask your instructor for instructions on how to publish your Web page so that others may have access to it.

APPENDIX A
Microsoft Word 2000 Help System

Using the Word Help System

This appendix demonstrates how you can use the Word 2000 Help system to answer your questions. At any time while you are using Word, you can interact with the Help system to display information on any Word topic. It is a complete reference manual at your fingertips.

The two primary forms of Help are the Office Assistant and the Microsoft Word Help window. The one you use will depend on your preference. As shown in Figure A-1, you access either form of Help in Microsoft Word by pressing the F1 key, clicking Microsoft Word Help on the Help menu, or clicking the Microsoft Word Help button on the Standard toolbar. Word responds in one of two ways:

1. If the Office Assistant is turned on, then the Office Assistant displays with a balloon (lower-right side of Figure A-1).
2. If the Office Assistant is turned off, then the Microsoft Word Help window displays (lower-left side of Figure A-1).

Table A-1 on the next page summarizes the nine categories of Help available to you. Because of the way the Word Help system works, please review the rightmost column of Table A-1 if you have difficulties activating the desired category of Help.

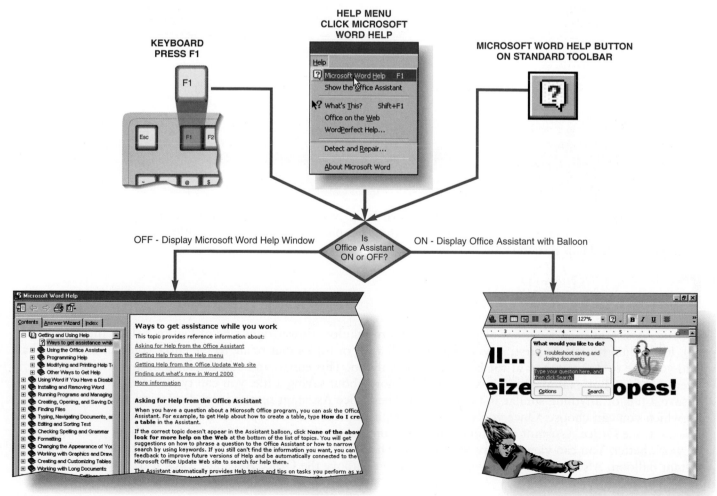

FIGURE A-1

Table A-1   Word Help System

TYPE	DESCRIPTION	HOW TO ACTIVATE	TURNING THE OFFICE ASSISTANT ON AND OFF
Answer Wizard	Similar to the Office Assistant in that it answers questions that you type in your own words.	Click the Microsoft Word Help button on the Standard toolbar. If necessary, maximize the Help window by double-clicking its title bar. Click the Answer Wizard tab.	If the Office Assistant displays, right-click it, click Options on the shortcut menu, click Use the Office Assistant to remove the check mark, click the OK button.
Contents sheet	Groups Help topics by general categories. Use when you know only the general category of the topic in question.	Click the Microsoft Word Help button on the Standard toolbar. If necessary, maximize the Help window by double-clicking its title bar. Click the Contents tab.	If the Office Assistant displays, right-click it, click Options, click Use the Office Assistant to remove the check mark, click the OK button.
Detect and Repair	Automatically finds and fixes errors in the application.	Click Detect and Repair on the Help menu.	
Hardware and Software Information	Shows Product ID and allows access to system information and technical support information.	Click About Microsoft Word on the Help menu and then click the appropriate button.	
Help for WordPerfect Users	Used to assist WordPerfect users who are learning Microsoft Word.	Click WordPerfect Help on the Help menu.	
Index sheet	Similar to an index in a book. Use when you know exactly what you want.	Click the Microsoft Word Help button on the Standard toolbar. If necessary, maximize the Help window by double-clicking its title bar. Click the Index tab.	If the Office Assistant displays, right-click it, click Options, click Use the Office Assistant to remove the check mark, click the OK button.
Office Assistant	Answers questions that you type in your own words, offers tips, and provides Help for a variety of Word features.	Click the Microsoft Word Help button on the Standard toolbar or double-click the Office Assistant icon. Some dialog boxes also include the Microsoft Word Help button.	If the Office Assistant does not display, click Show the Office Assistant on the Help menu.
Office on the Web	Used to access technical resources and download free product enhancements on the Web.	Click Office on the Web on the Help menu.	
Question Mark button and \What's This? command	Used to identify unfamiliar items on the screen.	In a dialog box, click the Question Mark button and then click an item in the dialog box. Click What's This? on the Help menu, and then click an item on the screen.	

The best way to familiarize yourself with the Word Help system is to use it. The next several pages show examples of how to use the Help system. Following the examples is a set of exercises titled Use Help that will sharpen your Word Help system skills.

The Office Assistant

The **Office Assistant** is an icon that displays in the Word window (lower-right side of Figure A-1 on the previous page). It has dual functions. First, it will respond with a list of topics that relate to the entry you make in the What would you like to do? text box at the bottom of the balloon. This entry can be in the form of a word, phrase, or written question. For example, if you want to learn more about saving a file, you can type, save, save a file, how do I save a file, or anything similar in the text box. The Office Assistant responds by displaying a list of topics from which you can choose. Once you choose a topic, it displays the corresponding information.

Second, the Office Assistant monitors your work and accumulates tips during a session on how you might do your work better. You can view the tips at any time. The accumulated tips display when you activate the Office Assistant balloon. Also, if at any time you see a light bulb above the Office Assistant, click it to display the most recent tip.

You may or may not want the Office Assistant to display on the screen at all times. You can hide it, and then show it at a later time. You may prefer not to use the Office Assistant at all. In this case, you use the Microsoft Word Help window (lower-left side of Figure A-1 on page WD A.1). Thus, not only do you need to know how to show and hide the Office Assistant, but you also need to know how to turn the Office Assistant on and off.

Showing and Hiding the Office Assistant

When Word is first installed, the Office Assistant displays in the Word window. You can move it to any location on the screen. You can click it to display the Office Assistant balloon, which allows you to request Help. If the Office Assistant is on the screen and you want to hide it, you click the **Hide the Office Assistant command** on the Help menu. You also can right-click the Office Assistant to display its shortcut menu and then click the **Hide command** to hide it. When the Office Assistant is hidden, then the **Show the Office Assistant command** replaces the Hide the Office Assistant command on the Help menu. Thus, you can show or hide the Office Assistant at any time.

Turning the Office Assistant On and Off

The fact that the Office Assistant is hidden, does not mean it is turned off. To turn the Office Assistant off, it must be displayed in the Word window. You right-click it to display its shortcut menu (right side of Figure A-2). Next, click Options on the shortcut menu. Invoking the **Options command** causes the Office Assistant dialog box to display (left side of Figure A-2).

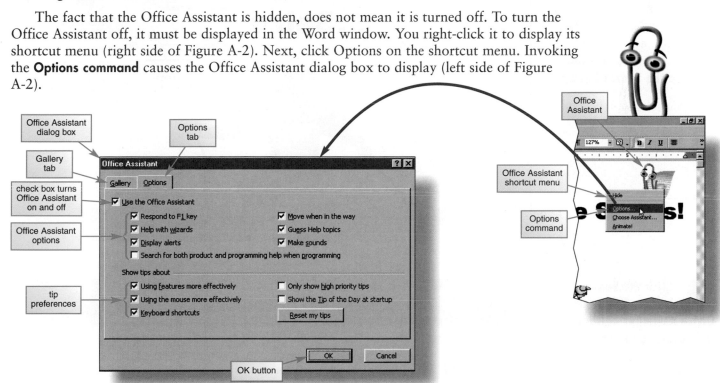

FIGURE A-2

The top check box in the Options sheet determines whether the Office Assistant is on or off. To turn the Office Assistant off, remove the check mark from the **Use the Office Assistant check box** and then click the OK button. As shown in Figure A-1 on page WD A.1, if the Office Assistant is off when you invoke Help, then the Microsoft Word Help window displays instead of the Office Assistant. To turn the Office Assistant on at a later time, click the Show the Office Assistant command on the Help menu.

Through the Options command on the Office Assistant shortcut menu, you can change the look and feel of the Office Assistant. For example, you can hide the Office Assistant, turn the Office Assistant off, change the way it works, choose a different Office Assistant icon, or view an animation of the current one. These options also are available by clicking the Options button that displays in the Office Assistant balloon (Figure A-3 on the next page).

The **Gallery sheet** (Figure A-2) in the Office Assistant dialog box allows you to change the appearance of the Office Assistant. The default is the paper clip (Clippit). You can change it to a bouncing red happy face (The Dot), a robot (F1), a professor (The Genius), the Microsoft Office logo (Office Logo), the earth (Mother Nature), a cat (Links), or a dog (Rocky).

Using the Office Assistant

As indicated earlier, the Office Assistant allows you to enter a word, phrase, or question and then responds by displaying a list of topics from which you can choose to display Help. The following steps show how to use the Office Assistant to obtain Help about online meetings.

Steps **To Use the Office Assistant**

1 **If the Office Assistant is not turned on, click Help on the menu bar and then click Show the Office Assistant. Click the Office Assistant. When the Office Assistant balloon displays, type** what are online meetings **in the text box. Point to the Search button.**

The Office Assistant balloon displays as shown in Figure A-3.

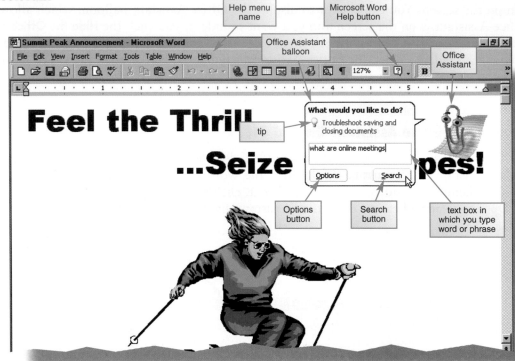

FIGURE A-3

2 **Click the Search button. When the Office Assistant balloon redisplays, point to the topic, About online meetings (Figure A-4).**

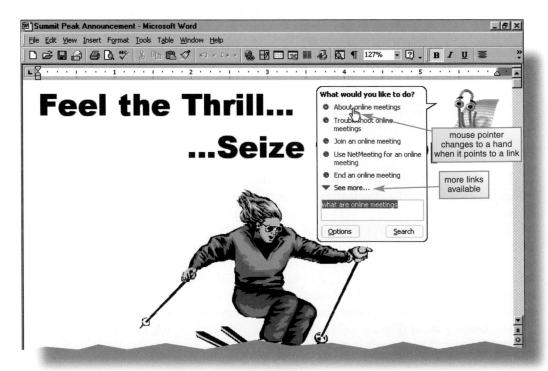

FIGURE A-4

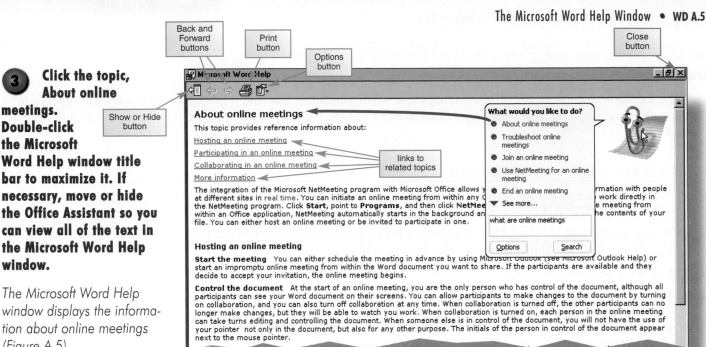

③ **Click the topic, About online meetings. Double-click the Microsoft Word Help window title bar to maximize it. If necessary, move or hide the Office Assistant so you can view all of the text in the Microsoft Word Help window.**

The Microsoft Word Help window displays the information about online meetings (Figure A-5).

FIGURE A-5

When the Microsoft Word Help window displays, you can choose to read it or print it. To print the information, click the Print button on the Microsoft Word Help toolbar. Table A-2 lists the function of each button on the Microsoft Word Help toolbar. To close the Microsoft Word Help window shown in Figure A-5, click the Close button on the title bar.

Table A-2	Microsoft Word Help Toolbar Buttons	
BUTTON	**NAME**	**FUNCTION**
or	Show or Hide	Displays or hides the Contents, Answer Wizard, and Index tabs
	Back	Displays the previous Help topic
	Forward	Displays the next Help topic
	Print	Prints the current Help topic
	Options	Displays a list of commands

Other Ways

1. If Office Assistant is turned on, on Help menu click Microsoft Word Help, or click Microsoft Word Help button on Standard toolbar to display Office Assistant balloon

The Microsoft Word Help Window

If the Office Assistant is turned off and you click the Microsoft Word Help button on the Standard toolbar, the **Microsoft Word Help window** displays (Figure A-6 on the next page). This window contains three tabs on the left side: Contents, Answer Wizard, and Index. Each tab displays a sheet with powerful look-up capabilities. Use the Contents sheet as you would a table of contents at the front of a book to look up Help. The Answer Wizard sheet answers your queries in the same manner as the Office Assistant. You use the Index sheet in the same manner as an index in a book.

Click the tabs to move from sheet to sheet. The five buttons on the toolbar, Show or Hide, Back, Forward, Print, and Options also are described in Table A-2.

Besides clicking the Microsoft Word Help button on the Standard toolbar, you also can click the Microsoft Word Help command on the Help menu or press the F1 key to display the Microsoft Word Help window to gain access to the three sheets. To close the Microsoft Word Help window, click the Close button in the upper-right corner on the title bar.

Using the Contents Sheet

The **Contents sheet** is useful for displaying Help when you know the general category of the topic in question, but not the specifics. The following steps show how to use the Contents sheet to obtain information about Web folders.

TO OBTAIN HELP USING THE CONTENTS SHEET

1 With the Office Assistant turned off, click the Microsoft Word Help button on the Standard toolbar (Figure A-3 on page WD A.4).

2 When the Microsoft Word Help window displays, double-click the title bar to maximize the window. If necessary, click the Show button to display the tabs.

3 Click the Contents tab.

4 Double-click the Working with Online and Internet Documents book on the left side of the window.

5 Double-click the Creating Web Pages book below the Working with Online and Internet Documents book.

6 Click the About Web Folders subtopic below the Creating Web Pages book.

Word displays Help on the subtopic, About Web Folders (Figure A-6).

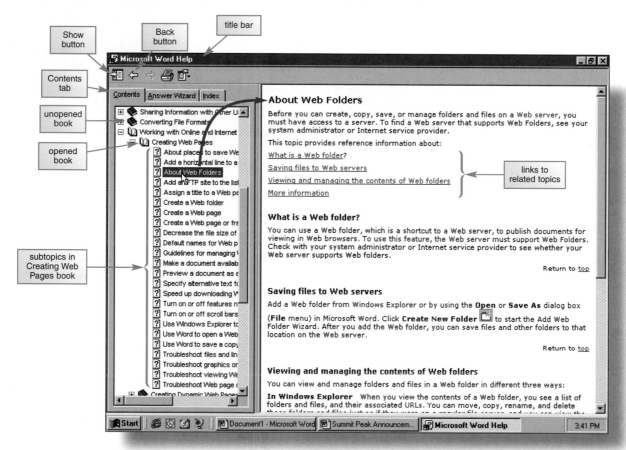

FIGURE A-6

Once the information on the subtopic displays, you can scroll through the window and read it or you can click the Print button to obtain a hard copy. If you decide to click another subtopic on the left or a link on the right, you can get back to the Help page shown in Figure A-6 by clicking the Back button as many times as necessary.

Each topic in the Contents list is preceded by a book icon or question mark icon. A **book icon** indicates subtopics are available. A **question mark icon** means information on the topic will display if you double-click the title. The book icon opens when you double-click the book (or its title) or click the plus sign (+) to the left of the book icon.

Using the Answer Wizard Sheet

The **Answer Wizard sheet** works like the Office Assistant in that you enter a word, phrase, or question and it responds with topics from which you can choose to display Help. The following steps show how to use the Answer Wizard sheet to obtain Help about discussions in a Word document.

TO OBTAIN HELP USING THE ANSWER WIZARD SHEET

1 With the Office Assistant turned off, click the Microsoft Word Help button on the Standard toolbar (Figure A-3 on page WD A.4).

2 When the Microsoft Word Help window displays, double-click the title bar to maximize the window. If necessary, click the Show button to display the tabs.

3 Click the Answer Wizard tab. Type what are discussions in the What would you like to do? text box on the left side of the window. Click the Search button.

4 When a list of topics displays in the Select topic to display list box, click About discussions in Word.

Word displays Help about discussions (Figure A-7).

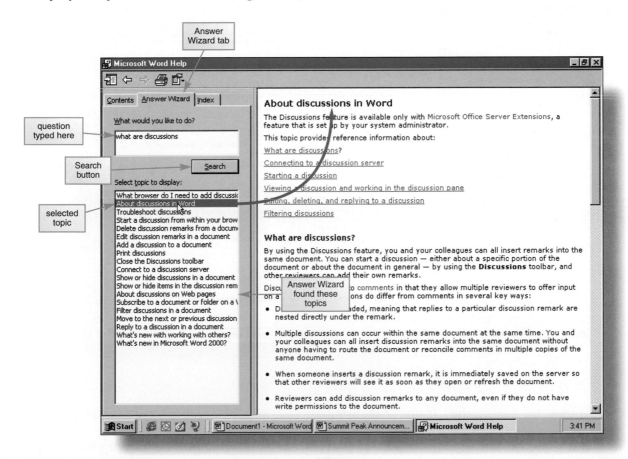

FIGURE A-7

If the topic, About discussions in Word, does not include the information you are searching for, click another topic in the list. Continue to click topics until you find the desired information.

Using the Index Sheet

The third sheet in the Microsoft Word Help window is the Index sheet. Use the **Index sheet** to display Help when you know the keyword or the first few letters of the keyword you want to look up. The following steps show how to use the Index sheet to obtain Help on understanding the readability statistics available to evaluate the reading level of a document.

TO OBTAIN HELP USING THE INDEX SHEET

1 With the Office Assistant turned off, click the Microsoft Word Help button on the Standard toolbar (Figure A-3 on page WD A.4).

2 When the Microsoft Word Help window displays, double-click the title bar to maximize the window. If necessary, click the Show button to display the tabs.

3 Click the Index tab. Type readability in the Type keywords text box on the left side of the window. Click the Search button.

Word highlights the first topic (Readability scores) on the left side of the window and displays information about two readability scores on the right side of the window (Figure A-8).

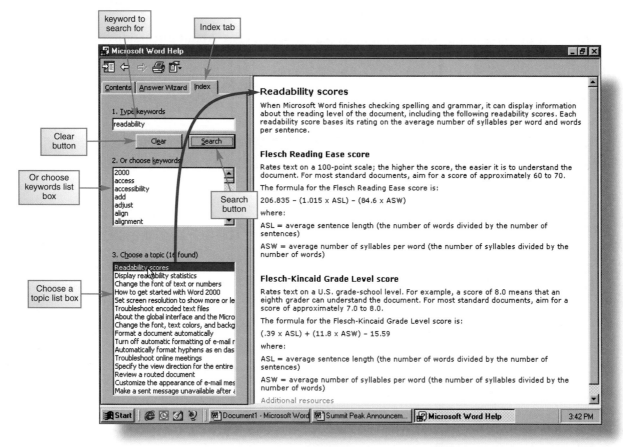

FIGURE A-8

In the Choose a topic list box on the left side of the window, you can click another topic to display additional Help.

An alternative to typing a keyword in the Type keywords text box is to scroll through the Or choose keywords list box (the middle list box on the left side of the window). When you locate the keyword you are searching for, double-click it to display Help on the topic. Also in the Or choose keywords list box, the Word Help system displays other topics that relate to the new keyword. As you begin typing a new keyword in the Type keywords text box, Word jumps to that point in the middle list box. To begin a new search, click the Clear button.

What's This? Command and Question Mark Button • WD A.9

APPENDIX A

What's This? Command and Question Mark Button

Use the What's This command on the Help menu or the Question Mark button in a dialog box when you are not sure what an object on the screen is or what it does.

What's This? Command

You use the **What's This? command** on the Help menu to display a detailed ScreenTip. When you invoke this command, the mouse pointer changes to an arrow with a question mark. You then click any object on the screen, such as a button, to display the ScreenTip. For example, after you click the What's This? command on the Help menu and then click the Zoom box on the Standard toolbar, a description of the Zoom box displays (Figure A-9). You can print the Screen-Tip by right-clicking it and then clicking Print Topic on the shortcut menu.

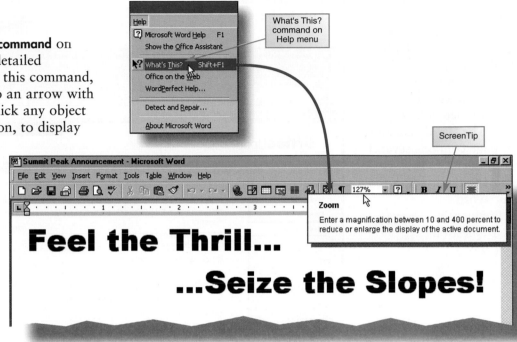

FIGURE A-9

Question Mark Button

In a response similar to the What's This? command, the **Question Mark button** displays a ScreenTip. You use the Question Mark button with dialog boxes. It is located in the upper-right corner on the title bar of dialog box next to the Close button. For example, in Figure A-10, the Print dialog box displays on the screen. If you click the Question Mark button, and then click the Print to file check box, an explanation of the Print to file check box displays in a ScreenTip. You can print the ScreenTip by right-clicking it and then clicking Print Topic on the shortcut menu.

If a dialog box does not include a Question Mark button, press the SHIFT+F1 keys. This combination of keys will change the mouse pointer to an arrow with a question mark. You then can click any object in the dialog box to display the ScreenTip.

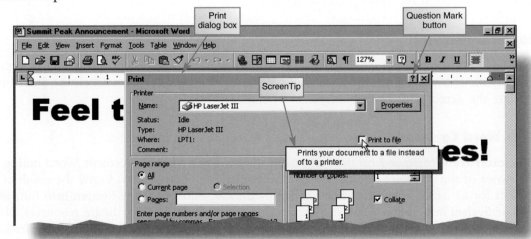

FIGURE A-10

Office on the Web Command

The **Office on the Web command** on the Help menu displays a Microsoft Web page containing up-to-date information on a variety of Office-related topics. To use this command, you must be connected to the Internet. Once the page displays, you can click the Word link on the left side of the window and then click the Assistance link (Figure A-11). The Word Assistance Web page contains several links such as Knowledge Base Articles about Word and Frequently Asked Questions about Word.

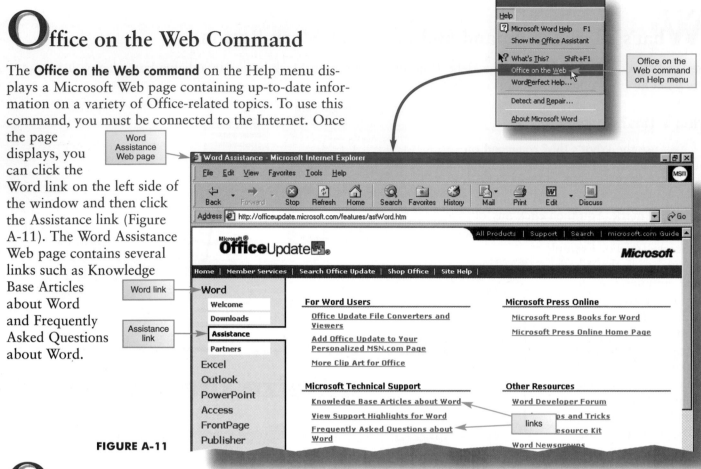

FIGURE A-11

Other Help Commands

Three additional commands available on the Help menu are WordPerfect Help, Detect and Repair, and About Microsoft Word. The WordPerfect Help command is available only if it was included as part of a Custom install of Word 2000.

WordPerfect Help Command

The **WordPerfect Help command** on the Help menu offers assistance to WordPerfect users switching to Word. When you choose this command, Word displays the Help for WordPerfect Users dialog box. The instructions in the dialog box step the user through the appropriate selections.

Detect and Repair Command

Use the **Detect and Repair command** on the Help menu if Word is not running properly or if it is generating errors. When you invoke this command, the Detect and Repair dialog box displays. Click the Start button in the dialog box to initiate the detect and repair process.

About Microsoft Word Command

The **About Microsoft Word command** on the Help menu displays the About Microsoft Word dialog box. The dialog box lists the owner of the software and the product identification. You need to know the product identification if you call Microsoft for assistance. The two buttons below the OK button are the System Info button and the Tech Support button. The **System Info button** displays system information, including hardware resources, components, software environment, and applications. The **Tech Support button** displays technical assistance information.

1 Using the Office Assistant

Instructions: Perform the following tasks using the Word Help system.

1. If the Office Assistant is turned on, click it to display the Office Assistant balloon. If the Office Assistant is not turned on, click Help on the menu bar, and click Show the Office Assistant.
2. Right-click the Office Assistant and then click Options on the shortcut menu. Click the Gallery tab in the Office Assistant dialog box and then click the Next button to view all of the Office Assistants. Click the Options tab in the Office Assistant dialog box and review the different options for the Office Assistant. Click the Question Mark button and then display ScreenTips for the first two check boxes (Use the Office Assistant and Respond to F1 key). Right-click the ScreenTips to print them. Hand them in to your instructor. Close the Office Assistant dialog box.
3. Click the Office Assistant and then type show me the keyboard shortcuts in the What would you like to do? text box at the bottom of the balloon. Click the Search button.
4. Click Keyboard shortcuts in the Office Assistant balloon. If necessary, double-click the title bar to maximize the Microsoft Word Help window. Click the Function keys link and then click the SHIFT+Function key link to view the set of shortcut keys using the SHIFT key and function keys. Click the Print button on the Microsoft Word Help toolbar to print the list of shortcut keys. Hand in the printouts to your instructor.
5. Close all open Help windows.
6. Click the Office Assistant. If it is not turned on, click Show the Office Assistant on the Help menu. Search for the topic, what is a netmeeting. Click the Use NetMeeting for an online meeting link. When the Microsoft Word Help window displays, maximize the window and then click the the Start an impromptu online meeting with Microsoft Word link. Read and print the information. Close the Microsoft Word Help window.

2 Expanding on the Word Help System Basics

Instructions: Use the Word Help system to understand the topics better and answer the questions listed below. Answer the questions on your own paper, or hand in the printed Help information to your instructor.

1. Right-click the Office Assistant. If it is not turned on, click Show the Office Assistant on the Help menu. When the shortcut menu displays, click Options. Click Use the Office Assistant to remove the check mark, and then click the OK button.
2. Click the Microsoft Word Help button on the Standard toolbar. Maximize the Microsoft Word Help window. If the tabs are hidden on the left side, click the Show button. Click the Index tab. Type undo in the Type keywords text box. Click the Search button. Click Reset built-in menus and toolbars. Print the information. Click the Hide button and then the Show button. Click the four links below What do you want to do? Read and print the information for each link. Close the Microsoft Word Help window. Hand in the printouts to your instructor.
3. Press the F1 key. Maximize the Microsoft Word Help window. Click the Answer Wizard tab. Type help in the What would you like to do? text box, and then click the Search button. Click Ways to get assistance while you work. Read through the information that displays. Print the information. Click the first two links. Read and print the information for both.
4. Click the Contents tab. Click the plus sign (+) to the left of the Typing, Navigating Documents, and Selecting Text book. Click the plus sign (+) to the left of the Selecting Text book. One at a time, click the three topics below the Selecting Text book. Read and print each one. Close the Microsoft Word Help window. Hand in the printouts to your instructor.
5. Click Help on the menu bar and then click What's This? Click the E-mail button on the Standard toolbar. Right-click the ScreenTip to print the ScreenTip. Click Format on the menu bar and then click Paragraph. When the Paragraph dialog box displays, click the Question Mark button on the title bar. Click the Special box. Right-click the ScreenTip to print the ScreenTip. Hand in the printouts to your instructor. Close the Paragraph dialog box and the Microsoft Word window.

APPENDIX B
Publishing Office Web Pages to a Web Server

With a Microsoft Office 2000 program, such as Word, Excel, Access, or PowerPoint, you use the **Save as Web Page command** on the File menu to save the Web page to a Web server using one of two techniques: Web folders or File Transfer Protocol. A **Web folder** is an Office 2000 shortcut to a Web server. **File Transfer Protocol (FTP)** is an Internet standard that allows computers to exchange files with other computers on the Internet.

You should contact your network system administrator or technical support staff at your ISP to determine if their Web server supports Web folders, FTP, or both, and to obtain necessary permissions to access the Web server. If you decide to publish Web pages using a Web folder, you must have the Office Server Extensions (OSE) installed on your computer. OSE comes with the Standard, Professional, and Premium editions of Office 2000.

Using Web Folders to Publish Office Web Pages

If you are granted permission to create a Web folder (shortcut) on your computer, you must obtain the URL of the Web server, and a user name and possibly a password that allows you to access the Web server. You also must decide on a name for the Web folder. Table B-1 explains how to create a Web folder.

Office adds the name of the Web folder to the list of current Web folders. You can save to this folder, open files in the folder, rename the folder, or perform any operations you would to a folder on your hard disk. You can use your Office program or Windows Explorer to access this folder. Table B-2 explains how to save to a Web folder.

Using FTP to Publish Office Web Pages

When publishing a Web page using FTP, you first add the FTP location to your computer and then you can save to it. An **FTP location**, also called an **FTP site**, is a collection of files that resides on an FTP server. In this case, the FTP server is the Web server.

To add an FTP location, you must obtain the name of the FTP site, which usually is the address (URL) of the FTP server, and a user name and a password that allows you to access the FTP server. You save and open the Web pages on the Web server using the name of the FTP site. Table B-3 explains how to add an FTP site.

Office adds the name of the FTP site to the FTP locations in the Save As and Open dialog boxes. You can open and save files on this FTP location. Table B-4 explains how to save using an FTP location.

Table B-1   Creating a Web Folder
1. Click File on the menu bar and then click Save As; or click File on the menu bar and then click Open.
2. When the Save As dialog box or the Open dialog box displays, click the Web Folders shortcut on the Places Bar along the left side of the dialog box.
3. Click the Create New Folder button.
4. When the first dialog box of the Add Web Folder wizard displays, type the URL of the Web server and then click the Next button.
5. When the Enter Network Password dialog box displays, type the user name and, if necessary, the password in the respective text boxes and then click the OK button.
6. When the last dialog box of the Add Web Folder wizard displays, type the name you would like to use for the Web folder. Click the Finish button.
7. Close the Save As or the Open dialog box.

Table B-2   Saving to a Web Folder
1. Click File on the menu bar and then click Save As.
2. When the Save As dialog box displays, type the Web page file name in the File name text box. Do not press the ENTER key.
3. Click Web Folders shortcut on the Places Bar along the left side of the dialog box.
4. Double-click the Web folder name in the Save in list.
5. When the Enter Network Password dialog box displays, type the user name and password in the respective text boxes and then click the OK button.
6. Click the Save button in the Save As dialog box.

Table B-3   Adding an FTP Location
1. Click File on the menu bar and then click Save As; or click File on the menu bar and then click Open.
2. In the Save As dialog box, click the Save in box arrow and then click Add/Modify FTP Locations in the Save in list; or in the Open dialog box, click the Look in box arrow and then click Add/Modify FTP Locations in the Look in list.
3. When the Add/Modify FTP Locations dialog box displays, type the name of the FTP site in the Name of FTP site text box. If the site allows anonymous logon, click Anonymous in the Log on as area; if you have a user name for the site, click User in the Log on as area and then type the user name. Type the password in the Password text box. Click the OK button.
4. Close the Save As or the Open dialog box.

Table B-4   Saving to an FTP Location
1. Click File on the menu bar and then click Save As.
2. When the Save As dialog box displays, type the Web page file name in the File name text box. Do not press the ENTER key.
3. Click the Save in box arrow and then click FTP Locations.
4. Double-click the name of the FTP site you want to save to.
5. When the FTP Log On dialog box displays, type your user name and password and then click the OK button.
6. Click the Save button in the Save As dialog box.

APPENDIX C
Resetting the Word Menus and Toolbars

When you first install Microsoft Word 2000, the Standard and Formatting toolbars display on one row. As you use the buttons on the toolbars and commands on the menus, Word personalizes the toolbars and the menus based on their usage. Each time you start Word, the toolbars and menus display in the same settings as the last time you used the application. The following steps show how to reset the menus and toolbars to their installation settings.

 To Reset My Usage Data and Toolbar Buttons

1 **Click View on the menu bar and then point to Toolbars. Point to Customize on the Toolbars submenu.**

The View menu and Toolbars submenu display (Figure C-1).

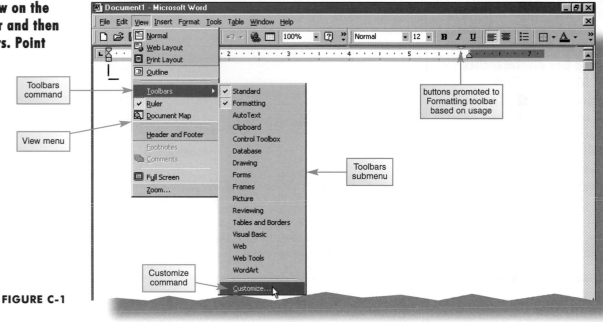

Toolbars command

View menu

buttons promoted to Formatting toolbar based on usage

Toolbars submenu

Customize command

FIGURE C-1

2 **Click Customize. When the Customize dialog box displays, click the Options tab. Make sure the three check boxes in the Personalized Menus and Toolbars area have check marks and then point to the Reset my usage data button.**

The Customize dialog box displays as shown in Figure C-2.

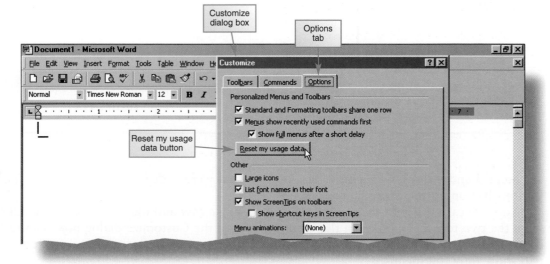

Customize dialog box

Options tab

Reset my usage data button

FIGURE C-2

③ **Click the Reset my usage data button. When the Microsoft Word dialog box displays explaining the function of the Reset my usage data button, click the Yes button. In the Customize dialog box, click the Toolbars tab.**

The Toolbars sheet displays (Figure C-3).

④ **Click Standard in the Toolbars list and then click the Reset button. When the Reset Toolbar dialog box displays, click the OK button. Click Formatting in the Toolbars list and then click the Reset button. When the Reset Toolbar dialog box displays, click the OK button.**

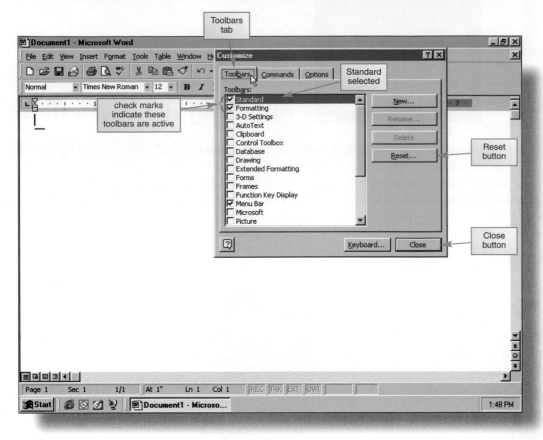

FIGURE C-3

⑤ **Click the Close button in the Customize dialog box.**

The toolbars display as shown in Figure C-4.

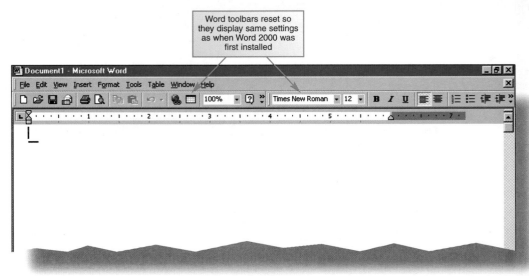

FIGURE C-4

Steps 3 and 4 display or remove any buttons that were added or deleted through the use of the Add or Remove Buttons button on the More Buttons menu.

You can turn off both the toolbars sharing a single row and the short menus by removing the check marks from the two top check boxes in the Options sheet in the Customize dialog box (Figure C-2 on the previous page). If you remove these check marks, Word will display the toolbars on two separate rows below the menu bar and will show only full menus.

APPENDIX D

Microsoft Office User Specialist Certification Program

The Microsoft Office User Specialist (MOUS) Certification Program provides a framework for measuring your proficiency with the Microsoft Office 2000 applications, such as Word 2000, Excel 2000, Access 2000, and PowerPoint 2000. Three levels of certification are available — Master, Expert, and Core. The three levels of certification are described in Table D-1.

Table D-1 Three Levels of MOUS Certification			
LEVEL	DESCRIPTION	REQUIREMENTS	CREDENTIAL AWARDED
Master	Indicates that you have a comprehensive understanding of Microsoft Office 2000	Pass all FIVE of the required exams: Microsoft Word 2000 Expert Microsoft Excel 2000 Expert Microsoft PowerPoint 2000 Core Microsoft Access 2000 Core Microsoft Outlook 2000 Core	Candidates will be awarded one certificate for passing all five of the required Microsoft Office 2000 exams: Microsoft Office User Specialist: Microsoft Office 2000 Master
Expert	Indicates that you have a comprehensive understanding of the advanced features in a specific Microsoft Office 2000 application	Pass any ONE of the Expert exams: Microsoft Word 2000 Expert Microsoft Excel 2000 Expert	Candidates will be awarded one certificate for each of the Expert exams they have passed: Microsoft Office User Specialist: Microsoft Word 2000 Expert Microsoft Office User Specialist: Microsoft Excel 2000 Expert
Core	Indicates that you have a comprehensive understanding of the core features in a specific Microsoft Office 2000 application	Pass any ONE of the Core exams: Microsoft Word 2000 Core Microsoft Excel 2000 Core Microsoft PowerPoint 2000 Core Microsoft Access 2000 Core Microsoft Outlook 2000 Core	Candidates will be awarded one certificate for each of the Core exams they have passed: Microsoft Office User Specialist: Microsoft Word 2000 Microsoft Office User Specialist: Microsoft Excel 2000 Microsoft Office User Specialist: Microsoft PowerPoint 2000 Microsoft Office User Specialist: Microsoft Access 2000 Microsoft Office User Specialist: Microsoft Outlook 2000

Why Should You Get Certified?

Being a Microsoft Office User Specialist provides a valuable industry credential — proof that you have the Office 2000 applications skills required by employers. By passing one or more MOUS certification exams, you demonstrate your proficiency in a given Office application to employers. With nearly 80 million copies of Office in use around the world, Microsoft is targeting Office certification to a wide variety of companies. These companies include temporary employment agencies that want to prove the expertise of their workers, large corporations looking for a way to measure the skill set of employees, and training companies and educational institutions seeking Microsoft Office teachers with appropriate credentials.

The MOUS Exams

You pay $50 to $100 each time you take an exam, whether you pass or fail. The fee varies among testing centers. The Expert exams, which you can take up to 60 minutes to complete, consist of between 40 and 60 tasks that you perform online. The tasks require you to use the application just as you would in doing your job. The Core exams contain fewer tasks, and you will have slightly less time to complete them. The tasks you will perform differ on the two types of exams.

How Can You Prepare for the MOUS Exams?

The Shelly Cashman Series® offers several Microsoft-approved textbooks that cover the required objectives on the MOUS exams. For a listing of the textbooks, visit the Shelly Cashman Series MOUS Web page at www.scsite.com/off2000/cert.htm and then click the Shelly Cashman Series Office 2000 Microsoft-Approved MOUS Textbooks link (Figure D-1). After using any of the books listed in an instructor-led course, you will be prepared to take the MOUS exam indicated.

How to Find an Authorized Testing Center

You can locate a testing center by calling 1-800-933-4493 in North America or visiting the Shelly Cashman Series MOUS Web page at www.scsite.com/off2000/cert.htm and then clicking the Locate an Authorized Testing Center Near You link (Figure D-1). At this Web page, you can look for testing centers around the world.

Shelly Cashman Series MOUS Web Page

The Shelly Cashman Series MOUS Web page (Figure D-1) has more than fifteen Web pages you can visit to obtain additional information on the MOUS Certification Program. The Web page (www.scsite.com/off2000/cert.htm) includes links to general information on certification, choosing an application for certification, preparing for the certification exam, and taking and passing the certification exam.

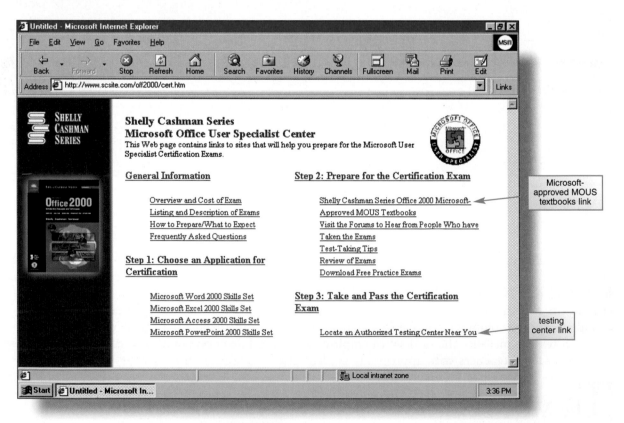

FIGURE D-1